Earth Tones

EARTH
TONES

The Poetry of Pablo Neruda

MANUEL DURÁN
and
MARGERY SAFIR

INDIANA UNIVERSITY PRESS
Bloomington

Permission to quote in translation from *Estravagario, Plenos poderes, Canto general, Fulgor y muerte de Joaquín Murieta,* and *Memorial de Isla Negra* granted by Farrar, Straus and Giroux, Inc. This translation © 1981 by Farrar, Straus and Giroux, Inc.

First Midland Book Edition 1986
Copyright © 1981 by Manuel Durán and Margery Safir

Manufactured in the United States of America

Library of Congress Cataloging in Publication Data

Durán, Manuel, 1925–
Earth tones.

Bibliography: p.
1. Neruda, Pablo, 1904–1973. 2. Poets, Chilean—20th century—Biography. I. Safir, Margery, 1947–joint author. II. Title.
PQ8097.N4Z616   861 [B]   80-8095

2 3 4 5 6 90 89 88 87 86

ISBN 0-253-16662-4 cloth
ISBN 0-253-20372-4 paperback

Contents

Forgive me
if when I want to tell my life
it's soil that I recount.
Such is the earth.
When it grows in your blood,
you grow.
If it dies in your blood,
you die.

—Pablo Neruda, *And Yet*

Preface

"On our earth, before writing was invented,
before the printing press was invented, poetry
flourished. That is why we know that poetry is
like bread; it should be shared by all, by
scholars and by peasants, by all our vast,
incredible, extraordinary family of Man."
                                    —Pablo Neruda

As a man, Pablo Neruda, Nobel laureate and political activist, was quiet and slow-moving, yet inwardly exuberant; as a poet, he was constantly moving, traveling, singing, writing, drinking, making love, celebrating love, playing, exuding energy. Both the man and his poetry come from the earth, from the clay, the stone, and the rains of southern Chile, from a reality that has always been there, but which with Neruda takes on a life and significance possible only through a subtle and refined process of awareness and discovery. Neruda, like Whitman before him, was a great poet in part because he was a great discoverer, uncovering the rhythm of common things, of everyday matter, elevating to epic proportions the working men and women of his continent.

Poetry is everywhere and belongs to everyman. A great poet, however, no matter how radical and populist his ideology, is inevitably an aristocrat within his society. Some of Neruda's poetry is obscure and very difficult; later, when Neruda makes a conscious effort to open up his verses, simplifying his style and structure, rejecting esoteric, hermetic poetry, he may have become the easiest, clearest, and most directly enjoyable of all contemporary poets. But he is still a poet, and as such, his work remains harder to assimilate than, for instance, a short story dealing with similar themes and concerns. A poet quite simply sees and awakens things that other persons, on their own, do not see. The poet is unavoidably separated from the mainstream of his society by his means of expression and his vision; he can bring the mainstream into his world, as Neruda so often and successfully does, but his way of seeing remains the poet's way of seeing, his the world into which others must venture.

This book offers an overview of Neruda's poetry and of the poet behind the work. The ideology guiding this book is contained in the epigraph that opens the preface. This is not a book directed to a public specializing in literary analysis, a public whose training and experience already allow them easy access to Neruda's work. Rather, this book is directed toward the general reading public; it attempts to construct a bridge providing passage for those who without it might not fully enter Neruda's world of earth tones. In this sense, the book could be subtitled "The Essential Neruda," for it provides the basics, outlining the most fundamental and often stated aspects of the style, structure, and content of Neruda's poetry as they develop and interrelate, and in their relevance to the life of the man who produced them.

For this task we have deviated from the conventional chronological presentation of the poetry and have chosen instead a thematic division, devoting a chapter each to Neruda the erotic poet, Neruda the Nature poet, Neruda the public and political poet, and Neruda the personal poet, as well as a chapter to the works published after the poet's death. Within the unifying theme of each chapter, the poetry is discussed in order of publication, and each chapter ends with a synopsis, so that the reader can trace the development of each theme from its earliest to its final manifestations in the poet's work. In addition, a system of cross-reference operates throughout the text. Thus in chapter 1, when *Twenty Love Poems and a Song of Despair* is first mentioned within the context of Neruda's erotic poetry, a note indicates that the same work is also discussed in another chapter. In this way the reader can see the complete trajectory of any one aspect of Neruda's poetry as an ensemble within a given chapter, while at the same time following any individual work as it is treated in various chapters throughout the book. A schematic chronological biography is presented at the beginning of the book, and each thematic chapter touches on aspects of Neruda's life as a frame of reference for discussing his works. We have also provided a selected bibliography for the reader interested in going further into the critical studies of Neruda.

Neruda's literary production was enormous: the latest edition of his *Complete Works* (1973) totals 3,522 pages in three volumes. Clearly, no single work of criticism can pretend to deal substantially with every work contained in these thousands of pages. All Neruda's books of poetry are mentioned in this book. Yet we have employed a guiding principle of selectivity: to focus most intently on those works that constitute crucial moments in Neruda's literary career, as well as those best known to the American public. Throughout the book Neruda's poems have been translated into English by Manuel Durán, in an effort to give the translated poems a consistency of style that would not have been possible if translations from various sources

were used. Except where otherwise indicated, all the translations
were done from the original Spanish *Obras Completas,* Buenos Aires:
Losada, 3d ed., 1967–68.

Pablo Neruda was, certainly, among the greatest poets of this century. He was also an extraordinarily vibrant and passionate man.
More than studied and dissected, his poems are to be lived, devoured, savored, experienced. This book has been written as an in-
strument to that end.

Manuel Durán and Margery Safir

The Man: A Biographical Outline

Long before the Swedish Academy awarded Pablo Neruda the Nobel Prize for Literature in 1971, it was clear to most poetry readers that Neruda was one of the undisputed giants of our time. Both volume and quality, both the individual lyrical voice and the collective political voice come forth to make Neruda's vast work almost without rival. Any enterprise begins with a birth, a soil that nurtures it, later becoming a vision, a project, a wave of hope and confidence. Neruda's life is a clear example of a curve projecting talent and ambition and commitment ever higher.

In discussing the general forms that Neruda's poetry took over the years—erotic poetry, Nature poetry, public poetry, and personal poetry—we shall refer to incidents, experiences, and persons that made their mark on the man and his poetry. This brief biography of the man provides a framework for those references. It is an exterior outline without detail, touching concrete movements more than intimate feelings. An "official" biography was written by Neruda himself. The final editing was interrupted by his death, but the manuscript compiled by his widow, Matilde, with the help of Miguel Otero Silva, is available in an English translation by Hardie St. Martin.[1] A real sense of the man does come through in what José Yglesias has called "these marvelous, exasperating memoirs," his playfulness, his commitment, at times his vanity.[2] Yet even Neruda's own account, written from the perspective of an enormously successful poet looking back, creating as much as remembering, is not always complete or wholly frank. The real interior biography is accessible only through Neruda's poetry. His poems are the drama of his life. "If you ask what my poetry is," Neruda once said, "I must say, I don't know; but if you ask my poetry, it will tell you who I am!"[3] This brief chronology is intended to serve as a backdrop to that poetry and to what it reveals about the man.

Neruda before Neruda

Pablo Neruda was born Neftalí Ricardo Reyes Basoalto in Parral, a small town in southern Chile, on July 12, 1904. His mother, Rosa, who was a schoolteacher, died of tuberculosis a month after his birth. His father, José del Carmen Reyes Morales, was a railroad man, fair-haired and stern, a man the child would soon learn to admire and fear. Later, as Pablo Neruda, the poet would remember "the golden beard of my father advancing / toward the majesty of the iron roads" ("I am," *Canto General*). The land in southern Chile was harsh, poor, cold. It was heavily forested and there was constant rain. It was Indian land, very much like Oregon or Montana at the end of the nineteenth century. Neftalí was not to spend much time in Parral. In 1906 the family moved to another village, Temuco, and the father soon remarried. The terrain remained the same, however, the cold, rainy hills of southern Chile.

Young Neftalí lived in Temuco for fifteen years. He learned to respect hard work and to love books and the dark woods. He day-dreamed constantly, took long walks in the woods, came to admire the Indians who in the hills and the forests were trying to preserve the traces of their ancient civilization. Instinctively, he identified with the oppressed. He refused to accept that only his Spanish blood was worthy of praise; he had Indian blood also that had to be expressed and listened to. His father's remarriage to Trinidad Candia Marverde was a blessing for Neftalí. As a child, he revered his step-mother, his "guardian angel" as he called her, a diligent, silent, sweet peasant woman, close to the earth the mature poet would continually reach back to. The town of Temuco was an old town of wooden houses with patios and small gardens. The Reyes home was modest but roomy, and there was privacy for the poet: "I go upstairs to my room. I read Salgari. The rain stampedes like a cataract. In one minute the night and the rain cover the world. I am there all alone and in my arithmetic notebook I write poems."[4]

In spite of his yearning for camaraderie and solidarity, the young schoolboy must have soon realized that he had embarked upon a lonely road. His classmates made fun of his love of poetry. A frontier society has no time for such things. Neither his friends nor his father would applaud or encourage him in any way. Neftalí was tall, shy, lonely. His reading was voracious and random: "I gobbled up everything, indiscriminately, like an ostrich," he later recalled.[5] Russian novels, Jules Verne, children's books, symbolist poets were all grist for his mill. And the principal of Temuco's girls' school was the poet Gabriela Mistral, who would be a Nobel laureate years before Neruda. It is almost inconceivable that two such gifted poets should find each other in such an unlikely spot. Mistral recognized the young Neftalí's talent and encouraged it by giving the boy books and the support he lacked at home.

Things began to happen. Neftalí translated Baudelaire. He fell in love, madly, time and again. He had his first sexual experiences. In 1917 an article by him, his first published work, appeared in the local Temuco newspaper. His first poem appeared in 1918 in a Santiago magazine, *Corre-Vuela,* which printed thirteen more of his poems the next year. Two literary prizes followed, then a third place in the Maule Floral Games poetry competition, and in 1920 first prize in Temuco's spring festival. His ambition began to grow as fast as his tall, thin body. He was ready to move beyond the frontier town.

Hunger and Love

In 1921, having finished high school in Temuco, he made up his mind to face the big city. He went to Santiago, the capital, to continue his studies and to become a French teacher. Leaving the fragrant woods and gray skies of the province for the fast pace and lights of Santiago, his head was "filled with books, dreams, and poems buzzing around like bees."[6] At the end of the long train journey, the young poet found the tumult and the loneliness of the streets of Santiago, where he was known by no one except hunger, a constant companion. A year earlier, after finding in a magazine the name of the Czech writer Jan Neruda, Neftalí had chosen a new name. Now he began a new life as "Pablo Neruda."

Most of Neruda's Santiago friends were bohemian writers and artists—there were even a few petty thieves and gangsters. His personal philosophy verged on anarchism. Love affairs, books, classes at the Instituto Pedagógico, daydreams, long hours spent looking at the sunset from his window on Maruri Street occupied most of his time. And writing. Neruda wrote feverishly, sometimes five poems a day. His first book, *Crepusculario,* appeared in 1923. Many of its delicate, subtle poems were in the mainstream of the symbolist-*modernista* tradition. *The Ardent Slingsman* was also written during this period, although it was not published until 1933. The quality of Neruda's work was already high. Nineteen twenty-three also saw the publication in magazines, especially *Claridad,* of some of the poems that, gathered together and published in 1924 as *Twenty Love Poems and a Song of Despair,* were his first real success.

Within the small bohemian circles he frequented, Neruda was becoming well known. Yet his poetry was not yet, and would not be for a long time, a steady source of income. In order to survive, Neruda did hasty translations and wrote magazine and newspaper articles. In

1925 be became the editor of a small literary magazine, *Caballo de Bastos*. And he had finished writing a new book of poems, *Venture of the Infinite Man,* in which the influence of the avant-garde movements, including surrealism, can be clearly felt. In 1926 Neruda published a prose book, *Rings,* depicting the subjective visions of an idle bystander, and a short novel, *The Inhabitant and His Hope,* which remains one of his least read works. In the same year, the second, definitive edition of *Crepusculario* came out—an unusual success for a young poet. He had by now also translated long fragments of Rilke's *Notebooks of Malte Laurids Brigge,* and he was writing the first, tormented poems of a new cycle, what would several years later become his first *Residence on Earth.*

Neruda at this time was fast becoming impatient with himself, with his friends, with his own poetry. From his perspective, life in Santiago had given him above all an unhappy love affair, a love affair that had inspired some of the best and most poignant of the *Twenty Poems.* As for success, fame, glory, he did not delude himself. He was totally unknown outside of Santiago. He was in fact despondent, without money or work. It was again time to take a bold step, to flee, to travel to the end of the earth. Perhaps like Mallarmé he felt that "the flesh was sad and he had read all the books." His readings of travel adventures, of Jules Verne and Salgari, the example of Rimbaud, came back to his memory. Perhaps, like Peter Pan, he did not want to grow up, to accept responsibility, to become a serious translator, a professor of French, a magazine editor. Or perhaps he thought that postponing success was the best strategy; only thus could he enjoy the anonymous life, which was the true life for a poet bent on expressing the voice of the collective people.

Escape, however, was not easy. He tried it first in 1925, abandoning his studies and fleeing with his friend Rubén Azócar, to Ancud, a village on a Chilean island. In 1926 he returned to Santiago, still poor, still anguished, despite the publication of his poetry, as we clearly see in those portions of *Residence on Earth I* that were written between 1925 and 1927.

Chile had a long tradition, like most Latin American countries, of sending her poets abroad as consuls or even, when they became famous, as ambassadors. Neruda made contact with the Ministry of Foreign Affairs, and in 1927 finally managed to pull the right strings to have himself appointed Honorary Consul to Rangoon in Burma. His knowledge of spoken English was sketchy, his familiarity with consular business nil. He was simply an adventurous, restless twenty-three-year-old poet, a lady's man with a gravel voice, a tall dark body, somber eyes, and a magnetic, charismatic presence;

above all, he was an accomplished writer about to reach the peak of his powers. He knew all about words, their meaning, their music, their rhythm; he had learned to combine what was in the books he had read with what Nature and his senses had taught him. He could touch his readers. He was a poet. Yet his second escape, this time to the Orient, would only increase his personal anguish.

Books published: *Crepusculario, Twenty Love Poems and a Song of Despair, Venture of the Infinite Man, The Inhabitant and His Hope* (prose), *Rings* (prose).

Wandering the Earth

In 1927, Neruda started his long journey to Rangoon. He traveled from Santiago to Buenos Aires, then to Lisbon, Madrid, Paris, and finally Marseilles, where he boarded the boat to the Orient. Short of money and long on hope, he sent reports and articles to *La Nación*, the Santiago daily, and letters to his friends. The Orient for Neruda was a mixture of chaos, poverty, and fascinating perceptions of the ancient cultures in contact with a degrading colonial present. Anguish and despair accompanied the poet, born partly of his sharing in the common grief of the poverty and oppression he saw everywhere, but also out of his own personal disorientation and loneliness. He was living from day to day, in abject poverty, and his solitude grew like a cancer. During this time he wrote some of his most somber poems. He tried to keep open his line of communication with a few friends in Chile and to establish new links with other poets and magazines halfway across the globe. He published poems in Spanish newspapers and magazines and sought friendships in Argentina and Spain. Yet everything seemed precarious, provisional, futile. Alcohol and poetry were escapes into turmoil, not beauty.

In Rangoon, a Burmese girl, Josie Bliss, fell in love with Neruda. Despite his attachment to her, Neruda was oppressed and frightened by her extreme jealousy, and he left her behind when he was suddenly appointed Consul in Ceylon in 1928. On the boat he wrote his "Widower's Tango" as a sad farewell to his jealous love. But Josie surprised him later by appearing on his doorstep in Colombo. Helpless in her love, she was unable to realize that Neruda at that time was largely incapable of giving or receiving such feelings. The second, and final, break between them, a source of remorse and sorrow for both the poet and the girl, took place in Ceylon. In 1929 Neruda traveled to India to attend a meeting of the Indian National Congress Party in Calcutta. There, the vast crowds only increased his feelings of loneliness, of looking at this world and yet being some-how separated from it. He continued writing the *Residence* poems. The Orient had become for Neruda a kind of Hell on Earth, a tor-turous entrapment that had to be endured and surmounted. Like Dante, Neruda became a traveler. Dante's travel was vertical, down into Hell and then up into Purgatory and Paradise; Neruda's was the travel of a poet without the benefit of theology, a horizontal trip that would take him from the Inferno of the Orient to the Purgatory of his return to the West, and finally, through political commitment, to the half-seen Paradise of a future world where all contradictions would be resolved in an ecstasy of community, a long-awaited and long-lasting brotherhood.

In 1930 Neruda was named Consul in Batavia, the capital of the Dutch East Indies, and he was trying to relate once more to the ex-ternal world, the world of sanity where poems get published and young people in love get married. He did manage to have some of his most exciting "nightmare" poems printed in Madrid by the pres-tigious *Revista de Occidente;* he did fall in love with a young Dutch girl, María Antonieta Hagenaar, and he married her. It was not to be a happy union.

In 1932, after a brief consular mission in Singapore, the couple undertook the long two-month journey back to Chile. The next year a second edition of *Twenty Poems* appeared in Buenos Aires, *The Ar-dent Slingsman* was published in Santiago, and a first limited edition of *Residence on Earth (1925–1931)* was printed in Buenos Aires. Nonetheless, Neruda could not live from his poetry, and he was forced to accept work in various government ministries. In 1933 he was appointed to a consular post in Buenos Aires. This was not a happy time for the poet; he detested his bureaucratic work, and his marriage gave him little reason to rejoice; yet in Buenos Aires he met a man who became an important and close friend, the Spanish poet Federico García Lorca.

Books published: *The Ardent Slingsman, Residence on Earth I.*

The Spanish Experience

In early 1934, the Nerudas were again traveling, this time to Europe. Neruda had been appointed Consul in Barcelona. Neruda's daughter, Malva Marina, was born in October, but the event was less cheerful than one would imagine. The birth was difficult and the child was sickly. Malva Marina would die in Europe in 1942, at the age of eight.

In other respects, nonetheless, Spain was exactly what Neruda needed at the moment. As Hernán Loyola has observed, "Spain seemed to be waiting for the Chilean poet."[7] Neruda didn't stay long in Barcelona, but moved on to Madrid, where in December of 1934, Lorca introduced him at a lecture and poetry reading. Neruda's success was instantaneous. While in Madrid, Neruda met a young Argentine, Delia del Carril; the love between them was immediate. Neruda and his wife separated in 1936, and the poet remained with Delia del Carril until the early 1950s. In 1935, Neruda was named Consul in Madrid. His literary success mounted; the second book of *Residence on Earth (1925–1935)* was published there and received with critical acclaim. In October 1935, there appeared a new poetry magazine, *Green Horse for Poetry,* edited by Neruda.

In Spain, Neruda found a congenial group of poets and critics, and a growing number of enthusiastic readers. For the first time he tasted international recognition, at the heart of the Spanish language and tradition. At the same time that his poetry was having an influence on the Spanish avant-garde, Neruda was being influenced by his politically active friends. Above all, poets like Rafael Alberti and Miguel Hernández, who had become closely involved in radical politics and the Communist movement, helped politicize Neruda, who was already convinced of the basic tenets of proletarian struggle and anti-bourgeois movements. When civil war came to Spain in 1936, Neruda became an ardent supporter of the Republic, losing his consular appointment because of his partisan support. All of the poet's strength and influence were directed to help the leftist fight against Fascism. His friend Lorca was assassinated by Franco's forces; Alberti and Hernández were fighting at the front; Neruda traveled inside and outside Spain to gather money and friends for the Republic. He founded the review *Poets of the World Defend the Spanish People,* gave lectures, established contacts with French writers such as Aragon and Eluard, and with César Vallejo, created intellectual centers at the service of the cause. *Spain in My Heart,* published in 1937, expresses the thoughts and feelings of a poet who is no longer alone; he has become part of an army, a political movement.

In 1937 Neruda returned to Chile and joined the political battle there. He traveled throughout the country in 1938, lecturing and giving poetry readings, defending Republican Spain and the new Chilean government, in which at last the forces of the Left seemed to have been victorious. It was a year of personal loss for the poet, however: his father died in May and his stepmother in August. Significantly, perhaps, it is at this same time that he began the *Song of Chile,* which eventually became *Canto General.* The following year

Neruda was appointed a Special Consul in Paris and given the task of supervising the migration to Chile of the defeated Spanish Republicans who had fled to France.

Books published: *Residence on Earth II, Spain in My Heart.*

Political Allegiance and Exile

In 1940 Neruda again returned to Chile. He continued working on *Song of Chile.* He was not to stay in his native land for long, however; in the same year he left for Mexico to serve as Chile's Consul General there.

Neruda's poetical aesthetics were changing. The Second World War had started, and it was urgent to fight Fascism. For Neruda, it was also urgent to think of a poetic definition of the American continent. From Mexico City, Neruda surveyed the whole expanse. He traveled to Guatemala in 1941 and to Cuba in 1942; he became familiar with the Mexican plateau and the Caribbean islands that are an integral part of the whole vast panorama. While he was still passionately interested in the outcome of European events (he gave a reading of his "Song to Stalingrad" in 1942), he realized more and more that for him the future of Man was linked to the Americas. On October 22, 1943, the poet climbed to the city of Machu Picchu.* The almost mystical fusion of Man, Time, and Nature that he experienced there would later develop into one of his key poems, "Heights of Macchu Picchu," the cornerstone of *Canto General.* Neruda would go back, time and time again, to this poem, recognizing in it one of the crucial moments of his poetic career. He would change and improve it, with love and care, just as one prunes and nourishes a plant or a tree.

In 1945, again settled back in Chile, Neruda was elected Senator. His election represented, however, only fleeting success, since the political situation was fast turning against the Left. The poet received the National Literary Prize; of more significance, he officially joined the Chilean Communist Party. In terms of his activities and beliefs, Neruda had in fact been a Communist for many years, since the Spanish Civil War. Yet it was only in 1945 that he joined the Party. Hernán Loyola, noting that the poet began writing "Heights of Macchu Picchu" one month after he joined the Party, considers the two events "twin expressions of the same internal reality."[8]

Neruda realized that even as a Senator, however, his situation in

---

*Machu Picchu is the English spelling. Neruda spells it Macchu Picchu.

Chile was at best precarious, since the strength of the political Right increased daily. But there was a glimmer of hope. A leftist presidential candidate, González Videla, asked for Neruda's help in the 1946 political campaign, help which the poet provided generously. González Videla won the election. On becoming President, however, González Videla promptly became a tool of the monopolists and foreign investors. When this happened, Neruda became an embarrassment to the President; the poet was suddenly a man whose voice had to be suppressed. In 1947 Neruda defied Chilean press censorship by publishing in Caracas a document entitled "An Intimate Letter for Millions of Men" and was indicted as a seditious rebel. In February of 1948 the Supreme Court of Chile upheld his having been removed from the Senate. His arrest was ordered. The Communist Party was outlawed, and its members were forced to hide or flee. The poet went underground in Chile for several months, living in different homes while he worked on *Canto General* and wrote pamphlets against González Videla. The fact that much of the *Canto* was written in 1948–49, while Neruda was being persecuted, is important. Loyola notes that the "rage, the indignation, the urgency of denouncing' treason" in the portions written under these circumstances colored the book's structure, form, tone, and language.[9] In 1949, manuscript in hand, Neruda crossed the Andes into exile.

It was to be a longer exile than he had anticipated. He attended a peace congress in Paris and then made his first visit to the Soviet Union, where he helped celebrate the 150th anniversary of Pushkin's birth. While in the Soviet Union, Neruda was honored by the Union of Soviet Writers in Moscow. His books were now being published in Germany, Czechoslovakia, China, Denmark, Hungary, the United States, the Soviet Union, and throughout Latin America. After a visit to Poland and Hungary, Neruda traveled to Mexico with the French surrealist poet Paul Eluard, and took part in the Latin American Congress of the Partisans for Peace. In Mexico he reencountered Matilde Urrutia, a compatriot whose intelligence and sensitivity had impressed Neruda when they had first met, in 1946. Now their love affair was to become a permanent fact of their lives, and she would inspire some of the most passionate and sensitive love poems written in Spanish in our century.

In 1950 *Canto General* was published, in Mexico, with illustrations by the renowned artists Diego Rivera and Davíd Alfaro Siqueiros. Neruda was fast becoming a living paradox: a poet outlawed in his own country, where *Canto General* appeared only in clandestine editions, he had become an acclaimed international celebrity, receiving official homages in Guatemala, Paris, Prague, Rome, and New Delhi, where he was received by Nehru. In November of 1950 he traveled to Warsaw to take part in the Second World Congress of Partisans for Peace. A new Soviet publication of *Canto General* was printed in an enormous edition of 250,000 copies. In 1951, Neruda was reading his poems in Italy, Berlin, Mongolia, and Peking. In 1952 Neruda and Matilde were in Capri. It was the first time they had lived together; during this period *The Grapes and the Wind* was begun and the first, private edition of *The Captain's Verses* was published. That same year the political situation in Chile changed. The order for Neruda's arrest was revoked, making it possible for the poet to return to his homeland.

Books published: *The Third Residence, Canto General, The Captain's Verses.*

Homecoming

Fame is a drug that only the strong can take and survive. Many writers have become paralyzed by success. Neruda was an exception. He returned to Chile in 1952, and this return to the land of his birth was only the beginning of a new period in his poetic evolution. Roots were growing again.

Neruda was received with honor upon his return. He set about decorating a house in Santiago, but continued to travel, first to his origins, the southern town of Temuco, and then to other parts of Chile, and to the Soviet Union as a member of the International Peace Prize jury. Most important, in 1952 Neruda started to write his *Elemental Odes,* a new departure in poetic exploration, and a successful one; never had raw matter, everyday life, familiar objects been so uplifted and dignified by the voice of a poet as in these deceptively simple verses.

In 1953 Neruda was awarded the Stalin Peace Prize, and by the next year, this new period of success was reaching a climax. At the University of Chile, Neruda read five lectures in which he explained—as much as a poet can explain the ineffable—the origins and evolution of his poetic insight; the lectures moved his audience to almost endless applause. The *Odes* were published in Buenos Aires and received with great critical acclaim. His fiftieth birthday was celebrated by a gathering of writers bringing greetings from around the world. Neruda donated his library to the University of Chile, which in turn subsidized the Neruda Foundation for the Advancement of Poetry. Foreign editions of his works continued to appear and were enthusiastically received. Neruda, the restless

traveler, the exile, began in these years to appear in a new light—
almost as the official establishment poet, although his allegiance to
the Communist Party never swerved. Applauded by Communist critics and readers, Neruda was likewise acclaimed and widely read in
the capitalist countries.

By 1955 Neruda had separated from Delia del Carril. He finished
building a house in a suburb of Santiago and moved in with Matilde
Urrutia, who later became his legal wife. They remained together,
deeply in love, to the end. Another trip, to the Soviet Union, China,
Brazil, and Argentina, gave proof that Neruda was still not ready to
accept a sedentary life. In 1956 another important book, *More Elemental Odes,* appeared, and the following year Losada published the
Complete Works. By this time translations of Neruda's poetry had been
published in virtually every language, including Japanese and Per-
sian. Neruda was as famous as Picasso.

Neruda was a vain man—he expected, even demanded, to be
praised by critics and friends, and was his own best public relations
man—but he was also charming, good-humored, and passionate, a
good conversationalist who was also good at listening. He had a
child's enthusiasm and, at times, caprices, and although he was shy
and not extroverted, he had an enormous *joie de vivre.* Like any
other man, he had his foibles and small obsessions. One of his ma-
nias was collecting—rare books, bric-a-brac, old bottles, shells,
carved figureheads from ships. The royalties from his books allowed
him to build new retreats, one in Valparaíso, and one that would be
his favorite during his last years, the wooden house on Isla Negra,
facing the stormy Pacific. The house on Isla Negra became a verita-
ble museum, filled with the objects he had collected. Some rooms
were so crowded with objects and furniture that visitors had to move
slowly, like ships maneuvering through a narrow strait. Neruda was
a complex personality—a Communist who filled his houses with material objects purchased with royalties from capitalist countries; a
marvelously free spirit who was, at the same time, capable of extreme Party dogmatism, as when in his role as Allende's Ambassador
to France, he refused to allow the Chilean Embassy to participate in
the showing of a Chilean film in Paris simply because the Party did
not approve of the film; Neruda, while insisting on the Embassy
boycott, freely confessed that he himself had never seen the film.

Neruda and Matilde journeyed frequently to other Latin American countries and abroad to Western Europe, the Soviet Union,
Eastern Europe, and China. In 1957 they set out on a sort of "pilgrimage," visiting the places where Neruda had lived before he knew
Matilde, especially Rangoon, Colombo, and other points in the

Orient. During the fifties new love poems, inspired by Matilde, appeared time and again. The first group, *The Captain's Verses,* was published anonymously in 1952, because Neruda feared hurting his companion of so many years, Delia del Carril, by the public demonstration of his love for Matilde. This book was later published with Neruda's name on it. *Extravagaria, One Hundred Love Sonnets,* and *Barcarole,* also inspired by Matilde, followed. This was a period of enormous production for Neruda, of mainly personal poetry; one volume came after another in rapid succession. Despite his constant travels and public activities, Neruda was no longer obliged to accept diplomatic work in order to live, and he could devote himself fully to his poetry. He began to spend more and more time at his Isla Negra retreat, and the peace that he found there is reflected in poetry that grew ever more intimate and meditative.

Free from anguish and financial concerns, Neruda turned his attention to his own life; several autobiographies appeared in these years. A series of articles published in 1962 in the Brazilian journal *O Cruzeiro Internacional* were the beginning of Neruda's prose memoirs. In these articles, Neruda presented a personal, subjective portrait of his youth and his hopes. The anecdotes are charming and we are told much, yet at the same time we feel that the ultimate truth has been left out of these articles. Neruda reworked the articles over the years, but the revised version, *Memoirs,* did not appear until after his death. In 1964 the autobiographical *Notes from Isla Negra* was published.

More travels. Wherever Neruda and Matilde went, crowds gathered to hear the famous gravel voice, to hear Neruda lecturing and reading his poetry; his powerful stage presence and moving poetry made him enormously popular. In 1963 a second edition of his *Complete Works* was published. In 1964 Neruda's Spanish version of *Romeo and Juliet* signaled a venture into the theater, a move which would be completed in 1967 with *Splendor and Death of Joaquín Murieta.* In 1968 still another edition of the *Complete Works* appeared. This was a time of plenty for Neruda, and everything seemed to be building to the crowning international recognition that the Nobel Prize would bring him.

Neruda's prolific writing at Isla Negra in no way meant that he had abandoned active political participation, and in 1969 he was again deeply involved in Chilean politics, this time as the Communist Party's candidate for the presidency of Chile. Neruda later renounced his candidacy, however, in order to support his friend Salvador Allende when Allende became the sole candidate of all the leftist parties. Neruda campaigned vigorously for Allende, and although Neruda reportedly had doubts about the ability of the new government to direct the country, Allende's victory at the polls did bring to the poet the hope of a new Chile in which social justice might at last abolish classism and poverty. In 1970 Neruda was already seriously ill with cancer, yet he agreed to represent the new government as Chile's Ambassador to France.

Books published: *The Grapes and the Wind, Elemental Odes, Journeys* (prose), *More Elemental Odes, The Third Book of Odes, Extravagaria, Voyages and Homecomings, One Hundred Love Sonnets, Chanson de Geste, The Stones of Chile, Ceremonial Songs, Fully Empowered, Notes from Isla Negra, The Art of Birds, A House by the Shore* (prose and poetry), *Barcarole, Splendor and Death of Joaquín Murieta* (theater), *The Hands of Day, Eating in Hungary* (mainly prose, with Miguel Angel Asturias), *And Yet, World's End, The Flaming Sword, Sky Stones.*

The Glory and the Sorrow

It was in France, on October 8, 1971, while he was working to renegotiate Chile's external debt, that Neruda received the news that he had been awarded the highest international recognition available to a writer: the Nobel Prize for Literature. Neruda traveled to Stockholm to receive the prize. In his acceptance speech he described his vision of a future City of Man, a new Utopia, a Paradise of everyday living, a universe in which poets would play a significant role.

Neruda, however, was now gravely ill. He knew that he was going to die soon, and he was coming to terms with oblivion. He was also aware of the problems besetting the Allende government in Chile. The message of his acceptance speech is positive, it is a message of hope; but he had moments of doubt, of anguish, of desolation as well.

Neruda returned to Chile in 1972, too ill to continue his work in France. A huge rally was organized in the National Stadium to greet him. Neruda's *Memoirs* refer to a "massive turnout" for this homecoming,[10] yet several Chileans now living in exile in Paris recall another version. Despite the Nobel Prize, despite Allende's putting all the press and communications apparatus of the country at the disposal of arousing the populace to greet the poet, the stadium of Santiago, they report, remained only half-filled. Perhaps Chile in 1972 was too preoccupied with the political tensions in its government to enjoy the luxury of saluting a great poet, even a poet fully engaged in the work of that government; perhaps at the end of his literary career, as at the beginning, Neruda was to know the sad irony of being more generously received outside his beloved Chile than within its borders. We have no independent way of verifying either this report or the more optimistic one presented in Neruda's *Memoirs*. As fact, we can state only that Neruda returned to Chile a world-renowned poet, but a very sick man, and he returned to a Chile whose leftist government was already threatened by internal opponents and external enemies.

Whatever doubts Neruda might have experienced upon returning to Chile do not change the fact that he was, by personal inclination, an optimist. He was also a "professional" optimist, committed to propagating the Party line of a Communist utopia. In conversations with friends, in between-the-lines confidences to his readers, Neruda at times departed from this official optimism, but the basic hopeful outlook usually remained intact.

The Neruda who emerges from conversations with those who were close to him also deviates somewhat from the myth, from the public Neruda, from the concept of the man gathered from seeing him externally, when he was consciously projecting himself and his image outward toward an audience. The vibrancy and exuberance that are associated with Neruda through his poems did exist in the man, but inwardly, in his attitudes and passions. Externally, he did not give the appearance of this vitality. On the contrary, Neruda's movements and gestures were slow, as was the rhythm with which his gravel voice spoke. In his private life, Neruda was in reality more shy than open, more retiring than company-seeking. He was not particularly given to socializing, preferring instead the solitude of his homes, especially his retreat in Isla Negra. For all his many travels and his youthful seeking of extravagant lifestyles, the poet was, for most of his adult life, more routine-bound than desirous of adventure; and despite his many public appearances pleading for political causes or simply reading his poetry, in reality he suffered crowds more than he sought them. He could be gay and playful among his close friends, donning a bartender's apron to ceremoniously serve marvelous concoctions of liquors at a birthday celebration, or carrying on serious conversations while an enormous stuffed horse peered over his shoulder. He was very astute, and equally narcissistic, yet capable of sustaining great love, as evidenced by his long relationships with both Delia del Carril and Matilde Urrutia.

Ironically, despite his country origins, Neruda, the poetic voice of the people, the working class, and the peasants, was never really in his adult life a man *of* the people. On the contrary, his friends were more literary than proletarian, and Neruda's only considerable professional experience outside the literary world was first bureaucratic, as a civil servant of the Foreign Ministry, and then political. Only once in Neruda's adult life did he really come into close contact with the day-to-day life of the working class. That was in the late 1940s, when Neruda, like thousands of other members of the newly out-lawed Communist Party of Chile, was forced to go into hiding in his own country to avoid arrest and persecution by the González Videla regime. Then, living in various safe houses provided by the Com-munist Party until he could escape into exile, Neruda did come again into real contact with the "Juans" of his country, with the workers and peasants, the urban and rural proletariat of Chile. Once safely in exile, Neruda was never again to know firsthand the everyday life and reality of the working man; he could write for this man, he could write of him, he could serve as a symbol and a spokesman, but his own life would be spent in the solitude of his comfortable homes or on the speaker's platforms looking at, but not forming part of, the masses he addressed. Nevertheless, Neruda's commitment to the proletariat was real and profound; and his case is not unique — Marx never worked in a factory, nor did Lenin or Stalin; Fidel Castro is, by class and by professional training, a lawyer; Che Guevara was a doctor; Salvador Allende, a doctor, an intellectual, and a politician. Leaders of the proletariat who have actually spent their lives among the proletariat are rare. Neruda's dedication to the working class of his country was absolute; but this dedication does not alter the reality of a life devoted to a class to which Neruda did not really belong by the way in which he chose to live his adult life.

In terms of his political activities, Neruda was a "man for all sea-sons." He accepted the official pronouncements of his Party and applauded every speech by its leaders, whether Stalin, Khrushchev, or their successors, without necessarily agreeing with every line. He must have been aware of Stalin's brutality, of the extent and horror of the purges, yet he said nothing publicly at the time. Only in the late 1960s, and particularly with the publication of *World's End,* is there a public moment of doubt in Neruda's political faith, and he acknowledges his anguish over the Soviet invasion of Czechoslovakia, and other excesses of the Party.

A similar, but this time private, moment of doubt existed for Neruda in 1973. Back in Chile and observing the situation there, Neruda certainly realized that Allende had committed serious politi-cal errors, losing his grip on the extreme Left and on the country's economy. Yet, unlike the late 1960s, 1973 was not the moment to criticize openly. Too much was suddenly at stake in Chile and elsewhere, and his physical strength was ebbing.

September, 1973: Neruda, bedridden, terminally ill with cancer, was working on his memoirs and the eight books of poetry he planned to publish on his seventieth birthday, July 12, 1974. He wrote appeals to his friends in Europe, in the Americas, in the Socialist countries, begging them to come to the aid of Chile, desperately trying to forestall the coup d'etat that everyone knew was imminent. "Hawker-Hunter planes bomb La Moneda [the Presidential palace]," Fernando Alegría writes, "Allende falls riddled with bullets. Workers are machine-gunned down the length of the country. . . .Neruda, wide-eyed, bearded now, wants to see all this death, and pulling himself half-way up, suddenly knows that at last he is 'face to face with truth.' The world he made, verse by verse, step by step, the country he worked from clay, foam, grain, rock, snow, that he named and sang over the years, the peasant and worker's country, falls in on him with all the dust and clatter of an old beamed ceiling and cracked adobe walls. Nothing is left but silence, the sea at his feet, a distant shore and a boat."[11] On September 23, 1973, Pablo Neruda was dead; his houses were vandalized and ransacked; and a new, military government ruled Chile.

Books published: *Barren Terrain, A Call for Nixonicide and Glory to the Chilean Revolution.* Posthumous: *The Sea and the Bells, The Separate Rose, 2000, Winter Garden, The Yellow Heart, The Book of Riddles, Elegy, Selected Failings, Memoirs* (prose).

Books by Pablo Neruda

Crepusculario / *Crepusculario* (1923)

Veinte poemas de amor y una canción desesperada / *Twenty Love Poems and a Song of Despair* (1924)

Tentativa del hombre infinito / *Venture of the Infinite Man* (1926)

El habitante y su esperanza / *The Inhabitant and His Hope* (1926; prose)

Anillos / *Rings* (1926; prose)

El hondero entusiasta / *The Ardent Slingsman* (1933)

Residencia en la tierra (I) / *Residence on Earth (I)* (1933)

Residencia en la tierra (II) / *Residence on Earth (II)* (1935)

Tercera residencia / *The Third Residence* (1947)

La ahogada del cielo / The Woman Drowned in the Sky
Las furias y las penas / Griefs and Rages
Reunión bajo las nuevas banderas / United under New Flags
España en el corazón / Spain in My Heart
Canto a Stalingrado / Song to Stalingrad

Canto general / *Canto general* (1950)

La lámpara en la tierra / A Lamp on This Earth
Alturas de Macchu Picchu / Heights of Macchu Picchu
Los conquistadores / The Conquistadors
Los libertadores / The Liberators
La arena traicionada / The Sands Betrayed
América, no invoco tu nombre en vano / America, I Don't
Invoke Your Name in Vain
Canto general de Chile / Song of Chile
La tierra se llama Juan / The Land Is Called Juan
Que despierte el leñador / Let the Rail Splitter Awaken
El fugitivo / The Fugitive
Las flores de Punitaqui / The Flowers of Punitaqui
Los ríos del canto / Rivers of Song
Coral de año nuevo para la patria en tinieblas / A New Year's
Hymn for My Country in Darkness
El gran océano / The Great Ocean
Yo soy / I Am

Books by Pablo Neruda

Los versos del capitán / *The Captain's Verses* (1952)

Las uvas y el viento / *The Grapes and the Wind* (1954)

Odas elementales / *Elemental Odes* (1954)

Viajes / *Journeys* (1955; prose)

Nuevas odas elementales / *More Elemental Odes* (1956)

Tercer libro de las odas / *The Third Book of Odes* (1957)

Estravagario / *Extravagaria* (1958)

Navegaciones y regresos / *Voyages and Homecomings* (1959)

Cien sonetos de amor / *One Hundred Love Sonnets* (1959)

Canción de gesta / *Chanson de geste* (1960)

Las piedras de Chile / *The Stones of Chile* (1961)

Cantos ceremoniales / *Ceremonial Songs* (1961)

Plenos poderes / *Fully Empowered* (1962)

Memorial de Isla Negra / *Notes from Isla Negra* (1964)

Arte de pájaros / *The Art of Birds* (1966)

Una casa en la arena / *A House by the Shore* (1966; prose and poetry)

La barcarola / *Barcarole* (1967)

Fulgor y muerte de Joaquín Murieta / *Splendor and Death of
Joaquín Murieta* (1967; theater)

Comiendo en Hungría / *Eating in Hungary* (1968; prose and poetry, with
Miguel Angel Asturias)

Las manos del día / *The Hands of Day* (1968)

Aún / *And Yet* (1969)

Fin de mundo / *World's End* (1969)

La espada encendida / *The Flaming Sword* (1970)

Las piedras del cielo / *Sky Stones* (1970)

Geografía infructuosa / *Barren Terrain* (1972)

Incitación al Nixonicidio y alabanza de la revolución chilena / *A Call for
Nixonicide and Glory to the Chilean Revolution* (1973)

El mar y las campanas / *The Sea and the Bells* (1973)

La rosa separada / *The Separate Rose* (1973)

2000 / *2000* (1974)

Jardín de invierno / *Winter Garden* (1974)

El corazón amarillo / *The Yellow Heart* (1974)

Libro de las preguntas / *The Book of Riddles* (1974)

Elegía / *Elegy* (1974)

Defectos escogidos / *Selected Failings* (1974)

Confieso que he vivido: Memorias / *Memoirs* (1974; prose)

Earth Tones

1. The Erotic Poet

P oetry, Neruda once said, is "an exploration of being." And Neruda's erotic poetry is just that. It is a slow, sensuous, methodical exploration of the being of a woman, a woman who is both specifically individualized and, at the same time, a woman who stands for all women, a symbol of femininity, Woman as Earth Mother and Mother Nature. Pablo Neruda is a poet of eroticism and earthy sensuality, and his initial fame was for those qualities—the spectacular imagery of *Residence on Earth* and the epic grandeur of *Canto General* were still to come.

From the very beginning, Neruda's verses included love poetry. His first published book, *Crepusculario** (1923) contains numerous love poems and erotic poems, as does another book written during these years, but not published until 1933, *The Ardent Slingsman*. This early love poetry is not always entirely successful, however. *The Ardent Slingsman*, for instance, has been criticized, even by Neruda himself, as being too given to hyperbole in expressing youthful passion. It has equally been rejected as too strongly influenced by the Uruguayan poet Sabat Ercasty. These two works announce love, passion, eroticism as major themes in Neruda's poetry. But it was *Twenty Love Poems and a Song of Despair,** published in 1924 when the poet was only twenty years old, that established Neruda's reputation as a love poet. It is with this book that we shall begin discussing the trajectory of Neruda's erotic and love poetry, a trajectory that includes *Residence on Earth I** (1933), *Residence on Earth II** (1935), *Canto General** (1950), *The Captain's Verses* (1952), *The Grapes and the Wind** (1954), *All About Love* (1953), parts of *Extravagaria** (1958), *One Hundred Love Sonnets* (1959), and the first section of *Barcarole** (1967). It is a voyage with stops, changes, revisions, but also with a remarkable continuity throughout Neruda's long career. Neruda was first and last an erotic poet. His love poetry opened his career to public acclaim; some of his final verses, published posthumously, were love poetry. And ripely sensual poetry regularly appeared in most of the many volumes in between.

*This book is discussed in more than one chapter. See Contents page.

Twenty Love Poems and a Song of Despair

The publication of *Twenty Poems* was one of the most important single events in Neruda's literary career. It would be difficult to overstate the impact of the publication of this slender book; and yet the impact cannot be fully understood without reference to its historical context, the First World War and its aftermath. In principle, wars have little to do with literary taste. In practice, they change the balance between ruling groups and masses, between opposing confederations of countries, and the consequences soon become evident even in the small details of everyday life, which literature captures and brings to our consciousness.

World War I toppled two empires and several kingdoms; it created a host of *nouveaux riches* and a multitude of destitute masses. The old-fashioned European culture was being changed, fundamentally as well as superficially. Fashions in clothes mirrored the changes in values. A woman's body was no longer a precious object to be adorned and put on a pedestal; it was a free agent, now liberated from corsets and long skirts, closer to the elements of Nature, closer to the water, the air, more dynamic. The surface details of fashion and modes represented a response to a deeper upheaval. Cynicism was rampant. The war had been fought with exaggerated idealistic slogans, and in the period that followed the war all slogans and every kind of idealism were challenged. Trust in the prewar system of values and the artistic styles that had reflected those values was simply lost in the postwar period. The impact of the war on literary styles was bound to be anti-academic, anti-traditional, favorable to experimentation and criticism. Experiments in literature were to be both an escape from the past and a rejection of its rhetorical devices, producing writers like Joyce and Kafka, men formed in the pre-1914 cultural period, and yet representing a complete break with it.

In lyrical poetry the new literary trends of the postwar years were especially apparent. The year *Twenty Poems* was published, 1924, was, coincidentally, the date of André Breton's first Surrealist Manifesto. It was a year in which literature was undergoing drastic changes. The avant-garde poetry written in this period signaled, in many cases, a radical departure from poetic traditions going back to Petrarch and the Middle Ages. It was a necessary break. The fact that many of this century's greatest poems were written in this period, adopting the new styles, confirms the necessity of the revolution. Necessity for the poets. But not always for their readers. Many readers were not prepared for radical changes; they found themselves baffled by the new poetry, which offered a kaleidoscopic image of a world in turmoil. The reader suddenly was subjected to a torrent of metaphors, often not related to one single subject, or even to a single angle of vision, at times resembling more a panorama of Nature as seen through a multifaceted eye, the eye of an insect, than a landscape seen and ordered by the human eye. A reader whose taste had been shaped by Tennyson or by Verlaine could only feel puzzled, if not downright repelled, when faced with a poetic personage like T.S. Eliot's Prufrock, a character full of strange fears and indecisions, who does not know how to part his hair and hesitates to eat a peach. The reader was equally unused to the prosaic, even vulgar, language that characterized early Dada and surrealist poetry. In Spain and Latin America, the new wave of shocking poetry was christened with two new and startling names, *creacionismo* and *ultraismo*, movements whose poetry was a confusing juxtaposition of images, in which punctuation, rhythm, and rhyme were cast overboard.

Originality was a primary goal of the new poetic movements. Yet originality was often an obstacle to the development of empathy between reader and poet. Without this empathy, even first-rate poetry falls into the hands of a coterie, of small groups of devotees, elites, and professional critics. And sadly, this indeed was the fate of most twentieth-century avant-garde poetry. It lost its appeal for the average reader. One has only to compare the social role of the great Romantic poets with the relative obscurity of today's best contemporary poets to realize that on the level of communication, the consequence of the stylistic revolution of the twenties was, on the whole, negative. It was negative not in terms of aesthetics, since there is no doubt that much great poetry has been written in the last fifty years. Rather, it was negative in terms of the sociological relationship between the writer and his reader, and today, as a result, the novel and other genres have largely taken the place once held by poetry as an integral social form of communication and expression. It is against this background that Pablo Neruda's *Twenty Love Poems and a Song of Despair* becomes such an exceptional and unique work. *Twenty Poems* is one of the great success stories of the avant-garde era. Over the years it came to dominate the Latin American literary scene and beyond. It was translated into many languages, and it achieved what few books of poetry in any language have achieved in this century: by 1973, the last year for which statistics are available, more than two million copies of the Spanish text had been sold.

Literary Latin America faithfully followed the major European literary movements, acting, at the same time, as a sort of distorting echo chamber for them. The educated literary groups in Chile were certainly aware of the new movements. The Chilean poet Vicente

Huidobro, founder of *creacionismo,* was a full participant in the new avant-garde movements. Neruda's friend, the poet Alberto Rojas Giménez, was equally in tune with the new European movements— so much so, Emir Rodríguez Monegal notes, that Neruda referred to him as "an archangel of revolution in poetry," who "knew by heart all the isms."[1]

Neruda not only knew these advocates of the new movements, but he also read widely on his own. He was clearly aware of what was happening in European literature. Yet Neruda's reaction to the events and his creative interpretation of the new trends were less conditioned by the experiments of the literary elite than by the needs of the general Latin American public, which was quite out of touch with postwar trends in Europe. The great majority of Chilean readers were less disaffected from traditional values than were the poetry readers of western Europe. The war was sensed as a great and glorious adventure that had taken place in remote lands. No clear image of devastated cities and muddy trenches, of toppled empires and fleeing aristocracies had reached the consciousness of most Latin American readers. As a result, there was a basic differ-ence of attitudes; and the sentimental vision that had been char-acteristic of popular European culture during the *fin de siècle* years but was being rejected in the postwar era was still valid in the Latin America of the 1920s. The golden age of tango, with its melodrama-tic lyrics, was only then getting started in the River Plate region. A whole generation was still being reared on secondary school patriotic platitudes and the pieties of Edmondo de Amicis' *Cuore (A Young Boy's Heart)*. The postwar bitterness that produced works as diverse as Brecht's *Threepenny Opera,* Mayakovsky's political poems, and the great outflow of French surrealist poetry was simply not felt by the great majority of readers in Latin America. For most Chilean and other Latin American readers, the moment of change had not yet come.

Nor had it really come for Neruda. For Neruda in 1924, despite his knowledge of the new avant-garde wave and his association with some of its Latin American proponents, what was critical was not the introduction of new styles, but rather treating in a personal way the timeless subjects of love, sensuality, and loneliness. His links to the Romantic and symbolist traditions were still strong. He could reject the abundance of literary allusions, the exotic scenes of the Paris of the *belle époque,* of Venetian canals, of classical Greek forests, so char-acteristic of the poetry of Rubén Darío and his *modernista** followers,

---

modernismo: A movement in Spanish American poetry that began in the 1880s and was strongly influenced by French symbolism and Parnassianism. The poets who wrote in the style of this movement are called *modernistas.*

while still accepting as valid the rhythm and rhyme they had used. He sensed that the Latin American general reading public was not ready for a complete change in style. Neruda's merit was that he could restate the basic truths of adolescent love in a simple, dignified, yet extremely effective style. Modern trends would be accepted in the metaphors and in a number of adjectives, without changing the logical continuity of each poem or destroying its unity of feeling. Above all, *Twenty Poems* is poetry that comes from deeply felt personal emotions. "I have never uttered insincere words of love. I could not have written a single line that departed from the truth," Neruda would later comment.[2] And in *Residence on Earth,* he restates this attitude: "I talk about things that exist. May God/ preserve me from inventing anything while I sing!" ("Statute of Wine"). With *Twenty Poems,* Neruda had the good fortune that his truth was his readers' truth as well. He was able to state what his public felt. The Argentine writer Julio Cortázar has said that Neruda "suddenly gave us back what was ours, he tore us away from vague notions of European muses and mistresses to throw us into the arms of an immediate, tangible woman, and he taught us that a Latin American poet's love could happen *hic et nunc* and be written that way."[3] Neruda, in 1924, had found the right mixture of traditional and new styles, the right poetic voice for his time.

Woman in Nature, cosmic woman, woman surrounded by the forces and attributes of Nature—this is the subject from the very beginning. *Twenty Poems* was written in Santiago, but the inner world described in it is still the world of Neruda's memories, the woodlands of southern Chile where he was born and spent his childhood and adolescence. The extraordinary nature of this book lies in its rare blending of a literary message which is both high in poetic quality and, at the same time, precisely in tune with its public. Perhaps the best general analysis of the book's special blend has been provided by Neruda himself. In a letter to the newspaper *La Nación* in the year *Twenty Poems* was published, Neruda wrote: "Ten years of lonely work, ten years that make up exactly half my life, have brought to my writing different rhythms, opposing literary styles. By fusing all of this, by weaving different styles, without finding something everlasting—because I know nothing lasts forever—I have managed to create *Twenty Love Poems and a Song of Despair.* These poems are as divergent as the unstoppable flow of thought. They are both bitter and sweet. They are my work; their creation has not been devoid of suffering."[4]

Most books of erotic love poetry are short: *Twenty Poems* is no exception. The tension is too high, it cannot be sustained. There is an intense climax, then a descent into sorrow and loneliness. Since

Catullus the formula has been the same. A great love poem contains certain specific ingredients: passion, sensuality, grief, reproaches, then the final and incurable loneliness. Achieving the right mixture is, however, a delicate task. It calls for great care in the proportion of each ingredient. Too much passion, too much sensuality, and the poem tends to become sweet and cloying, like many eighteenth-century neoclassical love poems; excess in the opposite direction—Musset's unending bitterness provides a good example—is equally debilitating, as evidenced by much of the poetry written during the nineteenth-century Romantic period. *Twenty Poems* is perfectly balanced. Passion is to be found everywhere, especially in the initial poems; it is then slowly overcome by regret, melancholy, sadness. The book is like a prism decomposing light into its primary colors: the fiercest, gayest colors appear more vividly near the beginning of the book, the somber colors and blue tones are more noticeable toward the end, while a judicious intermingling makes for a continuous, homogeneous whole. Sensuality is ever-present. The poet explores the body of his beloved, he rejoices in every second of his slow carnal knowledge. Yet shadows are also present. They will lengthen, the future will become more uncertain as the poet's heart "closes like a nocturnal flower" (Poem 13). And the book finally ends with a "Song of Despair."

If *Twenty Poems* is a book of two moods, it is also a book of two women. "Poets like St. John of the Cross and Juan Ramón Jiménez," writes Robert Bly, "describe the single light shining at the center of all things. Neruda does not describe that light and perhaps he does not see it. He describes instead the dense planets orbiting around it"[5]

Twenty Poems orbits around two women of contrasting tone. "There are basically two love stories in this book," Neruda has explained, "the love that filled my adolescence in the provinces and the love I would later find in the labyrinth of Santiago. In *Twenty Poems* they alternate page by page. Sometimes one can hear a call from the wild woods, at other times a background of dark honey appears."[6] In his *Memoirs*, Neruda gives these two women the names Marisol and Marisombra, literally "Sea and Sun" and "Sea and Shadow."* They define the dual tone of the book. Marisol, the woman from the countryside, evoking images of serene contemplation ("Wide open pine groves, the noise of waves breaking ashore,/slow interplay of lights,

---

*Information has come to light that identifies Marisol as Albertina Rosa Azócar, a schoolmate of Neruda's. Neruda's 111 love letters to her, written between 1921 and 1931, have been published as *Cartas de amor de Pablo Neruda* [*Pablo Neruda's Love Letters*], edited by Sergio Fernández Larraín (Madrid: Rodas, 1974).

lonely bell,/the sunset falling into your eyes" Poem 3), inspires ten poems, while the city woman, Marisombra, inspires the other ten. It is to her that the last poem of the book, the "Song of Despair," is addressed: "You have swallowed everything, like a faraway horizon./Like the sea, like time itself. Everything in you was ship-wreck." The poet, momentarily, has found only defeat in love: "Abandoned like the wharfs at dawn./It is the time to depart, O abandoned man." Here there is no hope, only the memory of a lost love, around which the sounds of the sea and the crying seabirds create a counterpoint of muted sorrow: "The river ties to the sea her obstinate lament." The interplay between the country woman and the city woman, which is in essence the interplay between the images of light and life that Marisol inspires, and those of darkness, of dis-quieting yet powerful and alluring forces evoked by Marisombra, is what gives the book its texture and richness. It is what defines the dual tone of the book, a complexity of emotional movement that one single subject alone could not have sustained.

The two women and the two moods of *Twenty Poems* are captured in the starkest and simplest of language. Neruda here is perched on the edge of contemporary poetic styles. He has not yet taken the deep plunge that will bring him to *Residence on Earth*. Intuitively he knew that the break with tradition must proceed in stages. As his images grew bolder and his adjectives more unexpected, his vo-cabulary, in a counterbalance, underwent a process of simplification. Very few words in *Twenty Poems* would not be found on a list of the two thousand most frequently used words in the Spanish language. If we compare Neruda's vocabulary in *Twenty Poems* with that of Rubén Darío, Herrera y Reissig, and Leopoldo Lugones—three of the outstanding poets who wrote in the *modernista* style—the contrast is startling. Neruda rejects the refined, exotic, and artificial sensual-ity of these poets. There are no obscure cultural allusions to mythological beings in Neruda, no words describing rare precious stones or exotic plants. He uses everyday language. As a result, even when the reader does not fully understand a metaphor, he can sense its meaning because he feels himself to be on familiar ground. This cultivated vagueness in which meaning is intuitive rather than "un-derstood" becomes, in Neruda's hands, a powerful poetic device:

> Between the lips and the voice something goes on dying.
> Something with the wings of a bird, something made of anguish and
>   oblivion.
> The way nets cannot hold water.
>
>   [Poem 13]

Neruda does not explain what this "something" is. The reader has to
supply meaning. The specific "what" is not essential; a mood of mystery and of sadness has been created through this cultivated vagueness. Common images are combined with poetic force. Nets cannot
hold water; that is everyday common knowledge. But "water" here is
not everyday water. It is, rather, the pure and intense love that is
now waning. A poetic dimension has been added to a commonsense
approach to language, the line has been enriched by the preceding
lines, both nets and water—common language—becoming a symbol
for the inability to keep emotion at its peak. Only a contradictory
statement—in technical stylistic terms, an oxymoron—can define
Neruda's use of the common and the poetic in his complex literary
personality: Neruda was, from the beginning, and to the very end, a
"sophisticated peasant."

The image serves not only to describe Neruda's use of language in
Twenty Poems; it serves as well to define the single overwhelming
consistency of imagery throughout the book. Woman, in *Twenty
Poems,* is Nature. Neruda, the sophisticated literary man, forms the
metaphors; the rural countryside of the peasant provides the material. The basic images of *Twenty Poems* equate a woman's body, her
moods, her mind, with some aspect of the natural world. We are
given an erotic love poetry that is robust, concrete, down-to-earth, a
poetry worthy in many ways of classical times: "I love you and my joy
bites into your plum-like lips":

> Nimble and bronze-skinned girl, the sun that
>   makes fruits grow,
> the sun that swells the wheat, the sun that
>   plaits sea-weeds,
> this sun has built your merry body, your luminous
>   eyes,
> your mouth that curves with the water's smile.
>
> [Poem 19]

In the process of linking woman to Nature, Neruda's metaphors
"explode" the human body, subject it to a peculiar tension, extend it
to the four corners of the earth: "Leaning into the afternoons I cast
my mournful/nets towards your oceanic eyes." These are the first two
lines of Poem 7. They set the mood for the following lines. The
tension and the explosion take place at the beginning of the poem
and the image is a hidden one. It depends on the interplay between
"I cast my . . . nets" and the word "oceanic" used to describe the
woman's eyes. The unexpected adjective sets in motion several mental reflexes in the reader. A woman's eyes have previously been
compared to "dark pools," and now the image is opened up to em-

brace the ocean. What is typical of Neruda's imagery is its expan-
siveness. The concrete moment has been discarded; we have an expansion of both time and space. Neruda is not only looking at his
love "here and now"; rather, his relationship transcends any given
time, any concrete afternoon. The poet is depicted as projecting into
a strange time that is a summing-up of present and past
experiences—he is "leaning into the afternoons." He is trying to
catch something—Blake's "Infinity in a grain of sand"—here in the
oceanic, vast, infinite eyes of his beloved. The economy of
language—inconceivable in, say, Baudelaire or Mallarmé—used to
effect the expansion and transition is remarkable. If the eyes of the
woman the poet loves are "oceanic," the sad tone of the initial line is
justified. The ocean cannot be apprehended. The poet, facing
superhuman odds, risks being devoured in this ocean (The idea of a
shipwreck appears in several other poems of the book and closes the
last poem). "You keep only darkness," he reproaches his love, and, all
in the same poem, he sees the "coast of dread" emerge from her
figure. A lack of concrete definitions, of anchoring in specific detail,
adds to the mystery of Neruda's lines. What is this "coast of dread"?
Where is it to be found? Once again, the poet says nothing. In
Neruda, the mystery is full, and never gratuitous. It is a part of what
he finds hidden in the heart of things, in the heart of beings, at the
core of existential situations. Robert Bly has accurately described this
side of Neruda's imagination:

> We tend to associate the modern imagination with the jerky imagina-
> tion, which starts forward, stops, turns around, switches from subject
> to subject. In Neruda's poems, the imagination drives forward, join-
> ing the entire poem in a rising flow of imaginative energy. In the
> underworld of the consciousness, in the thickets where Freud, stand-
> ing a short distance off, pointed out incest bushes, murder trees,
> half-buried primitive altars, and unburied bodies, Neruda's imagina-
> tion moves with utter assurance, sweeping from one spot to another
> almost magically. . . . Moving under the earth, he knows everything
> from the bottom up (which is the right way to learn the nature of a
> thing) and therefore is never at a loss for its name. Compared to
> him, most American poets resemble blind men moving gingerly
> along the ground from tree to tree, from house to house, feeling
> each thing for a long time, and then calling out 'House!' when we
> already know it is a house.[7]

The same flowing imagination, displaying real knowledge and
profound contact with Nature, appears in Poems 1 and 3, where the
body of the woman loved is once more defined in terms of the earth:

Body of woman, white hills, white thighs,
you look like the world in your attitude of surrender.
My savage peasant's body burrows into you
and makes a child leap from the depths of the earth.

[Poem 1]

Ah vastness of pines, murmur of waves breaking on the shore
. . . .
In you the rivers sing and my soul flees in them

[Poem 3]

Woman is a "vastness of pines," the "murmur of waves breaking" over the beach; the poet sees the woman's body as the ears of wheat "tolling in the mouth of the wind." Each poem builds a bridge between a woman's body and the natural world that surrounds her. One expansive jump of the poetic imagination will fuse both. A woman's body is like the world of crops, woods, stars.

Once this jump has been taken and the fusion made, the reverse movement must take place. The natural world must be humanized. Birds, rain, stars, crops, hills must be shown to be only one aspect of a woman's existence. This happens in Poem 14 where the cosmic element once again enters: "Each day you play with the light of the universe." Here the bridge is built between the human body, the female body, and the universe; the woman's body is felt to be an important part of the cosmos. In this context the dramatic interplay between the poet and his love proceeds. It is no longer an individual relationship; it is fraught with philosophical consequences. The beloved is a being endowed with supernatural powers. The poet, who can contend with the powers of men, cannot fight a storm that whirls dark leaves around and turns loose all the boats that had been moored to the sky.

Neruda's relationship with Nature is essentially sexual. As the progression of Poem 14 suggests, however, it is not universally positive. Romantic poets had often described the dark side of Nature, a Nature hostile to man, a Nature that unleashed huge waves and hurricanes. We sense in many of Neruda's poems that Nature is as inimical to man today, in its potential, as it was in the past. For the still adolescent poet, the fear and awe of sex have not completely disappeared either. An early incident, narrated by Neruda in a talk, "Childhood and Poetry," and included in his *Memoirs,* confirms that for the young poet, the experience of Nature—extended in his poetry to be the experience with sexuality—can be as terrifying as it is exhilarating: "I wander off into the countryside and I walk, walk,

walk. I become lost on Ñielol Hill. I am alone, my pocket filled with beetles. In a box I carry a hairy spider I just caught. Overhead the sky can't be seen. The forest is always damp, my feet slip. Suddenly a bird cries out, it's the ghostly cry of the chucao bird. A chill of warning creeps upward from my feet. The copihues, crops of blood, can barely be made out. I am only a tiny creature under the giant ferns. A ringdove flies right past my mouth, with a snapping sound of wings. Higher up, other birds laugh harshly, mocking me. I have trouble finding my way back. It's late now."[8] Woman is Nature and part of Nature, but it is possible to get lost, both in Nature and in erotic love and thus in *Twenty Poems* we find that "The sad wind gallops, slaughtering butterflies" (Poem 14) and the poet faces "the sad rage, the screaming, the solitude of the sea" (Poem 17), and the immense night is "still more immense" without the woman he loves (Poem 20).

Love poetry, sensuous, erotic poetry is, for Neruda, a gift. Sex is a way of entering the world, of conquering and being conquered by the world. Neruda, both as an adolescent and as a mature man, often deals with sexuality as a path to knowledge. Yet, as these poems indicate, the precise place of sex and woman expressed through Nature in Neruda's poetry is far from clear. And disturbing sexual images appear once again in Poem 13:

> I have slowly marked the atlas of your body
> with crosses of fire.
> My mouth was a spider that explored, trying to hide.
> In you, behind you, timid, driven by thirst.

There is a succession of images, most of them new or unexpected: a woman's body is a map, an atlas, the mouth is a traveler and a spider, exploring the map and marking it with crosses of fire. The language in this poem has taken one or two steps toward the *"non sequitur,"* the oneiric visions of surrealism:

> I who lived in a harbor from which I loved you.
> The solitude pierced by dreams and by silence.
> Cornered up between the sea and sadness.
> Silent, delirious, between two motionless gondoliers.
>
> [Poem 13]

Neruda here creates a climate of anguish, strangeness, disquiet, similar to the tense climate of some of the expressionist films of the 1920s, such as "The Cabinet of Doctor Caligari." We are truly on the threshold of surrealism, German expressionism, Dada, cubism,

Spanish *creacionismo*. Two basic elements of the poem specifically
point to these movements and remind us particularly of Giorgio de
Chirico's canvasses, in which mannequins and infinity are constant
presences. The mannequins in Neruda's poem are the motionless
gondoliers. They are obviously out of place on the wharfs of Santiago. Why they are there does not matter. The poet is adding a
touch of mystery, here a modern manifestation of mystery in the
form of existential anguish. The gondoliers are troubling doubles of
man, troubling because they are both artificial and dead. The idea of
infinity present in the poem is equally troubling; it is irrational, it is
beyond our scope, it disturbs us because we cannot comprehend it,
we are incapable of translating it properly into our everyday experience. The presence of these forces in this poem is a clear sign of
Neruda's first flirtation with the new European trends. This is true
above all in the case of the references to infinity, for infinity is the
hallmark of the irrational forces of surrealism. As the French critic
Maurice Nadeau notes in his *Histoire du Surréalisme,* the poet Louis
Aragon would underscore the importance of infinity and the arrival
of irrational forces to surrealism, exuberantly proclaiming "Knock,
knock. Who's there? All right, let Infinity come in!"[9]

Infinity and the irrational forces it brings with it are already making their first tentative approach in *Twenty Poems.* The barrier between the normal commonsense approach to reality, so evident in
certain of the poems, and the higher reality of dreams and delirium
is already crumbling in some parts of this early book. Thus in Poem
7, the birds of night peck at the first stars, stars that flash like the
poet's soul when he is in love. And in Poem 13, Neruda writes:
"Sing, burn, flee, like a steeple in the hands of a madman." We are
reminded of Marc Chagall's canvasses, where the lovers leap over
roofs and steeples and float in space near the moon and the stars.
These, like many of the other images in *Twenty Poems,* reach the bor-
derline of irrationality. They can be sinister or gentle. The possibility
of dark tones is there. But Neruda does not yet exploit the strong
negative potential of infinity, madness, and irrational images. Rather
than shrinking back in the face of infinity, he causes the force to lose
some of its awesome elements by bringing it closer to everyday life,
reducing it to human scale. This is the case in Poem 7, for example,
where a vast starry night suggestive of infinity is brought close to
earth and to human dimensions: "The night gallops on its shadowy
mare/shedding blue ears of wheat over the land." The poem thus
becomes what it was intended by Neruda to be, an attempt to find
the place of man and woman, together, in the cosmos. Dark forces,
nocturnal birds, black stars may surround and attack them. The net
of passion may not catch the river of time. Yet for a moment the

lovers are at the very center of the universe. Infinity, in its dark, surrealist tones, is knocking at Neruda's door; in this early book, however, the poet does not fully open the latch.

Twenty Poems is a book of dualities. It is a great work of exuberant erotic love poetry, filled with light; it is a book born of, and ending in, despair, an exaltation of woman and sexuality, an awe of the darker hues and labyrinths of Nature seen from the city. It was written out of grief and loneliness, yet Neruda asserts "It is a book I love because, in spite of its acute melancholy, the joyfulness of being alive is present in it."[10] But *Twenty Poems*, it must be remembered, is only a shortened title. The full title is *Twenty Love Poems and a Song of Despair.* This powerful, slender book of poems ends on the dark notes, with the song of shipwreck and desolation. And it is that final dissonant chord that carries us over the years to another important work, *Residence on Earth.*

Residence on Earth, *I* and *II*

There is always interaction between what a writer publishes and the way he or she lives. Literature is nurtured in experience. But in turn, literature—the written and published book—can influence the way the writer lives. Neruda's life was deeply influenced by the success of his erotic poetry. After the publication of *Twenty Poems,* and the initial enthusiastic reaction of both critics and masses of readers, Neruda was confirmed as a poet. And he would live like a poet. He had come to Santiago from his remote provincial Temuco to become a secondary school teacher of the French language and literature. That was now too bourgeois. Neruda forgot that many of the finest symbolist poets, his idols at the time, had lived sedentary lives and had traveled seldom, although some—like Baudelaire and Mallarmé—were capable of writing the most convincing "invitations to travel." Neruda adopted a more romantic notion. In a self-portrait, he expresses clearly his attitude toward lifestyles: "In my day-to-day life, I am a tranquil man, the enemy of laws, leaders, and established institutions. I find the middle class odious, and I like the lives of people who are restless and unsatisfied, whether they are artists or criminals."[11] With this attitude, and perhaps with Rimbaud and Jules Verne, rather than Baudelaire and Mallarmé, as his models, Neruda felt the need to break away from the city that had witnessed his unhappy love affair. He was seriously depressed. He felt compelled to burn bridges and to escape, first to a Chilean island, and then to a faraway land.

In Chile, as in all Latin American countries, literature is never too far removed from political spheres of influence. Neruda was penniless and distraught, yet his literary success had given him a certain amount of prestige. Pedro Prado, a fellow writer who had recommended *Twenty Poems* to the Nascimiento publishing house, now recommended Neruda to the Ministry of Foreign Affairs. On April 11, 1927, Neruda was appointed Honorary Consul of Chile in Rangoon. In Neruda's first prose memoirs, published by the Brazilian journal *O Cruzeiro Internacional,* the poet recalls his appointment: "In the Secretary's office we found a great earth globe. My friend Bianchi and I looked there in order to find the city of Rangoon. There was a deep fissure in the Asia section. We found Rangoon half hidden in it. Yet when I met my friends a few hours later and they wanted to congratulate me on my appointment, I had forgotten completely the name of the city I had been appointed to, and I had to explain amidst much laughter, that I had been appointed Consul in the Fabulous Orient—and that the city I was travelling to was to be found in a hole in the map."[12]

The Orient did not turn out to be so fabulous for the young Neruda. Since Neruda seldom allowed much time to pass between emotion and the transformation of that emotion into literary texts, the disillusion is clearly revealed in *Residence on Earth (1925–1931).* Published in 1933, it was the first of three volumes to carry the title *Residence on Earth.* The book was begun in Chile, but many of its darkest poems spring from Neruda's experience in the Orient, his first five months in Rangoon, months during which his salary was not paid and he was penniless in the midst of a vast alien city, where he knew practically no one, and where—despite his earlier translations of several English poems—his spoken English was inadequate. The overcrowded, hot, poverty-ridden cities of the Orient produced in Neruda a more acute depression, which was pushing him toward alcoholism. Later he would write of Ceylon: "I learned what true loneliness was, in those days and years in Wellawatte. . . . Solitude, in this case, was not a formula for building up a writing mood but something as hard as a prison wall; you could smash your head against the wall and nobody came, no matter how you screamed or wept."[13]

Loneliness was for Neruda the basic reality, although he was not often physically alone. The young Neruda was extremely handsome; he was very tall and slender, with an eagle face, intense eyes, wavy brown hair, a sensuous mouth, a long straight nose, delicate hands and feet, and a deep gravel voice. His friend Alvaro Hinojosa, the Chilean poet, had accompanied Neruda on the long trip to Rangoon; by the time Hinojosa returned to Chile, he left Neruda with a dog, a mongoose, and Josie Bliss, a Burmese girl who had fallen in love with the poet. Of her, Neruda writes: "I lost my heart to a native girl. In the street she dressed like an Englishwoman and used the name Josie Bliss, but in the privacy of her home, which I soon shared, she shed those clothes and that name to wear her dazzling sarong and her secret Burmese name." "Sweet" and "passionate" are the adjectives Neruda most frequently uses when talking about Josie Bliss. But it is clear that she was much more in love with Neruda than he with her. And her love was accompanied by fierce jealousy. Sometimes at night, a light would wake Neruda up, "a ghost moving on the other side of the mosquito net . . . .It was she, walking around and around my bed for hours at a time, without quite making up her mind to kill me. When you die, she used to say to me, my fears will end."[14] The next day she would carry out mysterious rituals to make him remain faithful. Neruda soon found Josie's jealousy as oppressive as the sweltering city itself.

When Neruda was suddenly appointed Consul in Ceylon, he wrote a hasty letter saying good-bye to Josie and took the first available ship for Colombo. Yet the same mixture of joy and despair so present in *Twenty Poem* still lingers in Neruda here. His sense of freedom at escape is immediately tempered by a sense of loss and regret. And still on board ship, he begins to long for Josie and to mourn her absence:

> I would gladly exchange this wind of the giant sea for your breathing
> heard during long nights without mixture of oblivion,
> cleaving to the air like a whip to a horse's skin.
> And for hearing you urinating, in the dark, at the other end of the
>   house,
> spilling a slender, shimmering, silvery, persistent honey
>   ["Widower's Tango"]

He also evokes "the swallow that asleep and flying inhabits your eyes," and, as a contrast, "the hound of fury that you shelter in your heart." In this poem we can see a few changes in Neruda's style. His love poetry follows the same evolution of style that can be found in the rest of his work; it becomes less traditional, less constrained by rhythm and rhyme. It is by turns "modern provincial" and "neoclassical" with modern touches. Here, we find an abundance of surrealist imagery, of contradictory, illogical language—the swallow in her eyes is both sleeping and active—and the presence of realistic, naturalistic details—a woman urinating—together with broken visions, bits and pieces of everyday reality, the jetsam and flotsam of his experience. It is a novel approach to erotic love poetry, one in which we can detect the influence not only of surrealism, but also of cubism and of the montages and collages of Dada and the type of cinema represented by Eisenstein's *Potemkin.*

Neruda stayed in the Orient for five years. During that time he made an ill-fated marriage to a Dutch woman, María Antonieta Hagenaar. He was poorly paid and constantly worried about money, and his general depression continued. It was not to end even when he returned to Chile in 1932. During these troubled years he wrote some of the most original and impressive poems of our time. Even when dealing with sexuality, however, few of the great poems in *Residence on Earth* can be called erotic; fewer still can be defined as love poems. A concrete example, the poem "Sexual Water," from the second volume of *Residence on Earth (1931–1935),* explains this judgment:

> And then I hear this sound:
> a red noise of bones,
> a sticking together of the flesh
> and legs yellow as ears of wheat meeting.
> I listen among the explosion of the kisses,
> I listen, shaken between breathing and sobs.

Here the sexual elements are like frenzied flashes of biological activity, much like the world of amoebas separating, dividing, and subdividing in a science film, much like the diagrams and color plates of a book for first-year medical students. The sexual elements are totally anti-erotic and menacing in their biological, naked presence:

> This is all like a hurricane of gelatin,
> like a waterfall of sperm and sea anemones.
> I see a cloudy rainbow hurrying.
> I see its water moving across my bones.

We touch the border of pornography here, and even of sadism: there is sexual activity and arousal in the absence of personal feelings, there is no I, no Thou. In Neruda's *Residence on Earth,* only material things exist, overwhelming the reader. The organizing eye of the poet, of the beholder, is strangely undefined. Even when the poet includes himself in the total picture, his presence is a passive one. Things happen to him, without his being able to direct the flow of experience in any meaningful sense. As for sadism and masochism, they are implied by this process of "objectification," in which the sexual partner is an object, is acted upon, as well as by the constant allusions to blood, to breaking limbs, to dangling internal organs. The poet's workshop has become a butcher's chopping block. As John Felstiner puts it: "'Agua Sexual' ["Sexual Water"] exudes a sordid, disrupted atmosphere dripping with tears, teeth, marmalade, blood, oil and sweat, without any human connection. Pastoral romance is gone." This is true of other poems of *Residence* as well. Neruda has read *The Waste Land,* and as Felstiner notes, "Gentleman Alone," like 'Sexual Water,' is a graphic nightmare vision of sexuality, exhibiting a totally urban scene of delirious widows, youthful tomcats, homosexuals, masturbating priests, incestuous cousins, adulterers. No pollen or plump doves here."[15]

Sexuality in *Residence on Earth* brings forth the dark Neruda. It is represented as a depersonalized force of Nature, a monstrous, mechanical, irresistible force without constructive aim, and thus the constant mention of nonreproductive sexual acts, acts enveloped by bourgeois taboos. Neruda's memoirs confirm this negative vision. The poet, isolated, anguished, was forced into himself, his love affairs were usually brief, either sordid or based on misunderstanding. In the poems cruelty and excess are often associated with the women he loves, and with the brillant, contorted images he chooses to express that love.

Erotic poetry demands a dialogue. *Residence on Earth* contains some of Neruda's most extraordinary and powerful poetry; it does not often contain, however, this dialogue. Neruda was simply not in the mental condition for real erotic or love poetry at this point in his life. He was, in *Residence on Earth I* and *II,* too much preoccupied with his own being, with survival, with maintaining sanity in an oppressive world portrayed in images of chaos, claustrophobia, and suffocating decay. And in *The Third Residence** (1947), having broken out of his own anguished solitude, the poet's passion becomes directed towards a political goal, the defense of the Spanish Republican cause.

Rarely in the brilliant volumes of *Residence on Earth* does Neruda return to the personal love poetry of *Twenty Poems.* Often the closest he comes to real love poetry in these works is when he directs his attention toward Nature, rather than toward an individualized woman. Neruda is a poet of matter, of the everyday material world that surrounds us, that can be touched and smelled. Frequently his poems to matter are also sexual poems, erotic love poetry to Nature. "Entrance into Wood," from the book *Three Material Songs,* first published in 1935 and later incorporated into *Residence II,* is such a poem. Wood is matter; it stands for the whole of Nature, of living

---

*See chapter 3.

Nature; it stands for the roots of trees, of plants, for the source of life. It is, in Neruda's unconscious mind, identified with the image of woman as Mother, and through this association with woman in a plane of sexuality as well. Wood under the rain is perhaps the basic image, the primordial image in Neruda's total poetic vision:

> Almost without my reason, with my fingers,
> with slow waters slowly flooded
>
> . . . .
> I fall into the shadows, in the middle
> of broken-down objects,
> and I stare at spiders, and graze forests
> of unfinished secret wood,
> and pass between damp uprooted fibers
> into the living core of substance and silence
>
> . . . .
> It is I with laments without origin,
> unnourished, wakeful, alone,
> entering darkening corridors,
> arriving at your mysterious matter.

John Felstiner has commented that "Entrance into Wood" reads

> like a hallucinated uterine descent in the bole of a tree. . . . *Materia misteriosa* . . . the phrase compels you to hear a pun on *mater misteriosa*. Both *materia* and *madera*, the poem's key words, are cognate etymologically with *madre*, "mother." Though *madre* does not appear here, it lies at the heart of the utterance. In the middle of 'Pores, veins, circles of sweetness,/weight, silent temperature,' the poet feels 'leaves dying inwards,/green matter amassed/to your abandoned stillness.' He implores the wood to clasp him to his life and death, and at the poem's climax—that is the word for it—he cries to this *madera-madre*, 'let us make fire, and silence, and sound,/and burn, and be still, and bells.' It is an entrance into wood to regenerate himself at the source.[16]

It is a return to a woman's womb. It is a song of sexuality and of love, with wood, the *materia mater* of the universe, occupying the place held by personalized and individualized women in *Twenty Poems*, the sentiment and impulses echoing Neruda's earlier work, the object toward which they are directed signaling the evolution of his poetic vision.

Canto General

The same repetition of sentiment and imagery, with the object having changed, is present in Neruda's great epic poem, *Canto Gen-*

eral, which sings of the American continent from its very inception to its present contemporary political reality. During the 1930s and 1940s Neruda became politicized in an active participatory fashion. In 1934 he arrived in Barcelona, where he had been appointed Consul. In Spain he was reunited with his friend the great poet Federico García Lorca, whom he had first met in Buenos Aires. In 1935 Neruda was transferred from Barcelona to the consulate in Madrid. He was in Madrid when the Spanish Civil War broke out in 1936 and García Lorca was tragically murdered by the Phalangist forces.

Neruda took an active part in the defense of the Spanish Republic, losing his position as consul in the process. From Paris he edited, beginning in 1936, the journal *Poets of the World Defend the Spanish People,* and in 1937 he and the Peruvian poet César Vallejo founded The Hispano-American Aid Group for Spain. In the same year, Neruda published some of his most powerful poetry, *Spain in My Heart,* * depicting the blood running through the streets of Spain as the Fascist forces of Francisco Franco moved against the elected government of the Spanish Republic.

The 1940s confirmed Neruda's already clear movement toward active political participation. In 1945, after his return to Chile, he was elected Senator from the provinces of Tarapaca and Antofagasta, and in the same year, he officially joined the Chilean Communist Party. Three years later, after a speech on the Senate floor entitled "I Accuse," Neruda was ousted from the Senate and forced to hide out in Chile, and finally to flee the country. In 1949, he made his first voyage to the Soviet Union and was awarded the homage of the Union of Soviet Writers. The following year, his enormous epic work, *Canto General,* written during this decade of political activism and exile, was published.

Canto General is clearly epic poetry and political poetry, and is discussed as such in chapter 3 in the context of Neruda's public poetry. It is the product of Neruda's unwavering commitment to social justice for Latin America and his option for Marxist ideology as the way to achieve the liberation of the continent. Yet Neruda's open political activity during these years and the epic nature of the masterpiece that emerged from it have tended to obscure the fact that much of *Canto General* is, in reality, love poetry. Much of what is best in this epic work, as in his earlier poetry to matter, is indisputably poetry sustained and informed by amorous and sexual imagery.

As with "Entrance into Wood," the love poetry in the *Canto* is of a different nature from that in *Twenty Poems.* The object of Neruda's love here is no longer Marisol or Marisombra. Nor is it the Josie Bliss

*See chapter 3.

of *Residence on Earth* nor generic maternal wood in any sort of universal form. It is America. *Canto General* is, in many of its most significant aspects, a love song to the New World, this particular Mother Earth from which Neruda's native land springs. "Love America" is the first poem of *Canto General* and the attitude its title reveals is the recurring note throughout the long, progressive history of the epic *Canto*.

Perhaps one of the finest poems of the *Canto* is the one which comes closest to real love poetry. It is "Heights of Macchu Picchu," written in 1945. Inspired by a visit to the ancient Indian sanctuary and fortress hidden in the heights of the Peruvian Andes, the poem falls into two principal parts. The first part, as interpreted by John Felstiner, narrates Neruda's search through a grey, everyday world for the "flower offering its seed," the "nuptial land" or true origin of modern Latin American society. The second part narrates the poet's encounter and dialogue with Machu Picchu, the ancient city. Phallic symbols abound: in Canto One, the poet is "a buried tower sinking its spiral," "like a sword sheathed in meteors/I sank a turbulent and gentle hand/into the genital quick of the earth." Before finding the sacred Inca city, he prefigures it as grain, a "tenderness in the germinal husks," with their "yellow tale of small swollen breasts." "On reaching Macchu Picchu, he names it 'cradle of lightning and man,' 'mother of stone,' and summons an *amor americano* to come up with him and 'kiss the secret stones.' At this point Neruda turns on the empty, ruined city and demands that it give back the people who worked and died there. The mother of stone is now the devouring mother, the earth that brings forth but also reclaims her children. 'Macchu Picchu,' he cries, 'Give me back the slave you buried!' 'Ancient America, sunken bride . . . were you hoarding hunger at your core, in the bitter gut?'"[17]

As the sketch of this poem suggests, it would be a mistake to think of Neruda's epic poetry as a departure from the early erotic love poetry. On the contrary, Neruda never stops associating the earth and woman. If in *Twenty Poems* the woman loved was seen in terms of the earth he loved, here the America that is his passion, is seen in terms of woman, it is the beloved. And thus the poem "The Coastal Night":

> Tell me who you are . . .
> . . . .
> mistress of all the metals, rose
> of the depths, rose moistened
> by the storms of naked love.

Neruda is not addressing a woman in this poem. He is talking to the night that falls on the coast of the Pacific. His field of vision is broader now. His verses are no longer orbiting around a single woman, but around an entire continent, which is his ultimate love. Neruda has not stopped being an erotic poet in order to become a politically committed epic poet. *Canto General* is a fusion, for Neruda's interpretation of Latin America's political history is a sexual one: the continent, seen both as sexual and maternal woman, was raped, not once but twice, first by the conquistadors, later by the United Fruit Company and the other multinational corporations based in the United States. *Canto General* is an exaltation of the pure, virginal woman, America, a poem of love to her; it is equally and powerfully a bitter accusation of her violators, both ancient and modern. It is, perhaps, Neruda's greatest work of love.

The Later Works

In the early 1950s, his *Canto General* completed, Neruda turned again to personalized, individualized, and non-epic poetry. The transition is evident in *The Grapes and the Wind,* which was begun in 1952 on a political note but came to include love poems as the presence of Neruda's new love, Matilde Urrutia, grew in his life. Among the many books written during the fifties and the early sixties, five in particular include important love poems and mark a significant development of this theme in Neruda's poetry: *The Captain's Verses* (1952); *All About Love* (1953), an anthology of Neruda's old love poems to which several new ones had been added; a number of poems from *Extravagaria* (1958); *One Hundred Love Sonnets* (1959); and the first section of *Barcarole* (1967).

Leaving aside Josie Bliss and Neruda's early loves, there had to this point been three "publicly declared" women in the poet's life: María Antonieta Hagenaar, whom he married in Batavia in 1930 and divorced six years later; Delia del Carril, an Argentine he met in Spain in 1934; and Matilde Urrutia, perhaps the great love of Neruda's life, his faithful companion, and finally his legal wife until the poet's death in 1973. Matilde inspired all the love poems of this period and these books trace the growth of Neruda's love for her.

The approaches to love poetry in the largely political *The Grapes and the Wind* are subtle, and it is really with *The Captain's Verses* that Neruda signals a deliberate return to a volume of clear love poetry. The book was originally published in a private, anonymous edition because Neruda, still linked with Delia del Carril, wanted to avoid hurting her by signing these poems filled with passion for Matilde. In *The Captain's Verses* we see clearly the influence of Neruda's political commitment, and if the return to personalized love recalls *Twenty Poems*, the object of his love is no longer presented in the same way. In *Twenty Poems*, Neruda yearned for the sensuous woman tied to the southern forests of Chile; now Neruda's love has become a part of the poet's social and political struggle:

> Get up with me.
>
> No one would want
> more than I to stay
> resting on the pillow where your eyelids
> want to close off the world for me.
> There I too would want
> to let my blood sleep
> surrounded by your sweetness.
>
> But, get up,
> you, get up,
> but get up with me
> and together we'll go out
> to fight body to body
> against the spiderwebs of evil,
> against the system that distributes hunger,
> against the organization of misery.

["The Banner"]

In *Twenty Poems* Neruda sought refuge in woman as a way of blocking out the anguishes of his existence; now he refuses to take refuge in a love that would cut him off from the outside world. Neruda now has a purpose larger than his own personal fulfillment and his love is incorporated into that purpose; the woman and the cause are fused in his passion and he wants the former to be his partner in fighting for the latter. We are a long way from the hermetic world of erotic love and idyllic Nature imagery that so characterized *Twenty Poems* when Neruda writes in "The Soldier's Love":

> In full war life carried you
> to be a soldier's love.
>
> With your pitiful silk dress,
> your fingernails of false stone,
> it was your fate to walk through the fire.
>
> Come here, my vagabond,
> come to drink on my breast
> red dew.

You didn't want to know where you were walking,
you were a friend of dancing,
you didn't have a cause nor a country.

And now walking at my side
you see that life goes with me
and that behind is death.

Now you can no longer dance
with your silk suit in a salon.
You're going to ruin your shoes,
but you're going to grow in the march.

You have to walk over thorns
leaving little drops of blood.

Kiss me again, beloved.

Clean that rifle, comrade.

["The Soldier's Love"]

We perceive in these verses a new strength and confidence in the poet. In his earlier love poetry, he sought to transform himself through the love of a woman. In *The Captain's Verses*, the poet has become the teacher; it is he who will transform his beloved and mold her into the combatant he needs to march along beside him. This is a book of fully realized love; there is eroticism and passion, without any of the anguish present in parts of *Twenty Poems*. It is also a book in which the poet's concept of love has been expanded and the lovers are no longer isolated as they were in earlier books; they are now together, and part of a cause. In *The Captain's Verses*, Neruda has found the woman for his life, and he is both loving her and training her for the life he wants to share with her. In the books of love poetry that follow, political overtones recede and a more purely erotic tone comes forth again; but the poet's love for the woman he has chosen never falters, and this sense of fulfillment permeates all the volumes of his mature love poetry.

By the time of the publication of *Extravagaria* (1958), Neruda's personal situation had changed. He was openly living with Matilde and could declare that she was the inspiration of his verses and could sign his name to them. During this period he wrote some of his finest love poems. The troubled young man has become a man sure of himself, and the militant has found freedom to return to a very private concept of love. We can see this by looking at one single example from *Extravagaria*, the poem "I Ask for Silence." In it, the poet's confidence and peace are revealed through a stark simplicity:

> I am going to close my eyes.
>
> And I only want five things,
> five favorite roots.
>
> One is endless love.
>
> The second is to see autumn.
> I cannot live without leaves
> flying and returning to earth.

The third thing he wishes for is "grave winter,/ the rain I loved," and the fourth is summer, "round like a watermelon." The fifth:

> The fifth is your eyes,
> Matilde, my beloved,
> I don't want to sleep without your eyes,
> I don't want to exist without you looking at me:
> I'll trade all of Spring
> for your glance.

This is a simple, direct approach to love poetry, its lines almost those of a popular song (several of Neruda's love poems have in fact provided the lyrics for songs in Latin America). The poet concludes this part of the poem with the same elegant simplicity:

> Friends, this is all I want.
> It is almost nothing—it is almost all.

Unlike *The Captain's Verses,* many of the poems written afterwards remind us of a more polished version of *Twenty Poems.* This is especially true of *One Hundred Love Sonnets* (1959). Sonnet xii from this book, for instance, begins very much like Poem 1 of *Twenty Poems* ("Body of woman, white hills . . ."):

> Complete woman, carnal apple, incandescent moon
> . . . .
> What primitive night do man's senses touch?

The setting for this and other poems in this volume is Isla Negra, the poet's huge frame house facing the ocean, the beach, the dunes, the sky lit by the Southern Cross. The book is divided into four sections, "Morning," "Noon," "Afternoon," and "Night." The characters are only two, the poet and Matilde. Everything else is landscape, the salty smell of the sea, the wind over the dunes, the poet's memories.

The sonnet has been associated with the expression of feelings of love ever since the late Middle Ages and Petrarch. Short, intense, concentrated, a sonnet can be crystalline and gemlike. Neruda had on the whole eschewed rhyme and formal poetry during most of his mature period, and the sonnets represent a clear departure. Neruda condenses his thoughts and his images: "Love is a voyage with water and stars," "love is a fight between two lightning flashes," he writes, for example, in Sonnet xII. Kiss after kiss, he travels through Matilde's "little infinitude," her shores and rivers, her tiny villages, her genital fire, a fire that races through the slender pathways of her blood, that surges from below as a nocturnal carnation between being and nothingness, leaving only a glow in the dark.

Paradoxes abound in this love poetry, since, almost like a mystic, Neruda finds the intensity of his experience too enormous to describe, and the only means of translation are, at times, in terms of the impossible, through startling juxtapositions of words and images that have no logical connection. At other times, however, the opposite occurs. Sometimes it is the simple and direct image, often equally unexpected, that best conveys the poet's meaning: "Naked, you are as simple as one of your hands," he declares in Sonnet xxvII.

It is not Matilde alone that Neruda sings in these sonnets, but also the things that make up his life with her. Their beautiful new house on the shore is thus also part of the poet's consciousness. In Sonnet xxxII he describes the house on a sunlit day, its inhabitants half asleep, with no clear purpose on their minds, "without a goal, adrift like a poor boat/ between the skylines of order and dream." The spacious house, the beach with its white sand and pebbles, the night pregnant with stars, are only extensions of the physical and emotional bodies of the poet and his beloved. The world is there only to make their embrace possible, and thus Neruda's love for Matilde fuses in these sonnets with his other loves: the sea and the wind, the delicate hues of the wild flowers that grow near the dunes, animals, and inanimate objects. *One Hundred Love Sonnets* was written as an affirmation of the poet's love: "I have told [Matilde] all I feel. Perhaps these poems make clear how much she means to me. . . . Everything I write and everything I have is dedicated to her. It's not much, but it makes her happy."[18]

This is the difference between the mature poetry and Neruda's earlier love poetry: in *Twenty Poems* love is described as both a joyous and a menaced experience. There is often a shadow in the background, an indefinable threat, a Romantic foreboding. In the mature Neruda there is only one tone. The images at times are more startling and disjointed, but it is pure joy, sensuality, fusion, ecstasy, triumph that inspire *One Hundred Love Sonnets*. Love, Neruda seems to now say, can be explored in its delights without the fear of suddenly losing it.

A similar optimism permeates the love poems of *Barcarole* (1967). The title refers to the songs the gondoliers used to sing while steering lovers around the canals of Venice. While the book contains much more than just love poetry, the first section of *Barcarole* is Neruda as love poet in full form, and once again all the poems are addressed to Matilde. The poems were in fact originally entitled "Loves: Matilde" and were first published in Neruda's autobiographical *Notes from Isla Negra** in 1964. With the publication of *Barcarole*, however, they were taken out of the earlier work and made the opening section of this one.

Complex phrases, highly musical, using an abundance of adjectives and images all searching for the same reality, glancing at the world from different angles—this is the love poetry of *Barcarole*. We see the lovers coming close, together, separating, yearning for each other, always seemingly surrounded by the water and cradled by the incessant movement of a ship: "Lover, I love you and you love me and I love you," the opening verse of this book reads:

> Short are the days, the months, the rain, the trains:
> Tall are the houses, the trees, and we are taller still:
> through the sand approaches the foam that wants to kiss you:
> and in my heart grow your roots of wheat.
>
> ["I Love You"]

These lines are typical of the love poems in this work, exuberant, joyful, optimistic. The lovers soar, they are taller than the houses and the trees. Once more the images of Nature abound: the sea foam wants to kiss Neruda's beloved, her roots of wheat grow in the poet's heart. The imagery is like that in *Twenty Poems;* the woman is always linked with Nature. Yet now the verses are long, at times narrative, and the tone is one of mature love found. Even when the poet speaks of doubtful moments in his love, there is a new confidence in the durability of that love. The verbs are in the past tense, and the perspective is that of someone who knows that the difficult moment has been overcome:

> It was the offense, perhaps, of hidden love and perhaps the
>   uncertainty, the vacillating pain,
> fearing the wound that would pierce not only your skin
>   and mine

*See chapter 4.

but would also come to place a hoarse tear on the
   eyelids of she who loved me,
what is certain is that we didn't yet have sky or shade or
   the branch of a red plum tree with fruit and dew
and only the rage of alleys that have no doors
   entered and departed from my soul
without knowing where to go or how to return without killing or
   dying.

                                  ["The Wounds"]

Neruda is speaking here of the time when he was still with Delia del Carril, but had already fallen in love with Matilde Urrutia. Thus the references to "hidden love," to the wounds that would touch not only the lovers but also "she who loved me." The poet recalls feeling caught in the entrapment of a dead end, an alley with no exit, the impossibility of his situation—leaving Delia would be "killing" and staying separated from Matilde would be "dying." There is sadness in this poem, but the anguish here, unlike that in *Twenty Poems,* is not intensely lived in the present. The poet acknowledges it himself when he says "we didn't yet have sky or shade . . . ." He is recounting to us the beauty of what they now have, while remembering a time before they were able to have it, and the anguish is but a memory.

We have noted that in *Barcarole* Neruda continues to apply Nature as the only metaphor worthy of describing his beloved. The extent to which this is true becomes evident in the poem entitled "You Among Those Who Seemed Foreign." Here, Matilde, "clear and obscure . . . dark and golden" is compared to wheat, to wine, to the bread of Neruda's homeland. The Nature images continue to flow forth in the following verses:

you made your hips sing and you resembled, ancient and earthly
   Araucanian,
the pure amphora which burned with the wine in that region
and you were known to the illustrious oil that filled the casseroles
and ten poppies growing in the pollen of ancient ploughs
recognized you and rocked and swayed
dancing in your murmurous feet.

The description of Matilde is remarkably similar in its essential elements to the description of the poet's fictionalized mother in *Canto General,* a woman also associated with the earth, with Nature, with the Indian heritage. Neruda, who was sixty-three years old when this poem first appeared, was still dealing in erotic terms with the fused images of matter, in the form of the earth, and mother, both now incarnated in the woman he loves. Likewise, as in *Twenty Poems* and the *Canto,* what the poet seeks from his love is above all a return, a return that we can consider a return to the earth of his homeland or, symbolically, to the womb of his dead mother buried in that land. To Matilde, in closing this poem, he says: "in your mouth you gave me the shadow and music of the terrestrial clay."

It becomes clear that what constitutes fulfillment for the poet in *Barcarole,* and in the other love poems written from the late 1950s on, has not changed from Neruda's earliest love poetry: fulfillment is still linked to his roots. What has changed is that now he has found those roots in the person of Matilde Urrutia. Neruda states it precisely in his *Memoirs:* "Now I'm watching her sink her tiny shoes into the mud in the garden, and then she also sinks her tiny hands as deep as the plant has gone down. From the earth—with her feet and hands and eyes and voice—she brought me all the roots, all the flowers, all the sweet-smelling fruits of happiness."[19]

Synopsis

Neruda's career as a poet began with love poetry and ended with love poetry. One of his very last works, written only days before his death, is "The End," a love poem to Matilde.* There were, of course, changes; there were deviations during the period of *Residence on Earth,* for example; there were turns and innovations during the period of political and epic poetry that began in the late thirties and culminated in 1950 with *Canto General,* but there was also a remarkable continuity. Erotic poetry and love poetry were for Neruda an important, essential part of his poetic life.

Pablo Neruda was one of the most prolific poets of our century. To trace the development of even one aspect of his poetic world is far from easy. Yet in the case of his erotic poetry and his love poetry the outline of that development is clear enough. The early Neruda, from his first published book, *Crepusculario,* and then especially in *Twenty Poems,* is a sensualist and a materialist in his approach to love and woman. As Luis Monguió puts it,

> What was new even in his first published book of verse . . . was the result of Neruda's senses being opened to the reality of the world around him, not an idealized world as his immediate predecessors the Modernists would have seen it, but to the world of surrounding

*See p. 172.

experience that had been imposed upon his sensibilities by the powerful nature of his early habitat. He intuitively captures it through all
his senses in perpetual vigil—sight, touch, hearing, smell. It is a
world of lilacs and brambles, moss and swamps; it is a world of iron,
ashes, bridges (let us not forget that his father was a railroad man
and that the world of the railroad was one of Neruda's first perceptions); above all it is a frontier-world of earth just opened up by the
plow, of furrows, trees, cut lumber, water, ever-present water; and
summing this sensorial world up, sensual love, physical love, expressed in images drawn from nature.[20]

A few touches of *modernismo* in *Crepusculario,* for instance, "A New
Sonnet for Helen" and the "Pelleas and Melisande" suite of poems,
do not change the accuracy of Monguió's remarks. Moreover, his
remarks serve equally well for *Twenty Poems,* where Neruda inten-
sifies the complete fusion between woman and Nature. Joy and despair, like Marisol and Marisombra, mingle and alternate in this
book, but whatever the emotion of the moment, the poet is constant
in his identification of woman with Nature, in his use of Nature imagery to describe woman, and in his conception of woman as a vehicle for a return to Nature. In these richly sensual poems, the style is
still on the whole "modern Romantic" with symbolist overtones and
the first few hints of the newer, more disturbing poetic styles. Yet
they remain "constructive" poems, in that they are organized around
experiences in which real human beings, Neruda himself and the
women he loved, provide a stabilizing platform upon which each
poem is built.

The period following *Twenty Poems* is largely a time of disintegration. The intensely passionate *The Ardent Slingsman* was published in
1933, but it had been written much earlier, at about the same time as
Twenty Poems. From 1925 to 1935 Neruda wrote very little erotic
poetry. Flashes of it appear now and then, for instance, in the poems
to Josie Bliss. Neruda was still a poet of sensuality, but in *Residence on
Earth* the sexual imagery is primarily used in a graphic, blatantly
anti-erotic form designed to show glimpses of a world in decay,
without aim, collapsing of its own stench and rot.

The poetry written in the late thirties and the forties is more loving and more erotic than that of the period 1925–35. In *Canto General* the poet is, as in his youth, drunk with Nature, earth, mankind,
but his passion is directed toward a continent, toward America,
rather than toward any individual woman in it. This is a period of
great love poetry, but one in which the primary thrust is political and
epic, the erotic and love images defining the tone, sketching the
hues, not providing the central impulse. Sexual elements abound in

Canto General, but they are ancillary—they help build the whole poem; they are not the whole poem.

The Grapes and the Wind and *The Captain's Verses,* while very different from each other, form a sort of bridge between this period of public poetry and the books that were published from the late 1950s on. In both books, Neruda continues his passionate commitment to a political cause, but now a specific woman also reappears in his verses in the person of Matilde Urrutia. The first of these books is still primarily political, and the perspective is that of a travel chronicle, with Neruda's growing love for Matilde entering almost in secondary fashion. In *The Captain's Verses,* Neruda returns to the clear intention of writing love poetry; the proportions are inverted and here the political militancy defines the poet's notion of what he wants from love and from his lover, but it is Matilde and his love for her that are consciously the center of the work. The image of his lover as a "fellow combatant" in this book is markedly different from the images in Neruda's earlier love poetry or those in his later books; yet this work is linked to both the earlier and the later works by the fact that once again a particular woman is at the core of Neruda's verses.

After this period of transition where, in differing degrees, political commitment and love poetry are fused, Neruda returned in the late fifties and the sixties to a tone of clear, romantic intimacy. His love for Matilde was by then an established, publicly acknowledged fact, and with the love poetry in *Extravagaria, One Hundred Love Sonnets,* and *Barcarole,* Neruda built a new vision of love. He wrote some of his finest poetry in this period. The style has become more supple, at times full of surprises and unexpected adjectives. Yet it is still recognizably linked to the style of the young Neruda, which has been subjected to a few limbering exercises. The late poetry openly expresses joy, confidence, and optimism, with none of the anguish of the early verse. It is also monogamous—there are no distressing alternations like those between Marisol and Marisombra in *Twenty Poems.* The differences are notable. But a continuity still remains, in the Nature imagery, always the essence of Neruda's eroticism, and in the presence of the poet's romantic self and the self of the woman he loves, providing again a solid ground.

We are faced, in other words, with one essential personality, a single literary *persona,* expressing his vision through varied techniques which respond to the different changes in his life, the accumulation of experience in living and in writing, yet echoing with constancy the same fundamental voice. Neruda's constancy has not always been recognized as clearly as his diversity. On the contrary, as Luis Monguió notes, "it has become somewhat fashionable among

certain critics to say that the poetry of Pablo Neruda is really consti-
tuted by two poetries: one, that of his early or hermetic period, up to
the 1930's, and the other, that of his social or political period, since
his conversion to Marxist militancy; and to speak of them as if they
were two separate water-tight compartments. . . . In general, such a
dichotomic view has resulted in high praise of one of the so-called
poetries and the undervaluing of the other, depending on the taste,
or the prejudices, of each reader, based more often than not on
extra-literary rather than literary concepts."[21] This tendency to divide Neruda's poetry into two irreconcilable halves and to analyze
them separately is critical drawing and quartering, a form of aesthetic sadism. There is a continuity in Neruda's work, and part of
that continuity is to be found in the constant return to erotic love
poetry, a return that encompasses different and evolving visions, but
which remains at its core constant, earthy, sensual, material.

The literary importance of Neruda's erotic and love poetry has at
times been overshadowed by the dazzling imagery of *Residence on
Earth* and the epic political vision in *Canto General*. For the average
Latin American reader, however, the reader that Neruda the committed Marxist most wanted to reach, there is no aspect of Neruda's
work more significant than his love poetry. Neruda's erotic love
poetry includes several indisputably brilliant masterpieces. His love
poetry is a thread running through his different works, his success-
ive styles and periods, unifying his whole poetic world and giving
clues to the relationships between the parts, the books, and the total
opus. Neruda's erotic poetry and his love poetry, and perhaps this is
one of their single greatest contributions, have served to acclimatize
an entire generation of readers to modern avant-garde styles. Many
of Neruda's readers acquired their taste for innovative language and
bold images from his early works, and they did not desert the poet
even when he beckoned them into the subterranean labyrinths of
Residence on Earth. Neruda gradually introduced the new styles, and
his readers were still with him when, in the forties, fifties, and sixties,
his style underwent a process of simplification and emerged as
clearly understandable to the average reader while never sacrificing
the use of bold, striking images.

Neruda in this subtle role of leader and teacher helped create a
large public of readers of poetry in Latin America. He gave poetry
social meaning, a place in the everyday reality of third-world nations.
Poets like Nicanor Parra and Octavio Paz, who never followed in
Neruda's footsteps either ideologically or stylistically, are, in part, the
beneficiaries of Neruda's influence, for he left them a willing public,
a public open to contemporary poetry as an integral part of contem-

porary reality. To acclimatize the reader to modern poetry, especially in the context of the hard realities of the Latin American nations, was an urgent task, one that Neruda carried out with rare success, largely through his erotic poetry and his love poetry, in all its varied and developing, yet constant, manifestations.

Neruda before Neruda, two years old

. . . and sometimes we remember
the child that lived with us,
there is something we ask him—that he remember us,
perhaps,
or know, at least, we were he and we now talk
with his tongue;
but there from the wreckage of his past
he looks at us and does not recognize us.

"Little Boy Lost," *Notes from Isla Negra*

The railroad company supplied my father with a cape of thick gray felt for his outdoor work, but he never wore it. I made it a feature of the poet. Three or four other poets also started wearing similar capes, and these constantly changed hands. This garment used to stir up the fury of good people and of others who were not so good ... These underworld characters— dancers and troublemakers— sniggered at our capes and our way of life. We poets fought back hard.

—*Memoirs*
(trans. Hardie St. Martin)

Neruda in 1921

Neruda in 1924

I love what I do not have. You are so far away.
My weariness wrestles with the slow twilights.
But night comes and starts to sing to me.

"Here I love you,"
Twenty Love Poems and a Song of Despair

I hear your wings and your slow flight,
and the flood of all who have died assails me,
blind doves dripping water:
                    you come flying.

"Alberto Rojas Jiménez Comes Flying," *Residence II*

Daydreaming is also a way of life. Neruda in
Ceylon in 1929

... Federico, do you remember
under the ground,
do you remember my house with balconies where
the light of June drowned the splendor of flowers in your teeth?

"A Few Things Explained," *Residence III*

Federico García Lorca and Neruda in Madrid shortly before the start of the Spanish Civil War in 1936 and Lorca's assassination by the Fascists

... they looked at the poet who was crossing volcanoes, waters, towns and plains ...

"Revolutions," III: The cruel fire, *Notes from Isla Negra*

1948. Neruda fleeing Chile on horseback

As a child in Temuco he had often admired a stuffed horse
in the window of a saddle shop. After a fire closed down the
shop, the poet bought the horse and made a place for it in
his Valparaíso home.

Neruda poses before Ben Belitt's English version (in poster form) of "Ode to the Lemon" at the University of Chile on the occasion of the poet's sixtieth birthday.

Lover, I love you and you love me.

Barcarole, 1967

In 1966 Neruda made his first visit to the United States, at the invitation of the P.E.N. Club. This picture was taken during a cocktail party offered in his honor by Grove Press. Ben Belitt is on Neruda's left. Photo by Fred Stein.

Neruda and Matilde at the Grove Press cocktail party. Photo by Fred Stein.

Neruda and a young visitor, walking on the
beach at Isla Negra

I want to tell you: The Ocean knows the answers—life in its treasure chest
is vast as the sands, numberless, flawless.
Between grapes of blood Time has polished
the flint in the petal, the glow inside the jellyfish.
Branches are threshed from the coral trees,
tumbling down out of a cornucopia of infinite mother-of-pearl.

"The Enigmas," *Canto General*

Watching the sea send me its greetings
or its insistence on turbulence,
I let my gaze flee on the shore
I fixed my eyes on the waves.
From this apprenticeship
I keep a bitter green smell.
It lives on in the whole of my motion.

"The Same," *World's End*, 1969

Neruda and Miguel Angel Asturias, another
Latin American Nobel Prize winner, looking
at the Pacific from the shore of Isla Negra

Neruda shopping in a flea market. This and the following
two photographs are from the film *I Am Pablo Neruda,* dis-
tributed by Films for the Humanities, Princeton, N.J.

Each week I become restless.
I look for aluminum clouds,
tormented screws,
bars of silent nickel,
unneeded doorknockers.
Hardware stores
know about my enthusiasm . . .

"A Citizen," *Extravagaria*

Neruda and Matilde create hats out of seaweed at Isla Negra.

Neruda, Matilde, and their dog at Isla Negra.

2. The Nature Poet

Nature does not refer solely or even primarily to descriptions of sunsets or rolling hills or ferocious storms. Rather, it encompasses every aspect of external reality. It refers to matter and to the material world which exists outside of man. Seen in this way, wood, dust, animals, vegetation, buildings, and urban landscapes are themes for Nature poetry, themes as valid as the more traditional contemplations of the sea or of uninhabited terrains. Poetry of Nature is, in short, material poetry. It is poetry dealing with the matter that constitutes man's external environment. As such, it includes not only the comforting and reassuring aspects of Nature, but also its menacing aspects, whether they be found in forceful drives of the elements or in threatening perceptions of urban squalor.

The Nature poet is essentially an observer of his surroundings. He is a man who describes what is to be seen or found at the other end of his senses. His musings, his stream of consciousness, his observations are inspired and directed by what he sees in the world outside his own psyche; and, at the same time this inner world of his own being is often defined in terms of the external world of Nature and matter, it is formed and expressed through images and metaphors taken, in a process of synthesis, from the poet's external environment. In this fashion, a modern poet of Nature is as well a poet of the human condition, in essence, an existential poet.

Like his love poetry, Neruda's Nature poetry runs throughout his entire career. It is constantly present in *Crepusculario* (1923), its stress is nostalgic in *Twenty Poems** (1924), surrealistic and sometimes horrific in *Venture of the Infinite Man* (1926) and the first volumes of *Residence on Earth** (1933, 1935), political, epic and mythical in *Canto General** (1950), joyous and appreciative in the *Elemental Odes* (1954), *More Elemental Odes* (1956), *The Third Book of Odes* (1957) and *Voyages and Homecomings* (1959), and alternately imaginative and contemplative in *The Stones of Chile* (1961), *The Art of Birds* (1966), *A House by the*

*This book is discussed in more than one chapter. See Contents page.

*Shore** (1966), and *Sky Stones* (1970). Nature poetry is also ever-present in the personal poetry that Neruda produced during the 1960s, and in the eight posthumous books. In short, whatever the major thrust of his poetry, be it love or epic or personal, Nature is present. Here we will limit ourselves to looking at some of the books where Nature plays a dominant role. As the poet's external environment changes, his relationship to Nature and his expression of it also change. It is the entire trajectory, and no one work alone, that brings forth his perception of the world of matter and defines Neruda as a poet of Nature.

Crepusculario and *Twenty Poems*

Neruda's first published collection of poems, *Crepusculario*, contains a number of poems that are clearly Nature poems, somewhat in the tradition of the best such poems written by the symbolists Verlaine and Rodenbach. This is particularly true of the section entitled "The Sunsets of Maruri." Maruri is the name of the street in Santiago where the young Neruda wrote many of his early poems. In an unpublished lecture, Neruda describes his life there: "On Maruri Street, in house number 513, I finished my first book; I would write two, three, four, up to five poems each day. In the afternoons, at the sunset, in front of my balcony a daily spectacle unfolded that nothing would make me miss. There was a sunset with a gigantic piling up of colors, with big chunks of light, with immense orange and scarlet fans. The central chapter of my first book bears the title 'The Sunsets of Maruri.' Nobody has ever asked me what Maruri meant. Perhaps some people are aware that this humble street is daily visited by the most extraordinary sunsets."[1]

The hallmark of the poems from "The Sunsets of Maruri" is their simplicity. They are short poems; the words themselves are often short, and the number of images is restricted to the minimum needed to create a mood. The poem "The Afternoon Over the Roofs" illustrates this. Carrying an epigraph—much like the musical notation "pianissimo"—which reads "Very slowly," the poem signals the slow, soft voice needed to allow the stark simplicity of the words to make its full impact:

> The afternoon
> falls

---

*This book is discussed in more than one chapter. See Contents page.

and falls
over the roofs . . .
Who gave it for this journey
the wings of a bird?

The words are short (the Spanish word for afternoon is *tarde*) because the subject itself is airy, light; it is air itself, in the winged
shape of a sunset, and the vague sadness that the approach of night
creates in the poet:

And this silence that fills out
  everything,
from what remote stars
  did it come?

And Neruda ends:

And why has this mist
  —trembling feather—
this kiss of sensitive rain

fallen in silence
  and forever
over my life?

The subject is air, space, sunset, approaching darkness, and their
impact on the observer, the poet. Yet the emphasis is clear: Nature
itself is the central focus of the poem. We see this again in "Southern
Beach":

The gnashing teeth of the sea bite
the open pulp of the shore
where the green water breaks like star dust
against the silent earth.

Silent sky and distance.
The horizon, like an arm,
encircles the flaming fruit
of the sun falling in the dusk.

The poet is not using Nature here primarily as a means of expression for his own inner feelings of nostalgia, absence, and longing.
Even later in the poem, when the speaker asks the wind to carry him
off, the central subject matter remains Nature, its power, its force,
the wonders it can perform that are denied to men.

To appreciate the dominant place that Nature—as Nature—is

given in these poems, it is worth looking for a moment at the role
that Nature plays in *Twenty Love Poems,* published only one year after
Crepusculario.

> You have deep eyes where night flails.
> Cool flower-arms and a lap of rose.

> [Poem 8]

These lines confirm what has already been said about this volume: it
is generally love poetry whose amorous and erotic images are drawn
from Nature. As Luis Monguió writes of *Twenty Poems,* "Nothing is
more material than the love of *Twenty Poems,* nothing closer to veg-
etative, germinative, animal nature, a nature onto which the poet is
entwined like a vine, planted like wheat or a pine tree. In these
poems, Neruda equates earth and woman, the seasons of love and
the seasons of the year; he makes one the cycle of planting, ger-
minating, fructifying, passing and beginning again in the vegetable,
the animal, and the human realms."[2] This materialistic intuition appears in *Twenty Poems* in a climate dominated still by symbolism, with
its indirect, refined, bloodless interpretation of the external world:

> Body of woman, white hills, white thighs,
> you look like the world in your attitude of surrender.
> My savage peasant's body burrows into you
> and makes a child leap from the depths of the earth.

> [Poem 1]

In this first poem of *Twenty Poems* it is impossible to separate what is a
vision of woman and what is a panorama of Nature. This is the
difference from the other poems we have cited from *Crepusculario.*
The opening poem of *Twenty Poems* is clearly erotic; it is not a Nature
poem. The focus is not the material landscape—the white hills—but
rather the body of a woman.

Nature in *Twenty Poems* is more often an expression of a special
form of nostalgia than it is a value in and of itself. Neruda has spent
another year in the city, cut off from the world of matter he knew as
a child in southern Chile, cut off as well from the consolation of a
family environment. The Freudian implications of the relationship
materia-mater clearly operate throughout *Twenty Poems.* Through woman, Neruda is seeking a return to the primary matter of his childhood; he finds through the positive aspects of love a return to that
world of Nature, and he describes the woman in terms of that world.
His use of material images in these poems cannot be divorced from a
sense of longing and nostalgia, a longing he finds, for the moment at

least, fulfilled in the body of the woman he loves. In contrast with some of the poems in *Crepusculario,* there is nowhere in *Twenty Poems* an observation of Nature as such; rather we find a nostalgia for the sense of security and warmth associated with both the material world of Neruda's childhood and maternal solace, both recovered in Santiago through the present love, or the recollection of past love, of a woman.

The titles of these two works reveal the difference in their orientation: titles like *Crepusculario,* "The Sunsets of Maruri," "The Afternoon Over the Roofs," and "Southern Beach," announce that the external natural element is the primary subject of the poems, just as the title *Twenty Love Poems* expressly denotes love as the central focus. The difference between the two volumes is clear and significant. Nature is a constant presence in both, but its role is not the same. In *Twenty Poems* and also in some of the poems of *Crepusculario* — "Kissing Woman," for instance — Nature plays an expressive role, it reflects the poet's internal nostalgia and moments of return; in many other poems from *Crepusculario,* however, we find something totally absent from the later book: Nature poetry in the strictest sense of the genre, the poet observing and feeling the natural world as the central focus of his work. From the beginning of Neruda's published books, his sensitivity to Nature is evident; the poetic use of that sensitivity is varied, ranging from the dominant vision of the work itself in parts of *Crepusculario,* to a medium for lyrical expression one year later in *Twenty Poems.*

Venture of the Infinite Man and *Residence on Earth*

The description of specific poems in *Crepusculario* as Nature poems is easy to accept. The subject matter of these poems, as in traditional Nature poems, is a sunset or other manifestation of what can clearly be defined as the natural world. This is not the case in the two works which follow, *Venture of the Infinite Man* and *Residence on Earth.* Here the overriding vision is one of chaos. Yet the poet remains a Nature poet. He is still, as in the earlier work, an observer of the external world that surrounds him, he is still sensitive to its impact on his own being, and he is still expressing that inner world in images taken from the external one. What has changed is not the poet's stance vis-à-vis the world of Nature. It is Nature, defined as the external environment, which has changed and those changes are reflected in a newly pessimistic poetic *persona* and a newly adopted poetic style composed of incomplete, disconnected sentences and startling, irrational images.

In discussing Neruda's love poetry, it was clear even from the beginning that Nature was perceived by the young poet in both its positive and negative forms. There was an enormous appreciation of and love for the natural world; there were also moments of terror and unsettling images. In these later works, the dual vision remains, but the proportion is radically altered. Positive visions of the external environment do exist in both *Venture* and *Residence,* but they are largely confined to the realm of nostalgia. Nature is comforting when the Nature described is not that actually in front of the poet, when the Nature delineated is a recollection of, once again, the double soothing essence of maternal and material elements. It is the Nature that is currently absent from the poet's external world which continues the positive, longing aspects present in the earlier work. But the overwhelming proportion of the poems deal with what is present: a negative vision of Nature, a horrific world of chaos, destruction, and decomposition. Neruda, in his early works, searched for the maternal essence in wood; here even the wood is at times rotting, in unending decay. Nature—now encompassing urban terrains—is part of a nightmarish vision in which overwhelming forces of infinity and destruction have been unleashed.

A great poem or book of poems can never be fully explained by reference, no matter how detailed, to the cultural milieu in which it was written. It is equally possible to err in the opposite direction, however. To describe Neruda's work from this period with words like "chaos" and "nightmare," to attribute the differences from his earlier work to purely personal emotional factors, and to ignore the possible influence of surrealism would be such an error. It would be, moreover, an error that Neruda himself has encouraged. Neruda rejected surrealism, and in later years he deliberately erased all traces of his connection with the movement. Neruda's rejection of surrealism was largely political, since the Breton group soon evolved toward an independent, semi-anarchistic position, later affiliated with Trotskyism. It was also political in that Neruda's Communism later led him to reject all hermetic forms of "elitist" poetry. Neruda's attacks on surrealism were fierce and vitriolic; he described its adherents as "a tiny, perverse clan, a small sect of destroyers of culture, of feelings, of sex, and of action."[3] Neruda's words, for all their passion and sincerity, cannot, however, deny the poetic reality of the work he wrote during this period. Whatever Neruda's animosity toward the surrealists, the fact remains that many of the essential feelings and stylistic manifestations in *Venture* and *Residence* coincide powerfully with those of the surrealist movement, and must be looked at within that context.

The early surrealists, led by Breton, saw that the complexity of Nature is such that our normal senses are insufficient to encompass it in its entirety. Reason, common sense, clear vision, Euclidean geometry put us in contact with one or several aspects of reality, but not with the whole. How would the world look if we could see ultraviolet and infrared rays, X-rays, cosmic rays bombarding space, electric tensions inside objects, and, at the same time, huge galaxies tumbling through space? Surrealism was launched to free the human spirit from what Breton called "the reign of logic." It advocated a style that excluded logical connections, punctuation, images that could be clearly visualized or rationally comprehended. It favored the world of dreams, or more accurately of nightmares, and the description of frantic movement: "Beauty shall be convulsive — or it shall not be," Breton had decreed.[4]

Surrealism's moving images, blurred by speed, were in part a legacy of an older literary movement, futurism, which had announced the cult of the machine, of energy, of violence, and which has often been judged, not without grounds, as a forerunner of Fascism. Surrealism also capitalized on the earlier avant-garde movement of Dada, the delirious hallucinations of Arthur Rimbaud, the works of writers such as Guillaume Apollinaire, Pierre Reverdy, Alfred Jarry, and, in the Hispanic world, the Chilean poet Vicente Huidobro. There is much in Breton's early writings that would have attracted the Neruda of the 1920s. Neruda was decidedly anti-bourgeois, anti-government, anti-tradition. Surrealism advocated the overthrowing of all shackles imposed by the state, the family, the church, and old-fashioned morality. Surrealism was, in essence, a new and radical humanism, its goals were startling and subversive. It is ironic that although Neruda attacked surrealism during the thirties and forties, some of Neruda's poetry of the twenties and thirties played a paramount role in sensitizing Latin American and Spanish readers to the values of surrealist styles in literature.

There is no evidence that Neruda had read Breton's manifesto when, in 1924 and 1925, he was writing *Venture of the Infinite Man*. Yet this work was Neruda's first attempt at a style that is clearly akin to surrealism. Of this work, Neruda has written: "It is the least read and least analyzed of all the books I have written, and yet it is one of the most important ones in my career. It is entirely different from my other books. It has seldom been reprinted."[5] The reasons for this neglect are not hard to fathom. For the average Latin American reader of poetry, the book was ahead of its time. Later, when surrealist styles became accepted, the book was overshadowed by the more dramatic and pathetic texts of *Residence on Earth*. Moreover, *Venture* is a single long poem, and it is difficult to isolate any one fragment for inclusion in an anthology. As a result, American and English collections of Neruda's poetry usually omit it. Yet its importance as a literary "exercise" cannot be overlooked. Without it, the style of *Residence* would have been vastly different.

Nature in *Venture* is the vast, infinite space of the cosmos. The final lines of *Twenty Poems*' "Song of Despair" announced a departure. *Venture* is a tale of a voyage through a night made "out of emeralds and windmills": "embarked on this nocturnal voyage/a twenty-year-old man grasps a frantic bridle." Here Neruda breaks away from every traditional norm. No more fixed rhythm, no more rhyme, and still more significant, no more punctuation, no capitals, no commas, no periods. In his first Surrealist Manifesto Breton had recommended that the writer seek a state of passivity, of maximum openness or receptivity; that he write fast and without any preconceived subject; and that, to preserve the fluidity of subconscious thought, punctuation be eliminated. Neruda's brilliant artistry precludes considering his work as "automatic writing" in any literal sense, yet the coincidence between Breton's thought and the form in *Venture* is notable. The lack of punctuation in *Venture* effectively and literally destroys the boundaries between one line and the next, one image and the image that follows. Hence a sensation of hurtling through space, of falling into night and infinity:

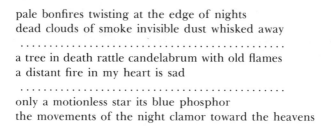

> pale bonfires twisting at the edge of nights
> dead clouds of smoke invisible dust whisked away
> . . . .
> a tree in death rattle candelabrum with old flames
> a distant fire in my heart is sad
> . . . .
> only a motionless star its blue phosphor
> the movements of the night clamor toward the heavens

What is conspicuously lacking is a fixed point of view: the "I" of the poet-observer dissolves into dust, into space. The main themes seem to be three: night, infinity, and sadness. Time and again they emerge through a jungle of disjointed metaphors. Yet the general impression is more one of astonishment than of melancholy. There is no time to be sad; things happen too fast, the poem is stylistically organized around active verbs expressing quick movement—"I jump," "it twirls," "they fall." The beholder is never fully identified nor is his sadness fully motivated. We are traveling through a never-never land, normal time and space have been replaced by the time and space of dreams. As Jaime Alazraki, one of the few critics who have dealt with *Venture,* observes, "dream time is independent from telluric time and from time as normally accepted by man. Dream time is chaotic and cannot be measured, normal time is ruled by a pitiless king, the clock. Thus when the poet wants to talk about normal time he writes specifically: 'dawn came however to the clocks on earth.' Time in [*Venture*] is closer to the chaotic time of dreams: in it 'weeks are closed down,' there is 'a deep clock' in which 'night isolates hours,' becomes 'a square of time perfectly motionless.'"[6]

If we were to describe *Venture* in strictly contemporary terms we might say that reading this book is like viewing the more spectacular sequences of the film *2001: A Space Odyssey.* It is a travel without beginning and without end, while "in the midst of great bursts of flame the mill turns around/and the night hours fall from the sky like bats." The poet advances through mist and shadows like a phantom vessel, and the final lines mark not an end but perhaps a new beginning: "sitting on this last shadow or still afterwards/yet still afterwards." An open beginning, an open end, a world of chaos in between. The poem was a project, an effort to reach the impossible. Breaking with all the poetic conventions of the past, Neruda plunges into the murky waters of the subconscious. A juxtaposition of unconnected images and things, belonging mainly to the natural world, creates by its tension a feeling of unending expansion. In what can almost be seen as the dream of a delirious sleepwalking astronomer, Neruda achieves the difficult goal of depicting man as an anguished traveler through infinite time and space. Any reader of science fiction, any aficionado of astronomy, can only applaud. Not even Vicente Huidobro, the great Chilean poet, was able to accomplish such a perfect nightmarish atmosphere in his best long poem, *Altazor, or a Parachute Jump.* Neruda's book is more spacious, more desolate, more charged with energy than Huidobro's poem, which, published five years after *Venture,* may well owe something to Neruda's vision.

Most Nature poets have known for a long time that the cosmos is made up basically of empty spaces and flashes of quick-moving particles charged with energy. Reality is often too harsh and unpalatable to be tamed into a poem. Yet Neruda's poem comes extraordinarily close to reproducing this reality. *Venture* was a first attempt to take into account the chaotic aspects of Nature; the second, fully successful attempt would bring Neruda, as a man, to a state of serious depression and, as a poet, to the masterpiece that ushers in his maturity, *Residence on Earth.*

The *Residence on Earth* cycle comprises three volumes: *Residence I,* covering the period from 1925–31, *Residence II,* covering the period from 1931–35, and *The Third Residence,* dated 1935–45. While the three volumes have often been published together under the general title *Residence on Earth,* it is primarily the first two volumes which are associated with the acute depression that the poet suffered both in Chile and during, and immediately after, his devastating stay in the Orient—in Rangoon, Colombo, Singapore, and Batavia; and it is the vision of the external world in these two volumes that we will consider here.*

When Neruda finally left the Orient in 1932, he returned to Chile, then served briefly in a consular post in Buenos Aires and soon was sent to Spain. In Barcelona, and especially in Madrid, Neruda was in contact with the new generation of Spanish poets, among them, Rafael Alberti, with whom he had corresponded from Asia and who had applauded the first unpublished texts of *Residence I,* and Federico García Lorca. This new generation of poets was engaged in an undeclared but bitter war with the well-established poets of the older generation. Above all, the battle was directed at Juan Ramón Jiménez, the leading advocate of "pure poetry." Jiménez regarded with suspicion the "wild experiments" of the young poets, a suspicion evident in his reference to Neruda as "a great bad poet."[7] The battle between the two groups was sometimes vicious, a fact made ironic today by the international acclaim given to the leaders of both groups—Jiménez received the Nobel Prize for Literature in 1956, Neruda received it in 1971.

To strike a blow against the old-fashioned aestheticism of Juan Ramón Jiménez and, at the same time, to explain the principles of his own style, Neruda issued in 1935 a theoretical consideration that can be considered a poetics for his *Residence on Earth.* This manifesto was published in the first issue of a new magazine, *Caballo Verde para la Poesía* [*Green Horse for Poetry*], which Neruda had helped launch. It was—in direct opposition to Jiménez's "pure poetry"—entitled "Towards an Impure Poetry":

> It is useful, at certain hours of the day and night, to look closely at
> the world of objects at rest: wheels that have crossed long, dusty

---

*In this chapter these two volumes will be referred to simply as the *Residence* poems, and quotations from them will be presented according to thematic, rather than chronological, considerations. We hope the reader will keep in mind, however, that the two works were written at different times and the largely common vision of the external world that unites them in no way negates the individual traits of each volume or the differences in other respects between the two. *The Third Residence,* containing Neruda's declaration of political solidarity with the Spanish cause, touches on subjects more related to Neruda's public poetry and is discussed in chapter 3.

spaces with their huge vegetal and mineral burdens, bags of coal from the coal bins, barrels, baskets, handles and hafts in a carpenter's tool chest. From them flow the contacts of man with the earth, like an object lesson for all troubled lyricists. The used surfaces of things, the wear that hands have given to things, the air, tragic at times, pathetic at others, of such things—all lend a curious attractiveness to reality that we should not underestimate.

This is the first paragraph of the manifesto. It may seem somewhat puzzling as a manifesto dealing with lyrical poetry. It is not puzzling, however, if we recognize that Neruda is speaking here as a true poet of Nature, for whom nothing that exists in the external world is worthless. Vincent Van Gogh, who also was an observer of Nature, and who painted with loving care an old chair, a pair of worn-out shoes, would have immediately understood the meaning of this opening paragraph. Neruda goes on in his manifesto to state that in these objects one sees "the confused impurity of human beings, the massing of things, the use and disuse of substances, footprints and fingerprints, the constant presence of the human engulfing all things, inside and out." The proper study of mankind is Man, according to Pope; for Neruda, the world of Nature cannot exclude the man-made world nor the "unaesthetic" facets of everyday life, since they too form part of the external environment in which man resides:

> Let that be the poetry we search for: worn with the rubbing of our hands, as if by acids, steeped in sweat and in smoke, smelling of lilies and urine, spattered by the trades that we live by, inside law or beyond the law.

> A poetry impure as the clothes we wear, as our own bodies, soup-stained, soiled with our shameful behavior, with wrinkles, vigils and dreams, observations and prophecies, declarations of love and of hatred, beasts, convulsions, idylls, political beliefs, denials and doubts, affirmations and taxes.

His credo is nothing if not modern. Marinetti and Mayakovsky would certainly have approved. Yet the manifesto ends on a curious Romantic note:

> . . . melancholy, old mawkishness, perfect impure fruits of a fabulous realm lost to memory, must not be forgotten as they have been by the frantic bookworms: moonlight, the swan at dusk, all hackneyed endearments: surely these are the poet's concerns, essential and absolute. For those who shun 'bad taste' will fall flat on the ice.[8]

This is the aesthetic credo of *Residence on Earth,* one of the peaks of Neruda's poetic career. Nature poetry, since its subject is the external world at large, is also existentialist poetry in its anguish for the human condition; and in its stylistic manifestations—unexpected combinations of words and images, the flow of obscure voices from the subconscious mind—it is surrealist poetry. The positioning of the poet vis-à-vis his subject is similar to that in Neruda's early poems, the external world of Nature he contemplates fusing with the poet's own inner world. The mood—loneliness, sadness, isolation—also repeats moments of the early works. The difference in degree, however, is radical. What in *Twenty Poems* was at times a melancholy longing or despair reaches the boiling point here. The poet's emotions explode like bombs, like depth charges inside a murky sea. We observe the world from inside it, we see its underbelly, the huge shape of a monster. And we are alone like "one single bottle moving across the seas" ("A Melancholy Family," *Residence II*).

The poet finds no middle ground between his self, corroded by anguish and self-doubt, and a complex, alien, external world that invades him with a chaotic presence. The result is exhaustion: "It so happens I'm tired of being a man," he writes in "Walking Around." The poem is a descriptive study of Nature—here the world of man-made matter—in an urban landscape; it is the poet on a walk through the streets of a city:

> I go to a tailor shop or to a movie—it so happens—
> feeling wizened and numbed, like a big felt swan,
> awash on an ocean of therefores and ashes.
>
> A whiff from a barbershop makes me start crying.
> All I ask is a little vacation from things, from boulders or woolens,
> from gardens, institutions, merchandise,
> eyeglasses, elevators—I'd rather not look at them.
>
> It so happens I'm fed up with my feet and my fingernails
> and my hair and my shadow.
> It so happens I'm tired of being a man.
> ["Walking Around," *Residence II*]

Traditional beauty—here the swan, the poetic symbol of the *modernistas*–is subverted, it becomes an anti-poetic object, a sort of grotesque hat navigating a sea of ashes. The external world of urban Nature that surrounds the poet is alien, disorienting, terrifying:

> There are sulphurous birds and a horror of hanging tripes
> nailed to the doors of the houses I loathe,
> there are dental plates lost in a coffee pot,

there are mirrors
that should have wept with the shame and horror of it all;
and everywhere, umbrellas, poisons, and belly buttons.

["Walking Around," *Residence II*]

The urban landscape as depicted by the poet is a vast, tortured flea market, a jungle of disparate objects, a chaos of sensations. The vision is overwhelming, it is quite literally mind-blowing for the poet, and for his readers.

As we pointed out in discussing Neruda's erotic love poetry and again in introducing his Nature poetry, Neruda at no point fails to acknowledge that the sensuous, comforting aspects of Nature do not negate its threatening and repulsive aspects. Neruda, like all great artists, grasps that Nature is not always pretty. It is vast, mostly alien to the human experience, often arid and cruel. Like Rembrandt, who did not shrink from painting a flayed ox or drawing a urinating dog, Neruda does not hesitate to boldly depict Nature's dark hues. The human imprint on the vast realm of Nature is necessarily limited. The imprint which does exist is directed mainly downward, toward the most accessible parts of Nature, the earth, its surface, its mud, the entrails of dead animals, the vast seas. Loneliness easily overtakes the poet in Nature's immensity of blurred limits, empty space, weariness, death, rejection, the delirium of undefined spaces:

I am alone among broken-down objects,
rain falls on me and looks like me,
like me the rain is delirious and lonely in a dead world,
rejected while falling, shapeless.

["Weakness at Dawn," *Residence I*]

One of the time-honored poetical techniques for dealing with the limitless vastness of the physical world is enumeration, the construction of lists. The technique appears frequently in Hebraic poetry and in the Bible, where it points to the variety and vastness of Nature, at the same time that it builds up a powerful rhythmic movement similar to that of a chant. In the eighteenth century, with the Age of Reason, the technique of enumeration was elaborated to become the technique of cataloguing, of ordering the elements of Nature into well-defined groupings. The great scholar Linnaeus used the technique to give definition to the entire world, listing, according to a strict system of categories and affinities, all the living beings on earth. Closer to Neruda's time and experience is Walt Whitman, who revived the Biblical technique of enumeration, adding a modern element: chaos. Whitman's exuberant poetry undid limits, crashed through Linnaeus' careful catalogues, and united, in a running enumeration, the most disparate elements of the American world. Neruda, who knew and admired Whitman's work, follows him in finding in chaotic enumeration a powerful poetic device for describing the natural world. Neruda's use of chaotic enumeration takes many forms. At times, it suggests the poet's groping and anguish as he reaches to express feelings which cannot be fully expressed. Most often, in *Residence,* it brings forth and expresses Nature's dark side, suggesting Nature's infinite disorder, more than its variety and richness.

Neruda's poetic descriptions in *Residence* in fact reflected accurately his external world. The physical world around him was disordered and foreboding. Not only the squalor of the Orient, but the collapse of Western nations, the financial disaster of 1929, the ruin of raw material producers in South America and Asia. Like his friend García Lorca, who was writing his anguished *Poet in New York* during the same period, Neruda was not, of course, documenting and cataloguing the collapse of international financial institutions in any objective way. He was involved in his own personal crisis. Yet both Neruda and Lorca could not have avoided an awareness of external failure, of the disintegration of an external material world, and both poets display an acute sensitivity to a new climate of fear. The poetic outcry is strikingly similar: both Lorca's *Poet in New York* and Neruda's *Residence* are permeated with chaotic catalogues and enumerations, startling and disjointed metaphors, reflecting the breakdown of natural boundaries, the natural elements in disarray, images of impending doom, feelings of guilt, premonitions of death and destruction. In both cases, the dramatic impact of the poems rests not on a rational understanding of the specific images and metaphors employed, but on an intuitive surrender to the powerful mood created collectively by them.

One example of the kind of strongly distorted imagery present in *Residence* can, perhaps, suggest the quality of the imagery used throughout the work. In "Ode with a Lament," from *Residence II,* Neruda writes: "You stand tall above the earth, full/of teeth and lightning." At first reading, the vision is not fully comprehended by the reader; yet intuitively the image is perceived as far from pleasant. We imagine a huge woman, perhaps a giant statue, surrounded by dark clouds and lightning. We are not sure where to place the teeth, in the mouth, out of it, in a necklace, coming out of her forehead, her arms, her bosom? These particular lines are instructive in defining Neruda's construction of images in *Residence,* because the lines cited are in fact a subtle reference to, and distorted transformation of, an image used by the great Spanish Golden Age poet Quevedo. In one of his sonnets to Lisi, Quevedo writes: "And when you laugh with a laughter/that is like red lightning . . ." There is a significant and revealing difference between Quevedo's image in these lines and Neruda's later transformation of it. Quevedo, a Baroque poet known for the obscurity of his imagery, uses an image that is far easier to understand than Neruda's, for Quevedo includes the key words—"you laugh"—in the poem. From these words, we can easily place the image; it is impossible to laugh without parting the lips, and because lips are red and laughter can be quick as lightning, the metaphor becomes clear. Neruda, on the other hand, omits the crucial word, laughter. He hides his metaphor. We can intuitively sense that it may be there, but we have trouble disentangling it from the rest of the poem. The image is felt, but it is never fully visualized or understood as Quevedo's is. Like Picasso, whose paintings of the cubist period and etchings and canvasses of the thirties are characterized by distortions of human—and specifically female— anatomy, Neruda in *Residence* displaces and hides his images in a way that produces an overall effect of strong distortion. Like Picasso, moreover, the Neruda of *Residence* does not want to describe the outside world as "attractive" or "pretty," and Neruda too sacrifices formal balance, traditional beauty, and explicit "logical" apprehension to the expression of a troubled and powerful vision.

This vision, which during the thirties becomes almost delirious, must be always intuitively grasped, rather than logically defined with the conscious mind. In *Residence,* Neruda's images never quite appear in a complete and defined form before our eyes. They are rather like different stages of a vast metamorphosis, much like the visual images confronted in a time-lapse film, run at high speed, depicting a larva struggling to become an insect, a mature butterfly. Only the larva does not reach its fulfillment in *Residence.* The struggle is present in Neruda's poems and the final emotion is one of frustration. The changes are swift and dramatic. We are projected into a never-never land in which intuition can never reach its goal. We are left with the suggestion of a powerful tension, a pent-up unreleased emotion, something unfulfilled, partially expressed, slowly boiling and festering inside the poet, inside the reader identifying with the poet. There is no release, no climax, no triumphant final image or final line that can carry the rest of the poem like a cavalry charge to victory. There are no victors in Neruda's *Residence* poems. It is a bitter war of attrition, and death, most often, has the upper hand.

Amado Alonso, the great Spanish scholar who later became the

leading figure in philological and critical studies at the University of
Buenos Aires, tried with partial success to disentangle the confused
web of images and styles in *Residence*. He came to two primary conclusions. The first is that Neruda's poetic vision in *Residence* always
starts with something finite, concrete, limited. Neruda believes in the
external world of Nature, in the objective facts and commonsense
definitions of our surroundings. As a "materialist philosopher" he
could do no less. Alonso's second conclusion is more disturbing. The
poet tends to leave this concrete world in which his senses are
confident. He takes steps toward what might be called "the road to
infinity." Boundaries fall or are ignored, the poet—or the people
and objects he describes—seem to soar above them, although often
the real direction of the movement is downward or sideways.[9]

Man becomes lost in an infinite world that he cannot grasp, and
that remains alien and menacing. The fusion and confusion of the
natural world is reflected in a series of images in which the logical
boundaries of the elements are broken: "between shadows and
space," "between garrisons and virgins" ("Ars Poetica," *Residence I*).
Here the words linked together are dissonant because they belong to
two different categories of Nature. Like the Golden Age playwright
Calderón de la Barca, Neruda here is expressing the disarray of the
natural world through a series of images in which something is
amiss, in which natural elements are appearing where they should
not appear. The images are distressing because they suggest that
something is not right in the natural universe; the logical order of
the natural world has been disturbed. And disruption of the order
of the natural elements bodes ill for the universe of man. The same
type of displacement of elements occurs with adjectives and descriptions. As Alonso points out, the "I," the poet and observer, experiences feelings that are suddenly ascribed to the object observed: "the
wounded morning," for example, appears where in reality it is the
poet who feels wounded, or a swan is called "painful" where again, it
is not the swan, but the poet who feels like crying out. Individual
identities are broken and man is confused with the natural world,
just as "shadows" above were combined not with "light," but with
"space," and "night," not with "day" but with "time." There is a complete fusion, the elimination of ordered boundaries in the imagery;
the ordered state of the natural world no longer functions.

And yet the crisis, the breakdown of clear boundaries, is also the
solution. The natural world is infinite and chaotic. The best way for
man to approach this world, to grasp it, is by erasing his inner
boundaries. The human mind has become too tightly com-
partmentalized; to move closer to the cosmos, it must become as

open and vast as the cosmos. The *Residence* poems are Nature poetry with a twist: the external world, itself in collapse, is seen by an observer whose own feelings of loneliness, rejection, failure, guilt have brought him to a state of acute depression. Both are in disarray, and yet it is the poet's sense of separation from the natural world that contributes to his depression. If the chaos of broken barriers is at times terrifying, it is only the breakdown of barriers between man and the natural world which offers an aperture. The poet constantly feels the barriers and seeks their destruction, preferring in the end the threat of chaos to that of claustrophobic isolation:

> People travel the tangible world
> hardly aware they have a body, ignoring its vigor,
> fear walks the world of the words which describe our bodies
> ["Ritual of My Legs," *Residence I*]

The human body, a subject often treated by Whitman, is brought by Neruda into the context of the barriers which govern the external world and which separate man from Nature. The human body is not free. A cloud of conventions, laws, and traditions bind it into slavery. Why is it so hard for a human body to touch the natural world? Why so many barriers, so many meaningless prohibitions?

> Always
> man-made things, stockings and shoes,
> or simply the infinite air:
> between my feet and the earth,
> exacerbating my solitude, my exile,
> something tenacious separates me from the earth,
> an invincible powerful enemy.
> ["Ritual of My Legs," *Residence I*]

The answer is not simple, for it is both Nature itself—the infinite air—and man-made matter that are barriers. The poet feels isolated both from Nature and by Nature. The ultimate goal is "constructive chaos," the elimination of barriers between objects, between bodies, between the body of the poet and the world, a quasi-pantheistic union in which a fusion of man and Nature does not encompass the sense of terror present in man's being absorbed by the infinity of Nature. But here, the goal is not reached. The world of Nature has been disrupted, there is a dismembering process present; the anguish is all that is present here, the anguish and the longing for the pantheistic union in which neither infinite air nor man-made matter will be barriers.

The absolute breaking down of barriers is not possible in the normal world, and, as we have mentioned, the overwhelming sensation of *Residence on Earth* is one of frustration, of a truncated process, of energy moving toward a reconciliation which remains an elusive absence. It is only in certain isolated moments of this work that the reconciliation occurs. Those moments are above all moments of oneiric vision, taken from the world of dreams, not lived reality. It is in the oneiric regions that chaos and depression can be overcome, that union can be realized, that ecstasy can once more be present. One such example is the poem "Dream Horse." The poem is said to have been written in Chile before Neruda's Oriental experiences, a fact which could explain its rapport with *Venture,* more than with some of the darker *Residence* poems. Neruda begins by describing "a country spread out in the sky/ a credulous carpet of rainbows" where crepuscular plants grow. He moves towards it with great difficulty, slowly. The poet is tired and dispirited: "a bad taste in my soul disheartens me." Yet positive notes begin to emerge: he welcomes the morning, thick like milk, and a red horse, the horse of the sun or perhaps the embodiment of male virility, neighs. The poet mounts the naked horse and, carried by it, soars over churches—once more the Chagall paintings come to mind—and gallops through barracks empty of soldiers. An impure army pursues him. The bell-body of the magic horse strikes a deep note, the gallop continues. The poem ends on a jubilant note—"I need but a spark, a spark that grows brighter"—and the poet hopes for a resplendent kindred, a child, perhaps, that will claim his inheritance. The poem, stemming from oneiric regions, overcomes what the poet's vigilant contemplation of Nature cannot. It moves from depression to ecstasy, from chaos to joyous fusion, from darkness to light.

There are also other poems in *Residence* where optimism prevails. These are the poems in which pure matter, largely isolated from other aspects of man's external environment, is described. This is the case, for example, in "Entrance into Wood" and "Hymn to Celery," which appear near the end of *Residence II.* These poems are an absorbing and triumphant exercise in sensitive description of the natural world. And here, as was the case in Neruda's earlier poetry, the essence of the optimistic Nature poetry is nostalgia, it is a return to a world of pure matter, untainted by cosmic disarray or urban decay, a return to Nature in its simplest, original form. "Entrance into Wood," which we discussed in detail in chapter 1, is a poem of initial destruction and ultimate re-creation: "I become myself when I see your color," Neruda says of wood. Wood, as we know, is a key word for the poet. The presence of wood, of what he calls here "sweet matter" and "rose with dry wings" brings him back to his childhood; for him it has the same forceful and mysterious effect that the famous madeleine had for Proust. Neruda's bonds with Nature were established in the woods around the village of Temuco. It is this, the solace, the certainty, the material and maternal warmth which he seeks in "Entrance into Wood." Here the pattern we have suggested holds true: when Nature is combined with nostalgia, with recollection and a return, rather than primarily with an observation of the poet's contemporary external environment, it holds its positive, comforting value. It is a nostalgic escape and return, an oasis of security in the desolate desert of modern urban life.

The same optimistic view of Nature is present when the poet contemplates the material sustenance provided by the earth and writes his "Hymn to Celery." Here too, the optimism is related to nostalgia, rather than to present reality. It too represents a return to a maternal presence, the nourishment provided by the earth, the life-giving female goddess, Mother Earth, present in virtually all cultures. Neruda's biography suggests a particular side of this common cultural vision of the earth as a life-giving maternal figure. The poet's mother died a month after his birth. Although Neruda was raised by a stepmother he adored, his natural mother always remained a figure to be sought; and, buried in the earth, she remains associated with the earth, it is there that the poet seeks her. As she had given him life, the earth in which she rests now provides sustenance, sprouting forth life-giving foodstuffs, among them the slender celery stalk to which his song is dedicated:

> river of life, essential strands,
> green branches, sunlight caressed,
> here I am in the night, I listen to secrets,
> to sleepless nights and loneliness,
> and you come in, among melted mists,
> you grow inside me, you let me know
> all about dark light and the earth's rose.
>
> ["Hymn to Celery," *Residence II*]

The poet longs to be part of the whole world; his memory of plants helps him to feel restored. It should be remembered in this context that numerous healing properties were attributed to celery by the ancient Greeks and Romans, and that furthermore, celery has often been seen as a phallic symbol and, thus, as an aphrodisiac food. Yet the poet here is not speaking solely of celery. He is describing the healing, uplifting effect of all plants, the whole vegetal kingdom, on a lonely and depressed mind. Neruda takes every aspect of the natural world seriously. He talks with natural objects, addressing all kinds of questions to them, as when, in an apt description, he asks of celery, "What do you want, you visitor with the flimsy corset?" When he communicates in this way with plants or with animals, the poet is lifted out of the nightmarish urban Nature that is his actual physical reality, and, in a process of nostalgic evocation, transported back to the positive, strength-giving aspects of Nature associated with his earlier life. What is important is that Neruda feels in this poem, as in the poem directed to wood, a union and an empathy with the natural world. While his vision is not the exuberant pure pantheism of Whitman, it does manage to break through barriers here that are anguishingly present in "Ritual of My Legs." It should be noted, however, that these moments of return are not long sustained. "Entrance into Wood" and "Hymn to Celery" together with another poem, "Statute of Wine," make up one section of *Residence II* entitled *Three Material Songs*. The "Statute of Wine"—as its more socially oriented and authoritarian title suggests—breaks the return to pure Nature and interrupts the uplifting movement of the other two songs. In this poem Neruda finds a kind of companionship with other men, but it is through the transport of alcohol, and contemporary reality comes forth in the poem as wine flows and runs through highways and churches.

Two different visions of Nature are thus present in *Residence on Earth*. One, offering sustenance, soothes the poet; the other, primarily relating to urban environments, offers mainly delirium, decay, and disorder. Amado Alonso has suggested that there is a pattern in the appearance of the positive and negative visions in *Residence*. "In the first part of *Residence* (the poems written between 1925 and 1931)," Alonso writes, "we can still find a good number of love poems in which the vision of the world is not one of disintegration nor does anguish dominate totally the poet; if disintegration exists, it does so as a stage set, as a background; through its slow piles of rubble an indestructible spirit is born again each time." This would be the case, for example, of the oneiric "Dream Horse" which we have cited. "In the second volume," Alonso continues, "destruction and pain are no longer mere atmosphere, they have become the main subject: Neruda speaks about a river that destroys itself by enduring, he speaks about what has been lost, what has been abandoned, about crying, about broken-down objects, about rotting dead animals, about an invisible fallout coming down from tree leaves; he has to mention death and destruction, and above all he wants to talk about the anguish in his heart."[10]

Alonso's scheme is generally accurate. It does not, however, account for the positive feelings present in "Entrance into Wood" and "Hymn to Celery." The more universally accurate scheme which is discernible, we believe, is that which we have identified in distinguishing between acutely observed and nostalgically recalled visions of Nature. It is generally the former which are anguished, the latter which are celebratory. A further pattern exists as well: where Neruda's Nature poetry is basically existential, that is, where it is geared to observing man in his external physical environment, it is overwhelmingly despairing. On those less frequent occasions, however, when the poet's verses are more traditionally "pure" Nature poetry, that is, when they are directed toward observing concrete, sustaining aspects of the physical world *without* man's societal presence or with only his minimal presence, the vision becomes optimistic. These remain, however, the less dominant moments of *Residence I* and *II*. Their fleeting, redemptive presence is not powerful enough, in either emotional intensity or brilliancy of poetic imagery, to alter the crushing sense of depression and oppression that is the prevailing mood of the works as a whole.

Nature is constantly present in *Residence on Earth,* but it is more often than not threatened by "a horse of shadows" near "women with cruel faces" ("Nocturnal Collection," *Residence I*). Neruda's dark vision and pessimism are the overwhelming presence in the first two volumes. It is a vision as dark as the most acute parts of T.S. Eliot's *The Waste Land.* The "sulphurous birds" of "Walking Around" are as threatening a vision of urban subversion of pure Nature as William Blake's "dark Satanic mills" created by the industrial revolution. Yet even where Nature is not pretty, Neruda remains a poet of Nature. Unlike the more spiritual Hispanic symbolists—Darío, Nervo, the other great poets of the *modernista* school, who followed the Pythagoric-Orphic tradition—Neruda is a materialist. In *Residence,* Jaime Concha notes, the *modernistas'* attitude "has become changed into a 'feeling the pulse' of the material energy of the world . . . in a telluric trip to the entrails of the world . . . everything is accumulated force, quantities that become energy."[11] What is significant is the continued presence of matter, even within the context of the poet's depression and acute sense of decomposition. His stance, as we noted at the beginning of this discussion, remains that of an observer sensitive to the natural world, influenced by his external environment. And it is to Nature that he looks for images to express his own sickened despair:

> I walk alone in the afternoon, I arrive
> somewhere, full of mud and of death,
> I bring with me the soil and its roots,

and its vague belly where you will see
sleeping cadavers covered with wheat,
and metals, and huge broken-down elephants.
                    ["Family and Melancholy," *Residence II*]

From *Canto General* to the *Odes*

Canto General is in many ways Neruda's greatest Nature poem, and
no overview of Neruda as a Nature poet can be complete without
examination of this key work. The vision of Nature in the *Canto* is,
however, inseparable from Neruda's overall epic perspective. As a
result, it cannot be discussed in any meaningful way independent of
that perspective which gives form and significance to the *Canto*. We
will, therefore, reserve our examination of *Canto General* for the discussion below of Neruda as a public poet, and refer the reader to
chapter 3 for commentary on the central role Nature plays in that
monumental work. Here, we will focus on the vision of Nature in
several other central works of Neruda's poetic maturity, beginning
with the *Elemental Odes*.

Nineteen fifty-four was a banner year for Neruda. Translations of
his poems were published in France (*Le Chant Général,* with illustrations by Fernand Léger; *Tout l'Amour,* in an edition by Pierre
Seghers), in Hungary, in Poland, and in Israel. Poets and writers
came to Santiago from China, Russia, Czechoslovakia, France, and
almost every Latin American country to celebrate Neruda's fiftieth
birthday. Lectures, speeches, and public readings of poetry took
place almost daily. Neruda had found an audience, and his public
seemed to be almost the entire nation. The poet donated his valuable
library to the University of Chile, and the establishment of the
Neruda Foundation for the Advancement of Poetry was publicly announced. Pablo Neruda's public role seemed to have reached a
climax. Yet the most important event of this year turned out to be
not the official ceremonies, but rather the publication of a new work,
the *Elemental Odes,* by the Buenos Aires publishing house Losada.
With this publication, a new cycle began. *Canto General* had been epic
poetry, with overt political overtones and motivations, an attempt to
encompass the history of an entire continent from a well-defined
ideological perspective. *The Grapes and the Wind** had also been
dominated by a political vision. But, while Neruda remained ar-
dently active politically, in the *Odes* the artistic emphasis has moved

*See chapters 1 and 3.

away from direct political statement and toward Nature poetry in a "pure" sense.

This change in direction was paralleled by certain aspects of Neruda's personal life. Neruda's second wife, Delia del Carril, was a militant Soviet-style Communist. The poet's new love, Matilde Urrutia, was less strident and politically motivated; perhaps she gradually influenced the poet's change in artistic direction. While it is possible to note these biographical factors, it is not possible to accurately gauge their real role in defining the change in Neruda's poetic direction. What can be stated unequivocally is that for artistic reasons Neruda felt an acute need for change, for a renewal of his poetic vision and his style. This had already become a cyclical pattern for Neruda. Before the publication of *Canto General,* Neruda had renounced his *Residence* poems, stating, "These poems should not be read by the young readers of our countries. These texts are drenched in atrocious pessimism, unbearable anguish. They do not help to live—they help the reader to die."[12] With the *Odes* Neruda changed as well from the *Canto:* "I have left behind me, one by one, all my books," Margarita Aguirre records his saying, "Every time I have replaced and rebuilt the meaning and the style of my poetry. I am myself the bitterest enemy of a 'Neruda style.' How can this style exist since I destroy it every time I publish a new book?"[13]

To suggest, however, that in leaving behind the overtly political thrust of *Canto General,* Neruda abandoned his political commitment would be a gross error. The *Odes* are not in any way directly ideological, it is true; yet they reflect attitudes that are ideological. The return to, and exaltation of, Nature in the *Odes* is itself a political commentary to the degree that in praising what is positive and basic, there is a silent accusation against those who would abuse and exploit the resources of the Americas. More important, in choosing this style for the *Elemental Odes* Neruda was clearly motivated by a deeply held political belief: a leftist poet must reject "elitist" styles, he must write simply and for the people. "For a poet, the main problem of our time," Neruda said, "is whether to write cryptically or clearly."[14] He associated the problem with political ideology. Rodríguez Monegal quotes him as asserting that "the ruling class has elaborated a false image of the poet. It has depicted the poet as a sort of blindfish swimming with magical agility through the waters of mystery." This concept is misleading, and its goal, Neruda believed, is "to isolate the writer from the human community. It aims at breaking the ties that bind the poet and his people; by destroying the poet's roots, he will be turned into a weak artificial plant."[15]

The poet, Neruda insisted, is not a "small god." He has not stolen the celestial fire. He is not a magician, a superman; he is a worker, a craftsman like all others. The poet belongs with the people, he is one with their collective voice. This definition of the poet is also a definition of the style his work must assume. The poet must write for the masses of people. "We are nations made up of simple people," Neruda said, "people who are learning to build, who are learning to read. It is for them that we must write."[16] This demand is, perhaps, the most difficult for a gifted artist to meet. And the politically committed Neruda was no exception. "It was very hard for me to come out of a cryptic style and into a clear and easy way of writing, because a hermetic style has often been among us very much like a badge of privilege, of the privileged caste of literati. Our class prejudices have made us despise as plebeian whatever was folksy, plain, simple. . . ."[17] This prejudice is a "vestige of the feudal system" and must be rejected; a poet of the political Left, Neruda concluded, can only opt for clarity. His poetry must be open and simple and it should reflect the everyday world.

Neruda saw in this new poetics a welcome return to the sources, his family, his native village, the modest lives of his childhood friends. In a lecture cited by Rodríguez Monegal, he said: "I started my talk by telling you how poetry is able to resist all its enemies. I shall end by stating that poetry must also resist an excess of sophistication, which is an attitude that tends to draw the poet away from everyday reality. . . . We must go back to what is simply human. This is at least my own way." And he concludes with the rhetorical question, "How could it be otherwise? I have told you where I come from, my humble frontier origins. You know about the people who grew up with me. If I were not a plain, simple man, if I did not try to write plainly and clearly, I would betray the very foundations of my poetry."[18]

The process is one of restitution. With the *Elemental Odes*, Neruda is, on a poetic level, following a pattern suggested in *Canto General* for the continent as a whole. He is rejecting the invasion of artificial sophistication and returning to basics, to simplicity, purity, and stark Nature. Simplicity is not, of course, new in the *Elemental Odes*. Most of Neruda's early love poetry is simple, at times deceptively so. In his *Canto General,* the poet is already the voice of the people and many of the poems do not offer difficult images or displaced adjectives. *The Grapes and the Wind* and *The Captain's Verses** show a similar process of simplification at work. It is only that this process reaches its most deliberate peak in the *Odes*. The *Odes* are consciously elemental

*See chapter 1.

in the two senses of the word: they are simple and they are basic. They are the essentials to which Neruda returns. From this moment to the end of his career as a poet, Neruda will not go back to the complex, oneiric, surrealist style of the *Residence* cycle. What he now seeks, and achieves, in both subject matter and poetic techniques is "a common language," Rodríguez Monegal observes, " . . . a language that without losing touch with lyricism is also the language of everyday life . . . a direct contact with all mankind."[19]

Together the three books of odes—*Elemental Odes* (1954), *More Elemental Odes* (1956), and *The Third Book of Odes* (1957)—contain more than 180 poems. A fourth book, *Voyages and Homecomings* (1959) is also often considered a part of the ode cycle. An ode, of course, is a poem of praise, and in these books Neruda's praise is directed toward every aspect of Nature. Neruda's concept of Nature is all-embracing. It includes not only the most obvious elements ("Ode to Air," "Ode to Energy," "Ode to Fire," "Ode to Summer," "Ode to Sand"), but also humble aspects of the natural world ("Ode to the Artichoke," "Ode to the Bee"), and the scientific and man-made aspects of Nature ("Ode to the Atom," "Ode to the Dictionary," "Ode to the Bicycle").

Each poem rings out with joy, with pleasure. Each poem also examines the object as if it were under a microscope, with loving attention, turning it around and exploring its facets, its uses, its power. Perhaps this very detailed approach, so particular to Neruda, is explained by the fact that Neruda was an accomplished naturalist, a specialist in marine life, and an avid collector of shells. (Neruda's expertise in this field did not go unrecognized, and in his *Memoirs* the poet recounts an apocryphal story that circulated in Chile years ago. When Julian Huxley, the renowned British biologist, wished to see Neruda during a trip to Chile, he was utterly baffled by the Chileans' reference to Neruda as "our great poet." "Oh, is he a poet?" Huxley is reputed to have asked. Huxley's only knowledge of Neruda was said to be as a "malacologist," a collector of mollusks and a specialist in seashells.[20]

In the *Elemental Odes,* of course, it is not only Neruda's scholarly knowledge of the natural world, but above all his enormous appreciation of it which comes through. As A. Comas has put it, "It seems as if the broken-down, dust-covered objects, the disintegrating bits of matter that he had described in his *Residence* poems, had suddenly recovered their full personality, had staked out their being, their need to exist. Neruda achieves in his *Odes* the complete objective view. The poet sings these aspects of reality by relating them to the need that mankind feels for them, and therefore his *Odes* become

true social poetry."[21] Every natural subject—autumn, stars, flowers,
the moon—is seen through a prism of joy. Neruda's verses celebrate
the world as seen by a happy man:

> I disdained you
> O joy.
> I was given bad advice.
> The moon
> made me take a wrong turn.
> The ancient poets
> lent me their eyeglasses
> and around each object
> I placed
> a dark halo,
>
> . . . .
>
> I took the wrong road
> yet today I beckon you, O joy.
>
> . . . .
>
> You and I together through the world!
> Together with my song!
>
> . . . .
>
> Let no one wonder if I want
> to offer every man
> the gifts from the earth
> for I learned in my struggle
> that it is my earthly duty
> to spread joy
> and I fulfill my destiny by singing.

["Ode to Joy," *Elemental Odes*]

Often Neruda's *Odes* unfold in what might be called a "spiral" pattern. The point of departure is small, almost insignificant, often not
fully poetic, the reader wondering what can be done artistically with
an artichoke, with vinegar, with the human liver, with a bicycle. Yet
Neruda establishes an emotional link with the object. He sees each
aspect of Nature as a gift and his poetry is a gift in return to a world
that offers him beauty and life. Neruda acknowledged this attitude
explicitly in a curious anecdote from his childhood. Loafing in the
backyard of his house in Temuco, he came upon a hole in the fence.
He looked through it and saw another backyard, uncared for and
wild. "I drew back a few steps, because I sensed vaguely that something was about to happen. Suddenly a hand appeared. It was the
tiny hand of a boy about my age." By the time he came close again,
the hand was gone. In its place there was a "marvelous white sheep."
Its wool was faded. Its wheels had fallen off. Yet Neruda had never

seen such a wonderful toy sheep. He went back to the hole, but the boy had disappeared. Then he went into the house and brought out a treasure of his own, a pine cone, full of woodsy smells. He placed it in the same spot and went off with the sheep. In his *Memoirs,* Neruda said

> That gift brought to me for the first time a treasure that would accompany me later in life: human solidarity. Life would place it in my path later on, this time highlighted against a background of trouble and persecution. It will not surprise you then that I attempted to give something resiny, fragrant and earthy in exchange for the brotherhood of other human beings. Just as I once left my pine cone by the fence, I have since left my words on the doorstep of many people unknown to me, people in prison, or hunted, or alone. This is the great lesson I learned as a child, in the backyard of a lonely house. Perhaps it was nothing but a game played by two boys who did not know each other and wanted to pass to the other some good things of life. Yet maybe this small and mysterious exchange of gifts remained like an indestructible sediment in my heart, lighting up my poetry.[22]

Poetry is an exchange, a gift, earthy and fragrant like a pine cone. It is a vehicle through which to reflect back to the world some of the beauty first given by the world to the poet's senses. Thus, the emotional link Neruda establishes with the commonplace objects of his *Odes* is often accomplished by reminding us of what he thought of the object as a child, or what his impression was when he saw the object for the first time. This gives a human dimension to the natural object which it did not have before. The spiral then takes a new turn: we are reminded of the link between the object and society, the link with history, the link with other—vaster, perhaps nobler— objects in the natural world, until from the initial, single object we have moved to reach toward infinity, now no longer threatening. A short passage can suffice as an example:

Book
handsome book
book
tiny grove
leaf
by leaf
your paper
smells
of nature
you speak

of mornings and nights
you are cereal-like,
oceanic . . .

[“Ode to the Book,” *Elemental Odes*]

A poem like this underlines the difference between Neruda's Nature poetry and the Nature poetry of a Shelley. For Neruda, Nature
is, as we have defined it, the entire external environment. The modern world has added so many features to the inherited world of sea,
sand, groves, valleys, and lakes, that it is no longer valid to sing only
of what in Nature is not marked by the imprint of man. When Vergil
in his *Georgics* describes man's efforts to cultivate the soil, to prune
trees and to extract honey from honeycombs, he too is celebrating
man's ingenuity and handiworks. But Neruda goes one step further,
celebrating as well man's crafts and the products of his industry
when they add to our joy. This last aspect is important, for in Neruda's Nature poetry, man-made objects are positive or negative depending on their role within the external environment. They are
negative when, as in “Ritual of My Legs,” they act as a barrier between man and the world in which he lives; they are positive, as in
the “Ode to the Book,” when they expand man's environment, when
they serve as apertures, when they broaden what can be seen as Nature. Then they, like the more traditional aspects of Nature, are de-
serving of celebration.

Nonetheless, perhaps the most successful of Neruda's *Odes* remain
those that deal with fundamental natural objects or beings, with the
basic properties of Nature, like the “Ode to the Smell of Cordwood”
or the “Ode to the Onion” or the “Ode to Salt”:

I saw the salt
in this salt shaker
when it was still in the salt flats.
I know
you
will never believe me,
but
it sings,
the salt sings, the skin
of the salt plains,
it sings
through a mouth smothered
by earth.

. . . .

Dust of the sea, our tongue

receives a kiss
of the night sea from you:
taste recognizes
the huge ocean in each salty morsel,
and therefore the smallest,
the tiniest
wave of the shaker
brings home to us
not only your domestic whiteness
but the innermost flavor of infinity.

["Ode to Salt," The Third Book of Odes]

What has changed here is once again the poet's attitude toward his external environment. Infinity, so menacing in the *Residence* poems, is here brought to human scale, where it no longer looms ominous.

No natural object is without beauty when seen through the eyes of the poet:

Onion,
luminous vessel,
your grace took shape
petal by petal,
crystal scales made you grow
and in the dark corners of the earth
your belly of dew grew large.
Under the earth
the miracle took place
and when your clumsy green stem
sprang forth
and your leaves
were born like swords in the orchard,
the earth gathered its power
showing your naked transparence
and like the faraway sea
duplicating a magnolia
in the breasts of Aphrodite,
the earth made you thus,
onion,
clear like a planet
and destined
to shine,
constant constellation,
round rose of water,
on
the table
of the poor . . .

["Ode to the Onion," Elemental Odes]

Neruda's "new" concept of how a poet should write, his exaltation of clarity, is manifest in these poems and throughout the *Odes* in three important stylistic details. The first and most obvious one is found in the titles of his compositions. With the *Odes*, we know exactly, and from the beginning, what the poem is about. Both its essence as a poem in praise of something—occasionally of somebody—and the subject described are explicitly stated and are instantly recognizable, since Neruda primarily deals with natural objects that we have seen a hundred times. Compare the titles "Ode to Copper," "Ode to Rain," "Ode to Wood," with the elusive, mysterious titles of the *Residence* poems: "Gentleman Alone," "Nocturnal Collection," "Burial in the East." Most poems of the *Residence* period, moreover, deal with several aspects of reality—both internal and external, objective and subjective—the subjects always multiple and seen through distorting prisms. Each ode centers on a single subject. The general tone of the poem and its subject are both known in advance and accessible to the reader.

The second stylistic detail important in the *Odes* is the typographical arrangement of the poems. Ever since Mallarmé's *Un Coup de Dés*, poets and critics have been aware of the importance of typography. The separation of lines, the white spaces between words, between stanzas, the very shape and size of the letters, influence the meaning of a poem in the same manner that silences and pauses form part of a musical composition. If we compare the division by lines in Neruda's early poems and the *Residence* poems with the line division in the *Odes*, we realize that a remarkable process of simplification has taken place. The earlier Neruda wrote in traditional meters or in long versicles reminiscent of the Bible and, later, of Whitman. Now Neruda makes use of numerous lines in which only one word appears. For instance, in a forty-two line section of "Ode to Rain," eleven lines contain only one word; thirteen have two words; the rest, three, rarely four words; only one line—"como un puñal de vidrio" ("like a glass dagger")—has five, and one—"a mí y a las raíces" ("to me and to the roots")—has six words. This line division is, of course, of great help to the inexperienced reader of poetry, allowing him to concentrate on one or two words at a time, to digest their meaning before going on. The simplified syntax works especially well when Neruda's subject matter is a description of Nature. In these cases, the description, proceeding step by step and facet by facet, is reflected in the typography in which each aspect is expressed by itself, standing out, each as a unit. Every line is a separate brushstroke contributing to the total effect, yet visible as an individual unit. This is the way, of course, that the finest Nature artists, Van Gogh or

Seurat, used their brush and colors. In several poems, the short line also works in a way that makes it suggestive of the subject matter, the poem about rain, for example, using lines as short and concise as raindrops themselves. The typography in the *Odes* quite simply creates an agreement between intention, content, and form. Neruda's poetics, now strongly based on clarity and simplicity, is effectively portrayed by, and revealed through, the typographical medium employed. It might be added that as a result of the employment of the short line and the consequent break with the traditional effects of metrics, Neruda's *Odes* are among his most easily and effectively translated works.

The third stylistic characteristic of the *Odes* is that the images have become clear and univocal. The images of the *Residence* poems were often based on strange visions in which concrete objects and abstract ideas were intricately fused, as in "Nocturnal Collection," where Neruda speaks of an "angel of sleep" which comes to him "wrapped in snails and cicadas . . . perfumed with sharp fruits," while the wind "rattles the months" and "an opaque sound of shadows" is heard. All of this creates a climate of oppressive anguish, tension, and nightmare. It is superb poetry, but if we want to take literally each sentence, each image, we cannot decipher the poem. Modern poetry like the *Residence* poems requires a certain training on the part of the reader, a willingness to accept what is apparently illogical or absurd but is actually necessary to create a mood by appealing to our subconscious mind and our subliminal memories. Many readers are not prepared for this kind of modern poetry and tend to reject it, claiming that it is "meaningless" or "impossible to understand." This is not so, although the precise meaning of some of Neruda's individual images in the early *Residence* poems has been vigorously debated by scholars—even the best-trained critics sometimes find the specific images of these poems obscure. No such accusation of obscurity can be levelled against the mature Neruda. From the Spanish Civil War on, his poetry becomes simpler and simpler, reaching its utmost clarity in the *Odes*.

In 1959 Neruda published *Voyages and Homecomings,* which he intended as a continuation of the *Odes* cycle. In the prologue the poet defines his work. Poetry is a craft. The poet is a worker, a craftsman:

> I just work and work,
> I must replace
> Our faulty memory,
> I must fill darkness with white bread,
> I must create hope anew (. . .)

["To My Obligations"]

Like the other volumes of *Odes,* this book for the most part presents Neruda as a joyful poet of Nature. The list of topics is inexhaustible, running the full gamut of the natural world and including as well a variety of man-made objects that appealed to the poet. One such example is "Ode to an Anchor." The choice of subject is not surprising—Neruda possessed several ship's anchors, all of them rusty and bent, which he kept at Isla Negra, some indoors and some out in front of the house. One of the loveliest odes in the volume is dedicated to swallows. The name of the bird does not appear in the title, "Ode to September Wings," but rather is introduced through a metaphor:

> Coming and going from every roof
> I saw today the sky's scissors.
> In their flight they cut the transparent breeze:
> Nobody will have to go without swallows.

Other odes, some of the best, are dedicated to animals: horses, the elephant, the cat. We also find odes to a chair, a dish, and even to French-fried potatoes.

Despite Neruda's intention and the evident similarities between *Voyages and Homecomings* and the other books of *Odes,* there are notes in this volume that set it apart somewhat. There is, for example, a long political poem, "Ode to Lenin," written in celebration of the fortieth anniversary of the Russian Revolution. This poem demonstrates Neruda's fidelity not only to the Communist movement, but also to his own concept of hero. If in *Canto General,* the liberators were linked to the earth and described as a tree, here everything in Lenin is directly related to Nature:

> Lenin, to sing of you
> I should say farewell to words;
> I should write with trees, with wheels,
> with ploughs, with grains.
> You are concrete like
> acts and like the earth.
> Never did there exist
> a man more earthly
> than V. Ulianov.
> . . . .
> Lenin kept a pact with the earth.

> ["Ode to Lenin"]

Another poem that deviates somewhat from the subject matter, and above all the mood, which we have come to expect from the *Odes* is

"Written on the Train near Cautín, in 1958." Here, Neruda reveals a melancholy not usually characteristic of his books of *Odes*. The subject is the impossibility of returning home; the poet, voyaging to the South, recognizes that now no one there knows him, no one is waiting there for him, with outstretched arms and honey, as they were years ago:

> Going away means returning when only the rain,
> only the rain waits.
> And now there are no doors, now there is no bread. There
>   is nobody.

What the poet recognizes in this poem can be applied on a different level to this volume of poems, that is, the difficulty of recapturing precisely the spirit of other volumes, already published. *Voyages and Homecomings* does largely belong to the cycle of *Odes;* yet *Extravagaria,** a very different sort of book, had been published in the intervening years, and a certain evolution in tone separates these odes from the three previous books of odes published earlier. The recognition of this evolution does not change the essential reality, however, that in intention, in poetic form, and for the most part in subject matter as well, *Voyages and Homecomings* represents Neruda's desire to continue producing odes that in their simplicity open up new perspectives on the material world in which man dwells.

With the *Odes,* as before with *Twenty Poems,* Neruda performs a feat that only a few modern poets have been able to duplicate. He manages to please both the crowd and the critics. This same difficult balancing act had been at the core of the success of a poet like Robert Frost, who was also a Nature poet, although more introverted and subject to mercurial changes in his view than is Neruda in the *Odes.* Frost writes his Nature poems wrapped in the garb of an old and wise peasant-philosopher; Neruda disguises himself as a bemused child for whom every natural object is a new and marvelous toy, very much like the toy sheep that was given to him in his childhood. The popular success of Neruda's *Odes* is an undeniable fact, and even critics frequently hostile to the Neruda of *Residence* or *Canto General* find the *Odes* captivating. The Chilean critic Alone (a pseudonym for Hernán Díaz Arrieta) who—partly for political reasons—had often attacked Neruda, wrote enthusiastically of the *Odes:* " . . . no longer hampered by sadness, obscure language and hatred, without tears, without hermeticism, without party slogans, we find [in the *Odes*] a poet beaming poems for the whole world, a

*See chapter 4.

poet easy to understand, the easiest, the clearest, most joyful and kindest of all poets. . . ." Most important, Neruda's clarity has been achieved without sacrifice of poetic quality. As Alone concludes, "Having eliminated bitterness, having proscribed complicated obscurity, it was to be feared that his poetry would seek to excess a common denominator and stoop toward prosaic language. And yet never has Neruda's poetry sounded so poetic and authentic."[23] It would be impossible to define the precise secret of Neruda's success in the *Odes*. A literary text can be explained, but the conditions that made it possible are locked in the writer. One source of strength, however, is identifiable and has been pointed out by Emir Rodríguez Monegal: "There is no poem [in the *Odes*] where the imprint of love does not appear. There is no poem in which we cannot find a trace, sometimes almost imperceptible, like a small gesture of complicity that only *she*, the woman he loves, can understand, and which for the average reader is transformed into a smile that runs through the poem and sheds light without our being fully aware where this light comes from."[24]

The Later Works

Love is equally a characteristic of another book, *The Stones of Chile*, published in 1961. Here the love is directed toward Neruda's native land and the entire book can, on a certain level, be seen as still another ode, this time with a single theme: the huge grey surfaces of granite and basalt which are the stones of Chile. Nonetheless, the tone is somewhat different in this work, as Eduardo Camacho Guizado notes: ". . . One would have to say that its tone seeks to be more transcendental on occasion than that which we generally find in the *Odes*. Poet and Nature meet here in solitude and the dimensions of the song become metaphysical, without ever ceasing to be concrete."[25]

In his preface to the volume, Neruda explains *The Stones of Chile* in the following manner:

> This flinty book, born in the wastelands along the coast and in the mountain ranges of my country, has lived for twenty years in my mind. . . . The poet must sing with his countrymen and give to mankind all that pertains to being a man: dreams and love, light and darkness, reason and vagary. But let us never forget the stones! We should never lose sight of these taciturn castles, the profile and bristling mass of our planet. . . . My compatriot Gabriela Mistral used to say that in Chile, it is the skeleton that one sees first of all, the profu-

sion of rocks, mountains and sand. . . . This book, adorned with portraits of rocks seen as individual beings, is a conversation that I leave open so that poets all over the earth might continue it and seek to encompass and define the secret of rocks and of life.[26]

The "portraits of rocks" to which Neruda refers are not only his own texts; the first edition of *The Stones of Chile* included splendid photographs by Antonio Quintana.

Hope is coupled with sadness in this volume where the poet recognizes the austere reality of the Chilean landscape. We see the two emotions in "The Great Hard Rock Table," in which the whole of Chile is seen as a bare table of stone, a table offering nothing to eat on its cold surface:

> . . . We sat down all of us, together, around the table,
> the cold table of our world,
> and no one brought us anything,
> everything had disappeared,
> everything had been eaten already by others.
>
> One single dish remains waiting
> upon the immense hard surface of this table
> of our world and its vast emptiness:
> and one child waits still,
> the child who is the truth of every dream,
> the child who is the hope of our earth.

Chile is a poor country, with few fertile valleys, a desolate coastal region in the North, rainy pine forests in the South. The beauty and power of its mountain ranges cannot hide or disguise in any way the stark landscape that the poet describes in this book. No matter: a poet can also be imaginative, even whimsical, when describing a wasteland, and here and there humor appears in Neruda's verses. His love for the land accepts its nakedness and its poverty and finds reason for rejoicing in the mythical origins of its stones and of the men who were born upon those stones, and the animals as well.

We can imagine the poet wandering along the coast or up the steep paths that lead to a summit and coming across a boulder that reminds him of a turtle, and soon, a poem is born. In the poem entitled "The Turtle," Neruda describes a mythical age-old turtle, wandering for years and years, looking at the world with her ancient eyes, a turtle that swam for seven centuries and saw the rebirth of Nature during seven thousand springs. An armor-plated turtle with amber warts, all yellow and silver:

> the turtle came to a halt,
> remained here
> asleep
> and is not aware of it.
> She was so old
> she hardened,
> she forgot about the sea and its waves
> and became rigid
> like a flatiron

The turtle then closes her eyes, the eyes that had dared so much ocean and sky, time and terrain,

> and then fell asleep,
> a boulder
> among other boulders.

Those other boulders, all the stones that constitute Chile's internal structure, its eternal skeleton, are described in the book: the lofty stones of the Andean peaks, known intimately only by the condors; the lichen-covered stones of Antarctica, at the very edge of the world, emerging boldly among glaciers and masses of snow; the castles of solitude in the southern plains; the calcinated rocks of the deserts in northern Chile; the stones that in their sheer massive power are a "theater of the gods."

The Stones of Chile is at once a private and a public statement. It is personal poetry inasmuch as it is Neruda, as an individual, who walks, physically or through his imagination, up and down the steep slopes of Chile's geography, and it is the poet's own solitary interpretation of each salient trait of the landscape that defines the poems. The subject matter, nonetheless, makes these private poems public poetry as well; *The Stones of Chile* examines a national landscape, the stones and mountains of an entire country, the resources belonging to an entire people.

The public side of *The Stones of Chile* points up one of the unique traits of several of Neruda's volumes of Nature poetry after 1950: the poetry is not just descriptive, but also narrative, and history is imposed on Nature. This was not the case in *Crepusculario,* where Nature was described in rather straightforward, even conventional, tones; nor in *Twenty Poems,* where Nature was employed primarily as a source of imagery, a metaphor for the expression of the poet's own inner feelings. While sporadic precedents in *Venture* or in the *Residence* poems are not lacking, it is really only with *Canto General* that Nature begins to take on a notably narrative quality in Neruda's poetry. It is equally in this work that the personification and mythification of Nature come to the forefront, with human qualities being attributed to Nature and the virgin landscapes of America being presented as a kind of paradise "in the beginning" of the continent's story, before the "fall." This tendency toward personification and narration in regard to Nature continues, albeit in a vastly different context and fashion, in the *Odes*. Material items, an apple or an orange, for instance, are addressed in the "human" form "you," and Neruda does not limit himself to a simple description of the natural product; he gives it a history as well, recounting, for example, the creation of the onion or the origin of salt in the flats.

In *The Stones of Chile* this narrative-historical element persists, even reminding us at times of certain early moments of *Canto General*. Thus this book, like that earlier one, begins with the story of creation:

> Because with sweat and fire they gave
> birth to the gods of the stone,
> and soon Saint Rain grew,
> Saint Sir of the battles,
> for the corn, for the earth,
> bird gods, serpent gods,
> ill-fated fecunders,
> they all were born from the stone:
> America lifted them up
> with a thousand tiny hands of gold,
> with eyes that were already lost
> wiped out by blood and oblivion.
>
> But my homeland was made of light,
> only man came and went,
> without other gods than thunder:
> . . . .
> The stones illuminated my country
> with natural statues.

["History"]

Here, as in the *Canto*, Neruda's natural world is dotted with history, with gods, with a continuing narration from "then" to the present, clearly touching mythical domains. While it is evident that this slender volume can in no way be compared to the monumental achievement of the *Canto*, it is important to note the continuation of the narrative-historical perspective in Neruda's treatment of Nature. The integration of Nature poetry and narrative poetry, of Nature and history, of Nature and mythical creation and attributes sets

Neruda's Nature poetry apart from that of many other poets dealing with the same subject. It is one of the distinguishing features of Neruda's approach to Nature, and while it is not dominant in all of his works, it reappears with insistence in some of the volumes published during the 1960s, and once more in some of Neruda's final verses, in particular the posthumous volume *The Separate Rose.**

From 1917, when Neruda published his first text in an obscure newspaper, until his death in 1973, hardly a year passed without the publication of one or two books by him; in each work, Nature is present in a central way. In addition to the works examined here, three more volumes in which Nature plays a dominant role were published during Neruda's lifetime. In 1966, *The Art of Birds* was published in a private edition by the Society of Friends of Contemporary Art, in Santiago. In this lavish edition, the poet describes the birds of his country, his texts accompanying color illustrations by several Chilean artists. Each poem bears as its title the name of a bird, and with the numerous illustrations, the book resembles a sort of Chilean Audubon in which the scientific explanations have now become poetry. The form of a field guide to birds is also imitated, since the Spanish name for each bird is followed by the Latin scientific name. In each poem, the poet defines and explores a bird's personality and habits, as if he were looking through field glasses. Some birds are comedians, always looking for a laugh while they pursue their prey. Others are tragic, like the lonely eagle or the huge condor, "living in his iron coffin/ among rusty stones/ eating only horseshoes." The penguin is seen as "an interrogating innocence/ dressed in night and in snow." And some birds are completely imaginary, such as the "I Bird," which carries the species label "Pablo Insulidae Nigra." As in the *Odes* and in *The Stones of Chile,* Neruda is once again observing Nature with a close-up focus, examining every aspect of the winged creatures who inhabit Chile's land and skies.

A similar close-up focus characterizes *A House by the Shore,* also published in 1966. Here, however, the subject matter is no longer exclusively a natural phenomenon; rather it is the poet's house at Isla Negra, seen in every facet of its construction. This volume was also published with texts accompanying graphics, in this case photographs by Sergio Larraín. A mixture of prose, of prose poems, and of some verse, the book reveals the intimate Neruda, reminiscing about his past, trying to express his personality through the building of a house. On the roof he had the names of some of his best friends, now deceased, written, almost as an invitation to the ghosts

*See chapter 5.

of Paul Eluard, Federico García Lorca, and Alberto Rojas Giménez, among others. Yet Nature also enters prominently in this book as Neruda speaks of the plants, the sand, the stones he contemplates. And above all, the sea. Twelve of the 56 texts in this short book bear the title "The Sea," and in them the poet never tires of describing its constant presence at Isla Negra, stretching out forever in front of the house: "the sea, the sea/ beating its heart beat/ just like yesterday, opening/ its iron fan,/ untying and tying/ the submerged rose/ of its foam . . ." ("A Sperm Whale's Tooth").

Finally, in 1970 the "sister" book to *The Stones of Chile* appeared. Entitled *Sky Stones,*[27] it is a minute examination of both rocks and precious stones. We are no longer in the immense dimensions of the huge boulder formations that constitute the landscape of Chile. The object of the poet's contemplations are the smaller stones, often the stones of everyday life, at other times more exotic stones: "When you touch the topaz/ the topaz touches you:/ the smooth fire awakens/ as if the wine in a grape/ came to life" ("When You Touch the Topaz"). In this book we find Neruda once again interrogating the natural world, seeking out every aspect, every secret that the silent minerals hold. At the same time, and in an implicit fashion, the poet is reflecting on Man; his observations of minerals are also observations on the differences between the solid, silent life of stone and that of Man. And once again, the poet's identification is with the natural world:

> I was stone: dark stone
> and the separation was violent,
> a wound in my alien birth:
> I want to return
> to that certitude,
> to that central repose, to the matrix
> of the maternal stone
> from which without knowing how or when
> they removed me in order to disjoin me.
>
> ["I Am This Naked Mineral"]

Synopsis

In his numerous books where Nature dominates, Neruda seems to have intuitively understood that Nature is so vast that no single angle of vision can do it justice. It is not surprising, therefore, that the poet's approach to Nature underwent significant changes through the years. In *Crepusculario,* Neruda looks at Nature in what can be called a traditional fashion: the poet contemplating the world and focusing on those aspects of it that have attracted poets for centuries—the sunsets, the sea, the wind. In *Twenty Poems* this stance changes somewhat, and a second stage of Neruda's Nature poetry is initiated. Nature does not enter for itself alone, but rather Nature and woman are seen as two aspects of the same reality. The beauty and strength—and mystery, at times terror—of Nature and the beauty, strength, and mystery of woman are but mirrors of one another. In *Twenty Poems,* nostalgia, love of Nature, and love of woman are united in a single strand and nowhere do we find the detached contemplation of Nature itself, as occurred in a number of the poems in *Crepusculario.*

A third vision begins with *Venture of the Infinite Man* and reaches its climax with the *Residence* poems. Neruda's loneliness impels him to flight, to look at the world from new angles, whether soaring as in *Venture* or immersed in the heart of darkness as in *Residence on Earth.* The poet invades matter and is in turn invaded by it. It is an uneven battle; the poet is crushed, his senses explode on the verge of delirium and madness, and yet his flight gives us a glimpse of the pure energy—and inhumanity—of the vast chaotic forces of our external environment.

A fourth approach to Nature springs forth in Neruda's epic period, which is examined in chapter 3. This is a time of commitment to interpreting the past of the poet's continent in order to understand its present. In *Canto General,* Neruda seeks original Nature. He looks to recreate the initial innocence, the lost paradise, to plunge into a primeval world in which plants and animals are still only emerging. Neruda's vision of Nature here is didactic and politically oriented; it is also colorful and sometimes spectacular. His American Genesis gives us a glimpse of creative Nature at work. In this volume Neruda defines a unique approach to Nature: the personification of Nature, on occasion its mythification, Nature poetry as narration as well as description. The poet sees not just Nature as it presents itself to us. He imposes his imagination on Nature and develops a history for each natural element from the instant of its creation. While the climactic moment for this approach is undoubtedly *Canto General,* it characterizes in differing degrees several of his later works as well: the personification and narrative history of origin in the *Odes;* the mythification in *The Stones of Chile* and in the posthumous *The Separate Rose.*

These post-*Canto* works exemplify a fifth stage that, with certain variations, also endures until the end of Neruda's life. In these books, one senses that the film of evolution has been arrested at specific frames, giving us time to examine a particular plant, a stone, a flower, a bird, an aspect of modern life, at leisure. We look at the object, handle it, turn it around, all the sides are examined with love, care, attention. This is, in many ways, Neruda as a Nature poet at his best. The close-ups are more vivid, more detailed, more refreshing than the sweeping panoramas and traveling shots of some of his early poems. This perspective, which we have sampled in the *Odes* and in *The Stones of Chile,* reappears in *The Art of Birds,* in the focus on the sea in *A House by the Shore,* in *Sky Stones,* and in *The Separate Rose.* In these books Nature poetry is again for Neruda the poetry of unity. As he puts it: "On our earth, before writing was invented, before the printing press was invented, poetry flourished. That is why we know that poetry is like bread; it should be shared by all, by scholars and by peasants, by all our vast, incredible, extraordinary family of Man."[28]

Neruda's desire to share what he finds in Nature is evident in these works. And yet in the *Odes* and in *The Stones of Chile,* their public aspects notwithstanding, or in *The Art of Birds, A House by the Shore,* or *Sky Stones,* we find the poet alone, a solitary individual contemplating Nature. In this sense, these books lay the foundation as well for a sixth stage that surfaces in some of Neruda's poetry of the 1960s and that is fully developed in the posthumous works: the poet's desire for silence and solitude, his retreat into Nature, his yearning to be left alone with the sounds and smells of the natural world around him. In Nature Neruda seems to find a permanence that cannot be found in human life. This is implicit in the historical treatment given the virgin American continent in the *Canto* and the rocks in *The Stones of Chile.*

As his own death approaches, Neruda's attachment to Nature and to the continuity it represents grows. More and more he sees Nature as a life force overpowering the feeble impermanence of human existence, and in the posthumous works the poet seeks, in solitude, contact with this force. Man's life is fleeting. Nature is the source. It is the "before" and the "after" in regard to man, the enduring element that remains constant. For the poet and for his poetry Nature is the point of perpetual return.

3. The Public Poet

M uch of the poetry discussed in the previous chapters is essentially lyrical poetry, a personal, intimate vision of the universe that reflects the poet's own inner world. Even where Neruda's poetry treats the external world of Nature, it often remains in essence lyrical, for Nature is seen not only as a force in and of itself, but at times as a projection and reflection of the poet. The lyrical poet usually deals with the here and now, with what he feels and perceives. Whether he chooses to express himself immediately or to wait until feelings coalesce and become clearer, the lyrical poet uses a sharp lens, narrowly focused. The resulting vision, at its best, can become the reader's vision as well; we can accept it as giving depth and meaning to our way of looking at the world and at ourselves. Yet however difficult, delicate, and subtle the process of lyrical poetry may be, few people are involved in it. The poet and his reader are the main actors in the drama. All others are fundamentally only intelligent and cooperative bridges between a poet and his reader. This is true even where, as in Neruda's case, a political ideology prompts stylistic renovation in the form of a rejection of obscure, elitist poetry and a new thrust toward simplification. Then too, while the form has changed, the actors remain individual, removed from an historical or collective vision.

In the 1930s, the emphasis of Neruda's poetry began to undergo a significant change, moving from the mainly lyrical to embrace as well poetry concerned with public themes, first political and then epic. It was, however, precisely that, a change in emphasis, for Neruda's political and epic vision is also a personal, lyrical vision, blurring the boundaries generally dividing these different poetic forms. As a political poet, Neruda left the realm of his singularly personal "I" to embrace a cause: in this stance he wrote a series of poems inspired by the Spanish Civil War and collected under the title *Spain in My Heart* (1937). The poet experiences solidarity with a movement and a people, in this work, but his focus is still directed toward the actual and the immediate. Later, as an epic poet, Neruda did not cease to be either a lyrical poet or a political poet; but the stress shifted from the personal or the immediate to embrace a larger reality, the genesis and evolution of an entire continent. It was essentially as an epic poet that Neruda wrote the monumental *Canto General** (1950). *The Grapes and the Wind* (1954), or his later public poetry of the 1960s and 1970s—*Chanson de Geste* (1960), portions of *Ceremonial Songs** (1961), *The Flaming Sword* (1970), and *A Call for Nixonicide and Glory to the Chilean Revolution* (1973)—all carry echoes of these earlier works, but do not rival their poetic accomplishments.

Spain in My Heart

Neruda's movement along the path of public poetry began with his commitment to the Republican cause during the Spanish Civil War. When the war started in 1936, Neruda was Chile's Consul in Madrid. As a representative of his country's government, Neruda should have been neutral in the war. Yet neutrality was not possible for him. His previous reluctance to commit himself politically and his desire to be left alone to devote himself to his poetry "were cast aside by the hurricane of the Spanish Civil War. His heart decided the issue: he would stand beside Rafael Alberti and the many other poets who had espoused the cause of the Spanish Left, he would fight for the survival of the Spanish Republic."[1]

Neruda's political position before the explosion of the Spanish Civil War, if vague and not defined in terms of partisan ideology, had been in fact leftist and radical for many years. A young intellectual could hardly have reacted otherwise to the socially stratified world of Chilean society, where the poor were very poor and the rich could afford every luxury, including that of despising the poor. In Neruda's case, however, there was also a complex personal factor that had, many years before, prefigured his later political stance. Neruda's father, a symbol of authority throughout the poet's childhood and adolescence, had strongly opposed Neruda's poetic vocation. To write poetry, Neruda at an early age had to reject and actively oppose the established and conservative force of authority his father represented. The poet's relationship with his father was subtle, ambivalent, and complex, and its precise influence on the poet's eventual political convictions is not always clear; but it can be noted that in the case of more than one true revolutionary, a father's rejection or disapproval has been as decisive in the end as any volume by Marx. In fact it can be noted that Neruda in his *Memoirs*

*This book is discussed in more than one chapter. See Contents page.

never mentions Marx and, like many other politically active artists, shows a marked distaste for theoreticians of all persuasions.

Other personal factors also influenced Neruda's position once war broke out in Spain. The poet's three closest friends in Spain, all poets also, were deeply involved in the political struggle. Federico García Lorca, as we have mentioned in discussing Neruda's erotic poetry, was tragically murdered, a victim of Fascist hatred. Rafael Alberti and Miguel Hernández, active members in the Communist Party, carried the struggle to the battlefield; Alberti's fate would be exile, Hernández's would be death in one of Franco's prisons. Through this combination of personal predispositions and external political factors, the Spanish Civil War acted as a catalyst for beliefs and ideas Neruda had previously felt but had not defined nor publicly committed himself to.

Neruda had been up till then something of a loner. Suddenly, in Spain he discovered solidarity, the heady feeling of being among friends, of sharing with others goals, hopes, and fears. Neruda realized that Republican Spain needed help from supporters in every country. In chapter 1, we chronicled some of his activities during this period: the loss of his diplomatic post, his travels to Paris to give lectures on Lorca and the Spanish cause, the magazine he founded there, which had the unambiguous title *Poets of the World Defend the Spanish People,* his fund-raising efforts with the great Peruvian poet César Vallejo. Neruda gave time, energy, and money to the cause. In July, 1937, he took part in a congress of writers and intellectuals from all over the Western world who had gathered to lend their support to the endangered Spanish Republic. Hemingway, Koestler, Yeats, Stephen Spender, W.H. Auden, Louis Aragon, and André Malraux, among many others, either took part in the gathering or sent their support to the embattled Spanish people. Spain was suddenly at the center of the lives of all who understood the menace of Fascism.

The congress of writers traveled to Madrid, which was already being besieged and bombarded by Franco's forces. While there is nothing precise in Neruda's life that can be compared to a "mystical experience," a religious rebirth, these days in Madrid produced a kind of awakening in the poet. Neruda, in a secular way, was "born again," awakened to the excitement and the risks of human solidarity. The "I" is now no longer alone as it was in his first *Residence* poems,* where the individual is different from, separated from the rest of mankind, where, with rare exceptions, even when the verses

*See chapters 1 and 2.

are not explicitly related to a lonely observer, the reader cannot usually understand the chaotic visions offered to his eye without relating them to a being who has in some degree lost touch with the collectivity of men.

The Spanish Civil War was so critical in Neruda's development as a man and as a poet, that it becomes attractively simple to divide Neruda's poetry into two clear-cut sections, parted by the great explosion of the war. To insist upon such a division, however, is to run the risk of making a dramatic black-and-white presentation of what was in reality a multi-hued and complex experience. Neruda continued to write "non-political" poems both during and after the Spanish experience. And yet, in the immediacy of the situation, a change is discernible when one looks at the poet's work, allowing two poems, one written before the war and one after, to carry the message of what the Spanish Civil War meant to the poet. Such a comparison is provided by "Griefs and Rages," dated 1934, two years before the war started, and "I Am Explaining a Few Things," dated 1937, both incorporated into *The Third Residence* (1947). In the first poem, the "we" appears through a jungle of confused visions, the hint of solidarity in a forest ablaze:

> In the bottom of our breasts we are together,
> in the heart's thicket we travel across
> a summer of tigers
> We lie in wait for a length of cold skin,
> for a glimpse of untouchable complexion,
> with our mouths smelling sweat and green veins,
> we meet in a damp shadow, in a rain of kisses.
>
> You the enemy of so much sleep broken in the same manner
> as bristling plants of glass . . .
>
> 　　　　　　　　　　　　　　　["Griefs and Rages"]

The solidarity, however, is neither real nor permanent. Neruda is still lonely, although someone—a love for one night, a love for sale perhaps, a love that will not endure—lies beside him in the shadows. The poem's epigraph is negative: "There are in my heart griefs and rages," a line taken from Quevedo. Looking back on this poem in 1939, Neruda wrote a preface to it: "This poem was written in 1934. So many things have happened since! Spain, where I wrote it, is now a belt of ruins. If only we could, with a drop of poetry or a drop of love, placate the world's anger. Yet this can be done only by struggling with a resolute heart." And it is not a drop of love that the world gives back to Neruda: "The world has changed. A drop of blood fell on my lines and will go on living with them, indelible like true love."²

Like "Griefs and Rages," Neruda's first collection of *poésie engagée*, politically committed poetry, was also written in Spain. It is entitled *Spain in My Heart*. One of the most characteristic poems of the collection is "I Am Explaining a Few Things," and the experience of the three years between "Griefs and Rages" and this poem is evident in every line. The later poem begins in a conversational, almost colloquial tone, and without any rhetorical frills. "I am going to tell you all that has happened to me," the poet announces as he commences the articulation of the changes he has undergone due to the war and how these changes have altered his poetic style. He explains that before the Civil War he lived in a suburb of Madrid, with bells, clocks, trees. From his home you could look out toward Castile's dry face, looking like a leather ocean. The poet's home was known as the "House of Flowers" for the red geraniums that burst forth everywhere. It was a handsome building, dogs and children played around it, Alberti and Lorca and other poets came to visit it. "Federico, do you remember under the ground/do you remember my house with balconies where/the light of June drowned flowers in your mouth?" Everything around the poet and his home was life, movement, happiness.

And suddenly, "one morning everything was burning," one morning bonfires leapt out of the earth. From then on only fire, gunpowder, blood remained. The bandit-generals arrived with planes and Moors, with finger-rings and duchesses, and the blood of children ran through the streets, "smoothly, like children's blood." The generals have betrayed Spain, have heaped crime upon crime, this is the vision Neruda presents. But the people will fight back, and now from every house on fire, burning metal flows instead of flowers, from every hollow in the countryside Spain emerges, "and from every dead child a rifle with eyes," and from every crime bullets are born, bullets that one day will find their mark in the guilty generals. The poem ends in a lyrical, anguished scream:

> And you will ask why doesn't his poetry
> describe dreams and leaves
> and the great volcanoes of his native land?
>
> Come and see the blood in the streets.
> Come and see
> the blood in the streets.
> Come and see the blood in the streets!
> ["I Am Explaining a Few Things"]

An obsessive leitmotiv three times repeated, the last lines are absolutely chilling in their simplicity and in the revulsion they communicate and provoke. Strikingly direct, these stark verses become a terrible and powerful cry of moral outrage. Lyrical poetry, Neruda's own revulsion at the immediate situation he contemplates, has become now a political weapon with which to help the bloodied victims of Fascism. To attain its goal, the poetry must reach a vast public, it must be clear, direct, unequivocal; it must excite indignation and admiration, inflame the heart, move the hand toward the gun. It must become a flag, a slogan, a marching song. The poet who had once described the ecstasy of love and the anguish of loneliness must now tell of battlefields and city streets drenched in blood. And he must make these red-stained scenes appear in nauseating vividness before his public.

In his *Memoirs,* Neruda recounts his experience as a committed poet in war-torn Spain. It is a tale of friendship, solidarity, high hopes soon to be betrayed by historical events; and it is in the midst of the almost inconceivable bloodshed of this bloodiest of civil wars that Neruda finds his public. The decision was made during the war to reprint *Spain in My Heart* in an attempt to boost morale. Manuel Altolaguirre, a friend of Neruda's, undertook the project, in 1938, setting up a printing press in an old monastery near Gerona, close to enemy lines. Paper was scarce and had to be produced and improvised. Amid intermittent bombardments, the right mixture for paper was created, made out of enemy banners, old shirts, sheets, bits and pieces of discarded paper. Somehow, the finished book was a perfect work of art. Years later Neruda saw a copy of the book in Washington, in the Library of Congress, exhibited in a glass case as one of the rare books of our century.

The ink was still fresh on the pages of this book when the retreat of the Spanish Republican soldiers became a rout. Half a million soldiers and refugees crowded the roads leading out of Spain into France. But Neruda's poetry had given a unity and articulated purpose to the exodus. "I learned that many [of the Republican soldiers] carried copies of the book in their sacks instead of their own food and clothing. With those sacks over their shoulders they set out on the long march to France. The endless column walking to exile was bombed hundreds of times. Soldiers fell and the books were spilled on the highway. Others continued their interminable flight."[3]

Spain in My Heart is an exceptional blend of political and lyrical poetry, for if the subject is ideological, the tone and the passion are lyrical. It cries out with the poet's own personal despair as he watches the blood of Spaniards run down the streets of Madrid, filling the streets like an endless and terrible river turned red. It is an immediate response, a personal cry for what the poet is seeing and feeling. Its poetry can be magnificently powerful, among the finest political poetry to come out of the Spanish Civil War. The collection of poems created a propaganda vehicle for the Republican side; yet its tone and language stay very close to the poet's real and actual horror at what he sees before him. In many ways, Neruda's poetry on the war in which his friend Lorca was murdered, is very close to Lorca's own lament on the death of his friend the bullfighter Ignacio Sánchez Mejías. The anguish Lorca experienced upon seeing his friend's blood stain the bullfight arena is extended in Neruda's poetry to embrace the anguish of seeing the blood of an entire people fill its land. Only Lorca, in 1935, cries his anguish through denial: "I do not want to see it!/ Tell the moon to come/ I do not want to see the blood/ of Ignacio on the sand." ("Lament" 2, 1–4). Neruda, two years later, politicized by the war that killed Lorca, would boldly turn to the world and say: "Come and see the blood in the streets."

In his *Memoirs,* Neruda unabashedly recognizes the role of his own work in the Spanish Civil War, an attitude that has often been criticized as vanity. As the novelist José Yglesias noted in reviewing the English translation of Neruda's *Memoirs,* the Spanish Civil War is often presented there as "but an incident in the life of Pablo Neruda." Yet even Yglesias must go on to recognize that Neruda's contribution to Spain was no less than the poet's presentation of it: "But who equalled his contribution?," Yglesias asks rhetorically. "He personally saved 1,000 exiles from French camps and found them a home in Chile."[4] Neruda's contribution, his poetry, his dedication, and his energy did not go unappreciated by the Spain for which he fought. Years later the Spanish people were to repay to Neruda what he had given to them. When Chile in 1973, like Spain in 1936, found its democratically elected leftist government overthrown by a bloody military coup, by another rebellious officer with Fascist leanings, the Spanish people remembered Neruda's service to their cause and a volume of poems was published in Spain. In it Spanish poets one after another paid homage to Neruda and his commitment and mourned the death of the poet and the overthrow of the Allende government he had supported and served. This volume, in direct remembrance of Neruda's gift to the Spanish Republic and in deep grief for his death and his nation's plight, was called *Chile in My Heart.*[5]

Canto General

In *Canto General,* Neruda returns to look at his own land. The lyrical and the political poetic forms present in *Spain in My Heart* are extended and expanded, this time to embrace the epic, a collective and historical vision of an entire continent, in which immediate feelings and events are replaced by a broader, all-encompassing vision of America. Neruda had not chosen to become a political poet in Spain; he had been forced into it by the events he witnessed there. As Selden Rodman quotes him: "Nobody has ever *asked* me to write a political poem. If the subject didn't touch me, I couldn't. I haven't written a poem about intervention in the Dominican Republic, for instance, but I am free to write one. Poets like T.S. Eliot and Saint-John Perse are not free to. They are hobbled by conventions. Their conventions inhibit them, tell them that such a subject must wait a hundred years to be usable. After a hundred years the blood will be washed away by the rain. I prefer the blood to the rain . . . I do not believe in social realism. That label, that way of looking at things, is prefabricated. I want to taste the wine before it is bottled."[6]

In the same way, Neruda did not choose to become an epic poet; he was forced into it by the social reality of his country and his continent. As Neruda defined the poet's role: "Our volcanoes and our rivers have been so far mired upon the dry lines of textbooks. Let their fire and their fertility be given to the whole world by our poets. We are the chroniclers of a retarded birth."[7] *Canto General* means general song, and in his *Canto General* Neruda simply recognizes and accepts the role he sees as belonging to the Latin American poet. He sees a need for a poetry that will express the vision, history, and goals of a people, a poetry that can connect past, present, and future around the destiny of millions of human beings. For this poetry, Neruda necessarily turns to the epic tradition.

Although often associated with the classics, the epic has, in reality, never disappeared altogether from the world of poetry; it was very much alive during the medieval period and later. Dante, in his *Divine Comedy,* was often an epic poet, as was Milton in *Paradise Lost.* Epic poetry was present during the Enlightenment and surfaced at random during the nineteenth century, as in Victor Hugo's "Les Châtiments" or "Napoléon le Petit," written in political exile and inspired by a violent opposition to Napoleon III. The examples of Mickiewicz in Poland and Petöfi in Hungary are equally significant, if less well known. When political poetry transcends the specific moment that gave it birth, when specific personalities are subsumed in a vast panorama, this poetry can no longer be called strictly political. It becomes patriotic, in the best sense of this much-abused word, and finally epic. It deals with the destiny of societies, peoples, and cultures, and it tries to come to grips with the eternal problem of man's role on earth and his place in the world of the future. Neruda's *Canto General*—not all of it, to be sure, but enough of it—belongs to this privileged category. In it the role of the poet in today's world is redefined and exalted.

Neruda's erotic poetry and his Nature poetry are primarily lyrical, *Spain in My Heart* is both lyrical and political, and *Canto General* is lyrical, political, and epic. It should be understood that we are here using the word *epic* in a generic way that defines poetry by its content and that does not demand strict adherence to formal structures or meters associated with the classical epic. *Epic* here is used to reflect the fact that *Canto General* is no longer only Neruda's immediate and emotional vision of the world. In the *Canto*, Neruda presents his history of the American continent, a history that describes the very beginning of the continent, its geography and flora and fauna before the existence of man, that goes on to catalogue its violent history of conquest, and ends by dealing with current political figures and problems, and with the life of the poet himself. It is the scope and attitude of the poem that classify it as epic, rather than any adherence to classical rules of epic form. And it is above all the poet's place in the poem that establishes this classification, for here Neruda rises to become the epic bard of the Americas.

Throughout much of *Canto General*, Neruda is no longer the single individual Pablo Neruda or his poetical projection or persona. He is the spokesman and chronicler for an entire people, he is the voice of the South American continent, much as his greatly admired predecessor, Walt Whitman, saw himself as the voice of the North American continent.* It is a break with the poetical themes of the Old World in order to establish a poetry, a vision, a mythology for the New World. In the Heroic Age of Greece, the chronicler of such vast histories, the epic bard, his disciples and imitators already "were marked as men possessing peculiar qualities of memory and vision. In fact, the purveyors and refurbishers of popular tradition concerning gods and heroes, they were credited with being able, by special inspiration, to transcend the limitations of sense . . . and to rescue the past from oblivion, restoring it to life and moving their hearers to pity and fear."[8] This is precisely Neruda's stance in much of *Canto*

---

*Emir Rodríguez Monegal has stressed this relationship between the two poets in a seminar at Yale University, "Neruda and Whitman."

General. It is the poet as epic bard who evokes the past and imbues it with palpitating life, who takes history and makes it immediate, almost journalistic in its presence. The poet is here as chronicler, observer, participant, and actor, and, above all, as the voice of a collectivity, a voice possessing all the special powers of evocation and creation of drama that form part of the magic of the classical epic bard.

And like that of the classical bard, Neruda's vision of history is not unlyrical. It is, in fact, more often personal than objective. The historical vision of *Canto General* has often been criticized on these grounds, especially for its simplistic division into black and white, good and evil, hero and villain. The vision *is* simplistic on the historical level. In it there are stars and scoundrels, and the line between them is implacably drawn: Nature, the indigenous American population, the common man of America are the heroes; the invaders, first the Spaniards and later the United States with its multinational corporations, are the villains. The heroes are too perfect, the common man, long-suffering, righteous, is elevated in Whitmanesque fashion to larger-than-life virtue; the Spaniards, in contrast, are presented as having no virtue. Even the imposition of their language (which the poet himself is forced to employ to communicate his rejection of it) is seen as a destructive rape of the indigenous and authentic American heritage. It is not only on this level that Neruda's historical vision is arbitrary. Certain political leaders, among them González Videla of Chile, are singled out for castigation, while others, like Trujillo, who were guilty of much greater crimes, are generally overlooked. Neruda seeks to present an epic of the South American continent, yet he largely ignores huge sections of that continent, most particularly the multiple spaces and personalities of Brazil. The poet's vision of the United States is likewise arbitrary. He defines the United States as an "outsider" in the Americas and ignores its very real accomplishments in order to focus exclusively on its imperialistic role in South America. Even in his narrow focus on the United States and his diatribe against modern invaders—the United Fruit Company and other multinational corporations—Neruda's vision is near-sighted and simplistic. As Emir Rodríguez Monegal has pointed out, Neruda singles out the United States, not only because it had in fact a large presence in South America, but also because Neruda was a strict Soviet-style Communist when he wrote the *Canto*, and as such, he shared the cold-war attitude toward the "Colossus to the North." But in this historical vision limited by ideology, other exploiters, true invaders in the Americas—France, Holland, and England all had colonies in Latin America at the time Neruda wrote—are strangely excluded from mention.[9]

Yet to acknowledge the personal and even inaccurate historical nature of Neruda's vision is not to lessen its impact as an epic work. In his *Satyricon,* Petronius makes clear that even for the classical epic bard historical accuracy is not a requisite or even the goal: "Things actually done are not to be put into verses, for historians treat them far better; instead . . . the free spirit is to rush; so there is evidenced rather the vaticination of a raging mind than the testimony of scrupulous statement by witnesses."[10] In other words, in presenting a personal vision of history, Neruda is well within the epic tradition. And in this tradition heroes and villains are customarily overdrawn. The heroism of El Cid, for example, and his generosity and his loyalty are matched only by the cowardice, niggardliness, and fickle ingratitude of the king he serves. In the epic, heroes are indeed heroes and villains are indeed villains. Neruda's treatment of the native American population and the invading Spaniards and North Americans follows that practice.

The ideological and propagandistic overtones of much of *Canto General* are also in the epic tradition. Ruling monarchs and noblemen often commissioned epic poetry to be written for the express purpose of presenting a particular version of historical or contemporary political events. The epic was used as a propaganda vehicle: the great deeds of former heroes were recounted in order to excite patriotic fervor and nationalistic zeal. The epic became the vehicle for putting forth a certain vision of reality, particularly in times of war, in order to spur on the listening public, to inspire its listeners to make great sacrifices and to perform acts of valor in the name of the realm. Neruda's often one-sided ideological vision may fail as history, but once again, it does not fail as epic poetry. On the contrary, it forms part of the popular epic tradition. Like Vergil's *Aeneid,* it "is deliberately conceived . . . to give meaning to the destiny of a people, asserting the implications of their history and recognizing the significance of contemporary events in relation to the past."[11]

Canto General, while largely an epic work, repeats the creative pattern established in Neruda's more lyrical works: it grew out of personal experience. Political activism and disillusion brought forth *Canto General.* After the disaster in Spain, Neruda returned to Chile. As chronicled earlier in discussing Neruda's erotic poetry, the 1940s were for Neruda a time of active political involvement followed by acute disappointment. Neruda had been elected a Senator in 1945, the same year that he joined the Communist Party. It was the Party that encouraged his writing of the *Canto,* which he had begun years earlier, and, in 1947, it was again the Party that gave Neruda leave from his parliamentary duties so he could devote himself fully to the *Canto.* He returned to the Senate, however, in 1947 and a year later made a blistering attack—"I Accuse"—on the government. Suddenly, Neruda found himself an "enemy of the State," forced to go underground and ultimately into exile. "But even in hiding," Rodríguez Monegal notes, "he continues writing that *Canto General* which will be converted inevitably into a weapon of political battle, not only in Chile, but internationally."[12]

What had been intended to be a history of Neruda's native land, a general song of Chile, became the epic of an entire continent. The finished work of these days of political battle was published in 1950. It is one of the few works of modern poetry to attempt in one volume a sweeping chronicle which spans time and space, history and geography to form a self-contained vision of a continent, its land and its people. It is divided into fifteen principal sections. Each section has a defined subject and tone, and each must be at least briefly considered for the reader to begin to grasp the scope and greatness of the work, for its fame rests not only on the excellence of many individual poems contained in it, but above all on the vastness of its vision, unique in modern poetry.

The first section portrays the birth of the American continent. If the epic is the basic model for the *Canto* in its entirety, in this first section, another ancient model prefigures and gives definition to the poet's words: the Bible. Like the Bible, and using verse forms and literary devices imitative of Biblical models, *Canto General* begins with a genesis. Nature is presented in its raw state, without the presence of man. Neruda goes back to the origins, to the chaotic world where twilight reminds us of the hues of the iguana's skin and monkeys in their frenzied flight among the trees seem to weave a thread of erotic violence. We witness the flight of a cloud of butterflies, we wade in the night of the alligator, surrounded by snouts moving out of the slime. We hear a clatter of armor, we catch a glimpse of huge primitive animals turning and twisting in the misty shadows. The jaguar appears and disappears, a phosphorous streak, faster than our eye can catch it. The eyes of the puma seem to blaze endlessly in the night, like the eyes of Blake's tiger; the "alcoholic eyes of the jungle," Neruda writes, burn in his head ("Some Beasts"). Badgers rake the river beds, red-toothed, ready for the final assault; below, surrounded by the vastness of water, as a dot in the circle of a continent, drenched in the ritual mud, rapacious and religious, the gigantic coiled anaconda appears.

Neruda introduces this virginal state of Nature with lines whose imagery and contrasts will hold constant for the entire *Canto*:

> Before the wig and frock-coat
> were the rivers, arterial rivers;

were the mountains, on whose frayed wave
the condor or the snow seemed fixed:
there was humidity and thicket, thunder
still without name, the planetary plains.

["Love America," "A Lamp on this Earth"]

Here the opposition present throughout the long epic is established. The "wig and frock-coat" represent the conquerors, the Spaniards who will be the invading force in this primeval garden. They are the "after" and they are designated by artificial trappings—false hair and man-made clothing to hide the naked reality of the body—which clash with the Nature they penetrate. The "before" is the eternal inheritance of America, what is lasting and authentic, America's roots, its rivers, its mountains, the condor, the native bird of the Andes. The poet's "before" is even before the invasion of language to categorize and limit, by naming; there is thunder before there is the word to designate it and separate it from the primal unity. In Neruda's portrait, Nature predates not only "civilized," artificial and invading man, but also language, the vehicle of social organization.

The verse is free, matching the motion of creation, the palpitation of unrestricted existence. This sense of active creation is reinforced by the mixing of natural elements: the mountains are described in terms of water, a "frayed wave," and the condor, a symbol of flight, is related to snow and transformed into an immobile statue which seems to almost form part of the "frayed wave," awaiting its moment of creation to soar into space. In the *Residence* poems, Neruda's mixture of natural elements in his metaphors signified a world in disorder; here it signifies a world before man's order, and it takes on a positive value. The metaphorical confusion of elements heightens the sense of a world just awakening; the elements seem alive and express a sense of becoming in an almost pantheistic universe where there are no divisions, only flowing, all-encompassing oneness and unity.

To describe America's genesis, Neruda employs poetic techniques like those Whitman used in *Leaves of Grass,* which have their origin in the Hebraic poetry of the Bible: the use of constructive parallels, a system of thought balance in which a verse cannot stand alone, but is dependent on the following verse to complete its thought; rapid enumeration characteristic of inspired speech; reiteration in varying form, and extensive alliteration, both designed to produce rhythm within the free verse and an almost chanting, hypnotic quality to the lines. Neruda's choice of verbs is also worth noting. The poet says the rivers "were." He could have said "there were rivers," but instead he chooses to give the rivers independent being; they were, they existed, they had life. This verb choice makes the rivers alive and immediate. It transforms them into quivering veins that reflect the "before," the "In the beginning" theme.

The entire first section of the *Canto* is devoted to this "before," to the raw, untamed Nature of the American continent. It is perhaps Neruda's greatest Nature poetry:

> A new perfume spread out and out
> filling through every pore in the earth
> the living lungs, turning them into smoke and fragrance.
> Wild tobacco was lifting into dawn
> its rosebush of imagined atmosphere.
> As a spear, as a sword ending in fire,
> corn came out: its slim vertical statue
> lost its kernels and was born again,
> its flour was broadcast, it cradled
> dead bodies under its roots, and later
> from its cradle it witnessed
> the slow growth of the vegetal gods.
>   ["Vegetations," "A Lamp on this Earth"]

In these lines, Nature exists on its own, the long enumeration of the variety of American vegetation becoming reminiscent at times of Andrés Bello's neoclassical ode to the richness of the Americas. And Neruda's genesis is specifically American. In it, only the lands, the minerals, the reptiles, birds, and mammals of the Americas are described. What is striking, moreover, in this genesis is that God is absent from the vast panorama. The animals spring to life within a tropical or arid landscape; they display their strength and their beauty among vast rivers—the Amazon, the Orinoco—and many-hued skies. The condor, both king and assassin, lonely friar of the skies, hurricane among the birds of prey, flies on and on over sharp summits and rivers of shadow. Fireflies send down their droplets of phosphor. This unfolding of mineral riches, vast jungles, birds is an autonomous, unmotivated, undirected surge of life. No Jehovah orchestrates from above the explosion of natural forces.

The particular symbolic value given to Nature in the opening of the *Canto* is the poet's own personal vision. It is he who assigns it a positive value, even where its more violent aspects are portrayed, in order to then set up the contrast with the men of "wigs and frock-coats" who will violate it. And it is he who presents the unfolding of Nature independent of any theological origin. Nonetheless, this vision, while personal, is no longer always strictly lyrical in its projection of Nature. It does not reflect the poet's immediate emotional state, as did the chaotic ruins of the Orient in the *Residence* poems. Now the poet is able to transcend the actual in order to arrive at a sweeping historical vision in which virginal Nature is the genesis, the point of departure in the destiny of a continent, the matrix for the man of Nature, the indigenous man of America, its sole legitimate heir.

Only after the raw continent has been described and all its vegetation, animal population, rivers, and minerals have been enumerated does this man of Nature appear as a central force in the poem. He *is*:

> like a vessel of clay it came,
> this mineral race, man
> carved out of stones and thin air,
> clean like a drinking vessel, full of music.
>
> ["The Men," "A Lamp on this Earth"]

Mayas, Incas, Araucanians, the Indian tribes of Mexico, Central America, and South America are listed one after another. Through the continual repetition of key images the poet makes it clear that the Indians are the only authentic possessors of the land. Earth, clay, air, copper, and stone are the raw elements of America, and these are also the key words used to designate the Indian. The male Indian is evoked as a "young warrior of shadow and copper," and the female as the maternal "nuptial plant . . . alligator mother, metallic dove" ("Love America"). Whether male or female, the indigenous American is described in earth tones; the copper of his body, the stone of his tools, artifacts, and cities, the earth from which he alone springs are metaphorically related to the strength or gentleness of America's native plants and animals. The Indian is the genuine offspring of Nature, the son of America; this authentic, indigenous, natural man is contrasted always with the inauthentic, artificial man of wigs and clothing, the rapacious invador, the *conquistador*.

We have noted that in Neruda's presentation of the Nature of the American continent, no divinity is present as the source of life. The same is true when man appears. Once again, it is in this fashion that Neruda's genesis departs from its Biblical model. In the Bible, as in the *Canto*, man is surrounded by mystery and fear, by vast forces he cannot control. But in the Bible man copes with the awe of Nature, of knowledge, of his own destiny by making a pact with God, a pact which—through Abraham, Noah, Moses—has to be clarified and renewed from time to time. The ensuing dialogue between man and God constitutes the central part of the Bible, both the Old and the

New Testaments, and forms also the core of the Biblical interpretation of the universe. When man appears in Neruda's poem, however, Jehovah remains absent from the heavens. Neruda is not about to fall back on Christian eschatology and theology. Nonetheless, the poet knows that mistakes, even disasters, can occur when man no longer understands the huge forces that surround him. In his own personal and secular way, he intuitively grasps the Biblical message that the pact between man and the forces of Nature, History, Destiny has to be established and reestablished, written and reinforced, time and again.

Such a pact is at the center of section II of *Canto General.* The genesis of section I closes with the appearance of man, and section II brings forth the "I" of the poet in one of Neruda's most acclaimed works, "Heights of Macchu Picchu":

> From the air to the air, like an empty net,
> I went among the streets and the atmosphere, arriving
>   and saying good-bye, . . .
> ["Heights of Macchu Picchu," I]

The poet, adopting the persona of the American man, walks among the ruins of the great Inca city, Machu Picchu, built high into the mountains near Cuzco in Peru as a last, and vain, retreat from the onslaught of the invading Spanish conquerors. It is a poem of symbolic death and of resurrection in which the poet himself participates as actor, beginning as a lonely voyager and ending with the manifestation of his full commitment to the collectivity, to the American indigenous people, their Indian roots, their past and their future.

Neruda had visited the Inca city in 1943. Unlike most other Indian ruins where only one or two individual structures, fragments of the whole, remain, Machu Picchu is a complete city. Hidden until one is virtually within the city itself, it suddenly appears, spreading before the viewer an entire urban landscape, tier on tier and row on row of terraced stone, an incredible sight to come upon in the remote and silent mountain terrain. One is compelled to imagine hordes of people going about their daily lives; it is this strong sense of human presence, even more than the vast stone, which strikes awe in the modern visitor to the city. Like others before and after him, Neruda in 1943 was open to this sense of awe and to the shadows of the city, whose mystery and allure penetrate in interstitial fashion. What sets Neruda apart is not his sensibility, his reaction to the contact with Machu Picchu—the city calls forth that response from everyone who sees it—but his ability to convert this personal experience into a collective rebirth for an entire people. "Heights of Macchu Picchu," written in the same year he joined the Communist Party, is perhaps Neruda's finest blending of the lyrical with the epic.

The hero of the poem is the "I" of the narrator. The poet explores the cosmos, penetrates the earth to its secret chambers, ascends toward light from the roots through the stems of plants, identifies with the stones of the huge sacred city. The poet as primitive man, as prophet and, ultimately, as semi-divinity, soaring through space and through history, brings the reader with him on an incredible voyage, an adventure to the end of the earth. A strange poetic time machine allows the poet to swim upstream in the flow of time, finding Nature, man, history, visions of the future.

A similar kind of movement is also present, of course, in the Bible and in Dante's *Divine Comedy*. Yet once again, Neruda's poem achieves epic scope and majestic rhythm without embracing theology. The Bible and Dante's work are the only kind of epic poetry that could have been produced by a deeply religious people or man. "Heights of Macchu Picchu" is perhaps the only poetry that could have been produced by a poet who no longer believes in God; it may also be the only kind of poetry fully comprehensible to the readers of our time, of an era that has been described more than once as the "post-Christian era." A Bible without Jehovah, a *Divine Comedy* without Vergil, Beatrice, Satan, and the Trinity. This is the sort of epic and philosophical vision Neruda offers.

In this vision, the poet experiences a vertical descent into the heart of matter:

> I placed my forehead among the deep waves,
> I descended like a drop among the sulphurous peace,
> and, like a blind man, I went down back to the jasmine
> of mankind's worn-out primeval spring.
>
> ["Heights of Macchu Picchu," II]

The attitude toward matter, the dark flow of time, the mysterious and violent spring of mankind is one thing that separates the poet from Dante. Neruda stresses what Dante chooses largely to ignore, the presence of matter, both inorganic and organic, as the inescapable reality. The poet touches stone, earth, roots, trees, rain, clouds, space. He is here, as elsewhere, the poet of "heroic matter," and each line, each metaphor brings this matter closer to human experience, specifically to human sexuality:

> deeper and deeper, in the gold of geology,
> like a sword wrapped in meteors,

I sank my tempestuous sweet hand
into the most genital recesses of the earth.
                    ["Heights of Macchu Picchu," II]

The tale that is slowly, serenely, majestically unfolded in Neruda's lines is the tale of the poet, alone, face to face with the vastness of matter. Dialogue is absent in this tale: we hear only the poet's voice, sometimes clearly, at other times muffled as in a dream or stream of consciousness. Both the Bible and Dante's work are, in contrast, rich in dialogue. Abraham, Noah, Job actually hear God's voice and respond to it, the patriarchs and prophets speak and are answered; Dante's dialogue with the inhabitants of the three vertically organized kingdoms fills out memorable pages of his book. Neruda, too, has his questions, but here, there is no God or gods beside him or above him. He will reach the high stone pinnacles of the sacred city, Machu Picchu, a city built by men to the greater glory of their gods, but the gods are departed. No mention is made of the divine forces that moved the Incas to haul huge stones in order to build the sacred city as a last refuge from the advance of the Spaniards and the religion they would impose. Only the stones remain, only an echo of the ancient fervor, the old faith.

Yet it would be a mistake to think that the poet's questions go unanswered. The dialogue between a poet and the world of matter, space, time cannot be defined except on terms established in the poem itself. In the *Book of Job,* God's answer to Job's anguished question is not the logical, expected one. Rather, God displays His awesome presence, His infinite power as a rebuke to the finite, ultimately self-centered questions Job asks. In Neruda's poem, the answer given is also in irrational or superrational language, an answer given by a Power that is at the same time the Power of Light and of Darkness:

All-powerful death invited me many times:
its words were like salt hidden in the waves
and what its invisible fragrance suggested
were fragments of wrecks and heights
or vast structures of winds and snowdrifts.

I had come to the steely edge of the blade, the narrowest
channel of wind, the shroud of field and stone,
the interstellar void of ultimate steps
and the vertiginous spiral way:
but not through wave on wave dost thou reach us, thou vast sea of
    death
yet rather like a gallop of twilight
or like the comprehensible mathematics of the dark.
                    ["Heights of Macchu Picchu," II]

The poet can travel vast distances, dive into the deepest seas of matter and history, because he is a visionary poet, endowed with all the powers such poets have. In this particular case Neruda makes full use of a special sort of poetic language, one associated with the surrealist school, the only modern school of art and poetry that has tried to come to terms with infinity. We find constantly the jarring juxtaposition of nouns and adjectives that are unexpectedly brought together, the strange metaphors that create a link between two aspects of reality no one else thought could be similar.

The poet's magic boots have taken him first down into the earth, through seas of darkness. Now he will go up the ladder. Climbing, the poet goes through thickets toward the tall city rocked in a wind of thorns, the city that is like a spade buried in primordial sand, the city made out of stone and the foam of condors, the abandoned city where the grains of corn grew to the heavens to fall again like red hail, up where men trod the thinning mist. And the poet beckons his reader:

> Climb up with me, American love.
>
> Kiss these secret stones with me . . .
> Love, love, until the night full of cliffs,
> from the musical flint of the Andes
> descends toward the dawn's red knees,
> come out and contemplate the snow's blind son.
>
> ["Heights of Macchu Picchu," VIII]

Echoes, sounds, chords, voices out of the mist come forth. There is a double presence of which we become aware, the overwhelming presence of Nature in all its power, and the ghostly presence of ancient men, of men who came to terms with Nature many centuries ago. Both presences fuse in a moment of love and recognition, and the past becomes as well the present. And here, the quasi-surrealist imagery of earlier verses gives way to a clear statement:

> Come to my very being, to my own dawn,
> climb toward crowned solitudes.
>
> The fallen kingdom goes on living.
>
> ["Heights of Macchu Picchu," VIII]

And again:

> We face a permanence: the stone, the word, endure:
> the city upraised like a vase in our hands,
> all the hands together, the living, the dead, the quiet,

death's fullness holds us here, a high wall, the fullness
of so much life is like a blow falling
a blow of petals of flint, an enduring rose, a dwelling:
all this in a stone reef, in a glacier in the Andes.
                    ["Heights of Macchu Picchu," VII]

What the poet finds in his vertical pilgrimage is not God or the gods
but something perhaps more moving, the traces of a destroyed civilization, the ashes of a ruined kingdom, its priests, its women, its children, its slaves. Everywhere the footprints of man are present,
everywhere matter has been penetrated. Within a confusion of
splendor and hope, the night of stone and hunger recedes. It is no
longer the wide rivers and the shiny boulders of the first contact with
Nature that occupy the poet. Beneath each stone the poet now
senses a presence from the past, the presence of a lost brother. And
the initial loneliness of the poem evolves toward exhilaration and
joy. The gods may have vanished, but the presence of man endures.
The ghosts invoked by the poet are the humble ghosts of laborers,
slaves, everyday men and women:

John Splitstone, son of Wiracocha,
John Coldbody, heir of a green star,
John Barefoot, grandson to the turquoise,
come up to be reborn with me, as my own brother.
                    ["Heights of Macchu Picchu," XI]

Come up to be born again, brother.
Give me your hand from the deep
recess of your scattered grief . . .
I am here to speak for your dead lips.
                    ["Heights of Macchu Picchu," XII]

Identity and brotherhood are the key words of the poem's climactic
end. Only thus are the ancient ghosts placated, not only the haunting figures of the ancient dwellers of these American lands, but also
the half-seen, frightful ghosts of Neruda's *Residence* poems, ghosts
that were only a reflection, in a dark mirror, of the poet's own isolation and despair.

Another word for "brotherhood" is "communion." Communion is
identity, companionship within a common goal. The future takes
over, it overwhelms with its light the dark night of the past. The poet
has identified with his ancestors, he *is* his ancestors. He asks them to
link their limbs, their memories, their lips, and from the bottom of a
long night he listens to their voices as if he, the poet, were anchored

to their bodies. He wants to hear every tale, every life story, step by step, he wants to receive from their hands each one of their tools, their knives, "a river of yellow sun rays," "a river of buried tigers." He asks for tears, for silence, for water and hope:

> Give me the struggle, the iron, the volcanoes.
> Cleave your bodies to mine like magnets.
> Flow into my veins, into my mouth.
> Speak through my words and through my blood.
> ["Heights of Macchu Picchu," XII]

In "Heights of Macchu Picchu," the poet has come into contact with death and with resurrection. It is the kindling of an identification and a commitment of solidarity with America's past, present, and future. It is also a rebirth for Neruda's own poetic sytle. When the poet is alone in the initial lines of this poem, the images are difficult, often depending on the radical juxtaposition characteristic of surrealism. As the poet moves toward his commitment to the collectivity, however, as he calls out to common ancestors, he speaks a language they can comprehend. The obscure and unexpected imagery of the early lines then gives way to the simple, easily understood language of Neruda's later poetry, making "Heights of Macchu Picchu" the death and regeneration as well of a form of poetic expression. It is one of Neruda's most important works of poetry. Like Neruda's days earlier in war-torn Madrid, the visit to Machu Picchu and the poem it inspired come close, on multiple levels, to achieving a kind of mystical communion and rebirth of purpose.

The three sections of *Canto General* that follow this poem move into the realm of history. The Biblical genesis of section I and the quasi-mystical awakening and commitment of section II are now replaced by the historical reality of a continent overtaken by men other than its own. Section III deals with the Spanish conquest, the *conquistadores,* as we have mentioned, being presented in unswervingly negative tones, as rapacious beasts, visiting destruction and violence on the native Indian past. "The butchers carved up the islands" is the opening line of this section, referring to the 1493 arrival of the Spaniards to the Caribbean. First it was Guanahaní and then Cuba:

> Cuba, my love, they tied you to the rack,
> they cut up your face with knives,
> they spread open your legs of pale gold,
> they broke open your pomegranate sex,
> they pierced you with swords,
> they tore you apart, they burned you.
> ["Now It's Cuba," "The Conquistadors"]

The continent is the virgin woman, brutally spread open, raped, and left dismembered by the red-bearded soldiers of Castile ("They Arrive at the Mexican Sea," "The Conquistadors"). The Spaniards here are not discoverers of a New World, they are the merciless invaders of an already established and beloved universe. The contrast between the strong yet gentle American man of copper and air, and the violent, destructive, raping Spaniard could not be more extreme.

In this portrayal of the indigenous population as authentic, good, and peaceful and of the Spaniard as villainous, false, and treacherous, some of Neruda's own personal psychology comes into evidence. The symbolic woman that the poet adopts as a mother figure throughout the *Canto* is without exception indigenous, and is associated always with the earth, the copper, America. Neruda, however, treats the paternal figure in a more complex fashion. Neruda's father, José del Carmen Reyes Morales, had been an authoritarian figure in his life, one who was associated with the industrial establishment through the railroad for which he worked, and above all, as we have mentioned, one who neither understood nor tolerated his son's vocation for poetry. It was to avoid the ire of his father, a man fair-haired like the invading Spaniards in the *Canto,* that Neruda first published his poetry under a pseudonym. This pseudonym, Pablo Neruda, would later become his legal name; the poet never reversed his rejection of his legal name, Neftalí Ricardo Reyes. But he did not omit the name of his father's family from his poetry. The family name, Reyes, appears several times in the *Canto.* While Reyes is a common Spanish name, there are many other common Spanish names that could as easily have been used, and Neruda could not have been oblivious to the implications of the choice of the name Reyes. It was his father's name and it is his father and his father's people who are being pointed to each time the name appears in the poem.

Unlike the constancy with which the maternal figure is portrayed in the *Canto,* the name Reyes appears in opposing contexts. At one point, the name is listed among the Spaniards coming to rape the American continent:

> Toward Veracruz a murderous wind is blowing.
> It is there that horses are brought to the shore.
> The ships are thick with claws
> and with red beards from Castile.
> There come the Arias, the Reyes, the Rojas and Maldonados,
> the sons of Castilian poverty,
> the ones that knew about hunger in winter
> and knew all about lice in country inns.
>   ["They Arrive at the Mexican Sea," "The Conquistadors"]

Or again when Neruda employs both his father's names, Reyes and Morales:

> See them falling down into the dust
> these harsh sons of hatred,
> the Villagras, Mendozas, Reinosos,
> the Reyes, Morales, Alderetes,
> see them roll down toward the white bottom
> of glacial American lands.
>
> ["The Expanded War," "The Liberators"]

Yet the identification of Neruda's blond father with the fair-haired and treacherous Spaniards is not absolute. In "The Land Is Called Juan" the name of Reyes appears once more, but this time in the list of martyred workers of "Catastrophe in Sewell":

> Sánchez, Reyes, Ramírez, Nuñez, Alvarez.
> These names are like Chile's deep foundations.
> They are the people and the people are the foundations
> of the fatherland.
> If you let them die our fatherland grows weaker,
> blood flows away, emptiness prevails.

The psychology involved is complex; Neruda includes his father's name both among the murdering Spaniards and among the martyred and exploited workers of Chile. As Emir Rodríguez Monegal has pointed out, this personal ambivalence toward the father figure assumes further significance through the fact that the poetry that would eventually become the voluminous *Canto General* was actually begun on the day that Neruda's father died: "The feeling, perhaps irrational, that his blond father belonged to the invading and conquering race while his mother is made of dark, indigenous clay, was to dominate Neruda's personal mythology from this moment on and would impregnate the *Canto General* with an extremely profound ardor."[13] The feelings are deep and difficult. It is not surprising that they come forth in the *Canto* in contradictory form.

Section IV, "The Liberators," is devoted to those who resisted invasion and colonization, from the Indian leaders who fought to defend their lands to the later colonial leaders who overthrew the imperial government established by Spain. These are the liberators who now appear:

> Here comes the tree, the huge tree
> of storm, the tree of the people.

Out of the earth its heroes emerge
as leaves drenched in sap.
and the wind shakes the foliage
a foliage that sends forth rumors of crowds
until once more the seed falls down
the seed of bread once more falls into the earth.

["The Liberators," I]

With the arrival of the liberators, the poetic imagery once more shifts back to Nature. The liberators will spring from the earth, they are the tree, the continent's roots. As throughout the *Canto,* the legitimate sons of America, whether they be the initial indigenous population or the later mixed population that fights the Spanish colonial hold on America, will be depicted in metaphors relating them to the earth, to Nature, to the primeval forces described in section I.

The image of the tree is of particular importance in this resurgence of Nature imagery, for it is a symbol that recurs throughout *Canto General.* The tree is solid and strong, and it is always related to the origins, to roots, as we recall from the triangle *materia-madre-madera* in Neruda's earlier "Entrance into Wood." The tree is the unifying force of the people, and it is an appropriate image for a people depicted as arising from and continually linked to the earth. It reaches into the earth and the past through its roots, it soars forward toward the air and the sky in its present, and it is constantly renewed, an eternal future, through its foliage, allowing this structure to connect the people's past and present and future growth through one single image. As Frank Riess has observed, it is through the image of the tree—linked to the people and their liberators— that "the natural cycle of continual rebirth is compared to the human or historical cycle. This comparison enables the poet to bring in the related themes of historical time which has passed away; the death of individuals who die in the defense of *pueblo* [the people], in the shape of the tree and its roots in the earth; or past layers of accumulated time. The individuals fall back into the soil to nourish the roots which keep the tree as strong and healthy as ever. The *libertador* [liberator] who dies for the sake of *pueblo* and *patria* [the fatherland] does not die in vain, but adds his effort and suffering to the eventual victory of *pueblo.* When the tree is re-formed or re-emerges out of the earth, it can be viewed as the eternal fruit of the union between *hombre* [man] and *tierra* [the earth]."[14]

By linking the image of the tree to the liberators here, Neruda establishes a continual time process in which each leaf is an individual liberator which may die or fall to the ground, but as it does so, it returns to the earth and becomes the seed and nurture for the eventual growth and further strength of the tree. Employing an image of Nature to paint those who fight for the authentic American heritage once again, Neruda paints a portrait in which the people can never be defeated, for as each individual falls, it is only to renew the life of the collectivity. "Each leaf is one man, and the foliage as a whole makes up the collective voice or story which is carried back into the ground to flower again and be communicated to the poet in the present."[15]

Among the heroes honored in this section of liberators are several Indians—Cuauhtémoc, Caupolicán, Lautaro, Tupac Amaru—and one Spaniard. The lone Spaniard is Bartolomé de las Casas, the controversial priest who defended the native Indians of America. In historical reality, las Casas' reasons for his passionate defense were not always the best. He opposed the enslavement of the Indian because he considered the Indian human and therefore open to religious conversion. But las Casas' long and arduous fight on behalf of the Indian was not in fact a fight against slavery and exploitation, for las Casas argued that Africans might be brought to America and used as slaves, thus freeing the Indian population for conversion. Neruda, in his personal history of America, chooses to overlook the historical details of las Casas' not always admirable arguments, and to accept instead the popular legend in which this Spanish priest stands out as a lonely figure, the only one among the Spaniards of the conquest and early colonial period to defend the native Indian population. It is in his capacity as defender of the native American that las Casas is honored by being included among those Neruda calls liberators.

After dealing with the colonial period, Neruda's parade of liberators moves toward the independence movements of the 1800s and its heroes: O'Higgins of Chile, San Martín of Argentina, Martí of Cuba. Independence from Spain is won. But for the poet, the battle does not end there. For Neruda, the Spanish invaders ousted in the nineteenth century have been replaced in this century by new invaders, no less rapacious than the first wave, and the new invaders carry the name of Wall Street. Section IV of the *Canto* ends with a new call to battle. The poet here is the prophet of a continent, beseeching his people to return to their roots, to take up the torch which is their inheritance:

. . . .
Blue Hussards fallen
into the depths of Time,
soldiers in whose freshly embroidered
banners dawn sheds its light,

soldiers of our own time, Communists,
fighters who inherit the fight
of the torrents of primeval metal,
listen to my voice. It was born
in the glaciers, it was raised
toward the daily bonfires
out of duty and out of love:
we are part of the same soil,
we are the same persecuted people,
the very same struggle is wrapped now
around the waist of our American lands . . .
the same ancient voices are calling us again.
Come down to the mineral roots,
come up to the peaks of empty metal,
touch mankind's struggle in the soil,
live through a martyrdom that tortures
hands that fate had wanted to climb towards the light.
                    ["The Day Will Come," "The Liberators"]

"The Liberators" ends with this call to battle, to reclaim the heritage
and the struggle of the indigenous American, the man of earth.

Section v is "The Sands Betrayed." Here Neruda's passion is directed less toward appealing to his brothers than toward constructing diatribes against those he perceives as threats to those brothers:
the oligarchies of South America, the "gentlemen" patrons of the
posh Jockey Club in Buenos Aires, South American lawyers who
work to protect the interests of foreign enterprises, and, of course,
the multinational corporations based in the United States. Three
corporations are singled out and their names are the titles of poems:
"The Standard Oil Company," "The Anaconda Copper Mining
Company," "The United Fruit Company." This last poem is perhaps
the best known of the group:

When the trumpet sounded,
everything was prepared on earth
and Jehovah divided the world
among Coca-Cola Inc., Anaconda,
Ford Motors, and other corporations.
For the United Fruit Company Inc.
the juiciest was reserved,
the central coast of my land,
the sweet waist of America.

Here Neruda brutally reverses the genesis of section I of the *Canto*.
There all was untamed Nature, undivided elements, indigenous and

devoid of an overseeing God. Now gigantic industrial forces divide and abuse the land, the entire invasion and dismemberment directed by Jehovah. The artistic value of many of the poems in the *Canto* that deal with contemporary political reality is questionable. The poems in *Spain in My Heart* were political poems and no less partisan than those present in "The Sands Betrayed" portion of the *Canto;* yet in the former the poet's outrage was impassioned and burning, and the lyrical quality of his cry made a political statement poetry. Now, Neruda is no less outraged, yet his tone is cold, the sarcasm bitter, and the political statement remains largely that, touching prosaic zones at least as often as poetic ones. It is simply not always Neruda's best artistic poetry. And yet for many, it is his most important contribution. There can be no denying the impact of "The United Fruit Company," for instance, and today, some thirty years after the publication of *Canto General,* this poem remains one of the works most quoted and invoked by young Latin Americans who share with Neruda the desire to banish from their countries all corporations based in the United States. This section of the *Canto* ends with Neruda's very personal and politically inspired chronicle of the year 1948 in South America.

Next come "America, I Don't Invoke Your Name in Vain" and the "Song of Chile," in which Neruda describes his nostalgia and love for his native land, feelings that came to the surface when the poet returned to Chile in the late 1930s after a long absence. In section VIII, "The Land Is Called Juan," the poet employs a series of biographies of common men—a Bolivian miner, a Columbian fisherman, a popular poet, a shoemaker—to bring forth the *pueblo,* the collective populace of America, as hero of the epic. The land belongs to this populace, its name is everyman's name, Juan, the worker so often overlooked by history, although he was there, always. He is celebrated in the title poem of the section, poem XVII:

> Behind the Liberators you could always find Juan
> working, fishing, also fighting,
> in his carpenter's shop, in his deep wet mine.
> His hands have ploughed the soil, they have measured
> every road.
>   His bones are buried everywhere.

"His bones are everywhere," and yet he has never been defeated. He receives the blows of invading armies, but the land is his and he will continually arise from it:

> But he is alive. He came back from the earth. He is reborn.
> He is born again like an eternal plant,

and today he opens again in our dawn his indomitable lips.
They tied him down, and yet he is once more a brave warrior.
They wounded him, and yet he is as healthy as an apple.
They cut off his hands, and yet his fists today strike his enemies.
They buried him deep, and yet today he comes to join us and sings.

In these lines the anonymous laborer "is brought to the forefront and given a name which is symbolic of the common man," Riess notes. "He is the hero behind great traditional heroes like Recabarren or Tupac Amaru; and it is through his activity, be it fighting or working, that he achieves this ritual contact with other men, both present and past. Through work, and contact with the soil and its parts, the achievements of past men are resurrected out of the earth and are reborn and fulfilled in the present. The man's body becomes the parts of the earth and his achievements through collective work bear fruit in the *planta eterna* [eternal plant] or the *árbol del pueblo* [tree of the people], which is so frequent a reference in the *Canto General*."[16] This American man will prevail as long as he is faithful to his roots in the land:

Juan, you own the gate and the road.
The earth
is yours, you are the people, truth was born
with you, from your blood.

It is not only the common man of South America that Neruda beseeches to be true to his roots in the land. In section IX, the poet turns his attention once more to the United States, here recognizing some of the past virtues of this nation, contrasting its present with this past, seeking a rebirth for North America as well. Return to your heritage, Neruda cries in "Let the Rail Splitter Awaken," to your pioneer spirit, to your great men such as Lincoln, to whom the title refers, to the America exalted by Whitman, its singer and chronicler. Here, as everywhere in the *Canto*, North America's past, like South America's, is evoked through earth images. Lift up your axe, Neruda calls to Lincoln, raise it against the new enslavers, against "the poison of the press, against the bloody merchandise they want to sell," "against the walls of gold, the manufacturers of hatred." Wood, roots, the past are contrasted with the exploitative machinery of contemporary North America. Wake up, America, Neruda implores, return to your heritage.

In "The Fugitive," section X, Neruda recounts his own experiences as a political refugee within his country, the months spent underground in hiding in 1948 in order to avoid political persecution.

Section XI contains once more the poet's expression of love for the South American continent and of solidarity with the common man and the poor masses. In section XII, he exalts as well some of his fellow poets, both South American and Spanish, and in section XIII he discusses the destiny and the enemies of the Chile for which he yearns. Nature poetry appears once more in section XIV, this time in the form of a total mythology of the Pacific in a poem entitled, "The Great Ocean." Finally, this monumental work ends with section XV, the autobiographical "I Am," which traces the poet's life from 1904 and his roots in southern Chile—"The first thing that I saw were trees"—to the present:

> Thus this book of poems ends, here I bequeath you
> my *Canto General* which I wrote
> while persecuted: I sang under
> the clandestine wings of my fatherland.
> Today the fifth day of February, this year
> of 1949, in Chile, in Godomar
> de Chena, a few months before
> reaching the forty-fifth year of my life.
>
> ["Here I End"]

These pages have outlined briefly the content of the vast *Canto General*. Literary critics—seeking identifiable structures in such a varied work—have often divided the *Canto* into two principal portions, suggesting that the first five sections of the work are the most nearly epic, while the remaining sections evidence a movement toward the more personal and autobiographical. This division is accurate in terms of stress, of what is placed at the forefront; but once again, like any division of a complex work, it cannot be considered in any way pure. In this sense it repeats the situation of the classification of Neruda's earlier works as lyrical or political and this as epic, for in both cases, the contrast made is one of emphasis only. Neruda is more given to the autobiographical in the later sections of the *Canto,* and he is more given to the epic and historical throughout the *Canto* than in most of his earlier works. Yet Neruda is always present as a personal force, even in the most nearly epic passages of *Canto General,* and he never completely divorces himself from being a lyrical poet for whom what he sees and describes reflects an inner passion. As a result, it is somewhat misleading to accept wholly that the *Canto* can be easily divided into two distinct parts, sections I-V being objective and sections VI-XV being more personal. As Rodríguez Monegal notes:

> In reality, the poet has created a much more subtle and personal
> structure, since as much in the first as in the second part, the objec-
> tive and subjective elements appear inextricably linked. Many times,
> when the poet is making an historical evocation, he introduces his
> personal figure (dramatic, impassioned) in the midst of the chronicle;
> in the same way, when he speaks of himself, he personifies or
> dramatizes his figure in such a way that he ceases to be Pablo Neruda
> in order to convert himself into Brother Pablo or another person. . . .
> Because of this, on top of the diversity of both parts the unity of the
> inner vision imposes itself: *Canto General* is, at the same time and not
> successively, epic and lyrical, a chronicle and an autobiography, an
> historical dramatization and a personal dramatization.[17]

Neruda's stance toward the poetry he produces in the *Canto* is thus
much like the stance which Walt Whitman, also the spokesman for a
continent, adopts in his *Leaves of Grass*. Both are observers and
chroniclers of what they see or evoke, and yet both appear at times
as actor in the events portrayed. Above all, Neruda, like Whitman
before him, experiences a complete identification with everything he
writes about, the mother he evokes is a mother of clay and stone, the
Indian roots become his roots, the blood that is shed is "our" blood;
he is at once the prophet of a continent and its appointed voice.
Time and again, Neruda, like Whitman, projects himself, his poetic
persona, as the vehicle through which a continent's story is to be told:
"I am here to tell the story," in variations and echoes is the refrain
repeated throughout the *Canto*. A division of emphasis can be made
between sections i-v and the remainder of the poem; yet it is only a
division in terms of stress and Rodríguez Monegal is correct in asserting that the poet is present simultaneously, and not progressive-
ly, in his multiple roles of actor, chronicler, prophet, journalist,
spokesman, and individual. In *Canto General,* the "chronicler and the
sufferer, the witness and the victim end up inextricably confused
and erase, once and for all, the rhetorical distinctions between epic
poetry and lyrical poetry, between narration and evocation, between
song and story."[18]

In this limited consideration of *Canto General,* we have attempted
to give an overall feel for the subject-matter, character, and tone of
the work, rather than focusing on the specific poems or poetic devices it comprises. The *Canto* is so vast and varied a work that one
cannot speak of any one or two poems as representative of the
whole. The first *Residence* poems, *Spain in My Heart,* and the volumes
of *Odes** —each has a homogeneous mood and poetic style, but *Canto*

*See chapter 2.

General is a heterogeneous work, ranging from prehistory to contemporary social problems, with many stops and detours on the long road between these two points. The *Canto* is also a very uneven work, containing some of Neruda's most brilliant poetry, and much of his weakest. Where Neruda becomes too bogged down in the immediate and the political, he tends to produce diatribes rather than poetry, ironically giving eternal life through his verses to mediocre political figures who on their own would never have entered the annals of history. Where, on the other hand, Neruda maintains the always personal yet somewhat removed perspective of the epic bard, where his poetry embraces a whole people and its heritage, it can be nothing less than brilliant. "The Day Will Come," from the section devoted to the liberators, for example, is both a strong political appeal and superb poetry; it is simple in its structure and chilling in its power, as his earlier verses to Spain had been.

Because of the fluctuation in content, tone, and especially the quality of the poetry in this work, what can be pointed to in *Canto General* is less a consistent poetic style or level than a purpose, an organization, and a series of leitmotivs employed in their service. The purpose is epic, tracing America's roots from before man to the present. As Neruda states it: "Many writers before me have felt a basic duty to express the geography and the citizenship of our American continent. To unite our continent, to discover it, to build it, to recover it, such was my purpose."[19] The organization of the heterogeneous material employed toward this end is essentially the sonata form, structuring the fifteen sections of the poem around four emotive centers. The first deals with the origins, the genesis, the creation of Nature and of man, a slow majestic unfolding of forces. The second center is faster, violent, explosive; it is the intrusion of outside forces. A slow interlude follows, and then come the frantic descriptions of present-day reality and violation. Four rhythms are present, the basic sonata with its four movements, alternating slow and fast rhythms. The leitmotivs that unite the epic depiction and the four movements are earth tones, the images of Nature tied to the indigenous man of America. Riess has pointed out that in the *Canto* earth, rivers, vegetation, minerals, ocean, waves, rocks, trees, beasts, birds, and mountains all come to point to man, the continent's rivers flow in parallel form to man's body and his arteries bringing life-giving blood.[20] And the man to whom all these natural elements point is the only legitimate heir to Nature in the *Canto*, the native American, opposed first to the bewigged and beclothed Spaniard, later to the machine-laden technology of the multinational corporation, both invaders, both violators of the authentic American space.

Pablo Neruda is one of the few literary figures who, for the most part, has been able to be both ideological and poetical. As with the visionary murals of the Mexicans Diego Rivera and Davíd Alfaro Siqueiros—both of them Neruda's comrades-in-arms in the Communist struggle—Neruda's commitment to an ideology, his talent placed at the service of a high moral endeavor, usually does not lessen seriously the artistic quality or the emotional impact of his work. And often, Neruda in his *Canto General* receives the uncommon grace of being at once an ideologue, a prophet, and an immensely powerful artist. He is passionately political, and this colors the entire *Canto,* but at his best his politics rarely challenge his essential being: he is a poet. In the high points of *Canto General,* Neruda indeed displays the magical powers, the gift of the epic bard, unfolding through his verses the destiny of a people and of a land.

The Later Works

Canto General is the masterpiece that even the most gifted poet produces only once in his life. It is not surprising, therefore, that while certain strains of the *Canto* were replayed later in minor keys, Neruda never produced another work comparable in epic scope and achievement to the *Canto.* In 1952 Neruda began writing a book that contains both public and personal poetry. *The Grapes and the Wind,* published in 1954, essentially recounts his travels, largely while in exile, through Europe, China, and the Soviet Union.

Two crucial factors operate in this book: Neruda's cold-war political militancy and his still "clandestine" love affair with Matilde Urrutia. Neruda sings joyously of the socialist solidarity he finds abroad, and explains his book in the following words: "After my *Canto General* and my travels around the world, I wrote a book . . . in which I recollect what I loved most in the old Europe and the new. What I call the "new Europe" is Socialist Europe. I want this book to be my contribution to peace. . . ."[21] In fact Neruda's book was not received as he wished. On the contrary, its partisan poems have usually been considered one-sided and even aggressive, the product of the prevailing Party line of the early 1950s, and their literary quality has been severely questioned. Nonetheless, *The Grapes and the Wind* is a book Neruda continued to love, considering it "a book of wide spaces and abundant light," which contrasts sharply with the dark vision of *Residence on Earth.*[22] Despite its militant perspective, however, it would not be entirely accurate to speak of *The Grapes and the Wind* as exclusively political poetry. In the second part of the

book especially, Neruda's political declarations are interrupted by
love poems, and the book as a whole is somewhat softened by
Matilde's increasing presence in Neruda's heart and life. As we have
noted earlier, this movement within *The Grapes and the Wind* is instructive in that it signals a transition. The beginning of the book is
related to the most partisan poetry of the *Canto;* yet it progresses on
occasion toward the more intimate poetry that characterizes most of
Neruda's work after 1950.

Neruda, as we have seen in the previous chapter, felt a constant
need to change poetic styles and attitudes. In the same year that he
began writing *The Grapes and the Wind,* the love poems of *The Captain's Verses** appeared, followed two years later by the *Elemental Odes.*
From the late 1950s until his death was for Neruda essentially a
period of personal poetry. Moments when he returns to the stance
of public bard are rare and are primarily concentrated in four
books: *Chanson de Geste* (1960), the most clearly epic of these works;
isolated sections of *Ceremonial Songs* (1961); the Biblical overtones
and global scope of *The Flaming Sword* (1970); and the blatant political diatribe of *A Call for Nixonicide and Glory to the Chilean Revolution*
(1973). These books are not among Neruda's finest work. It is in
order to trace the surfacing of Neruda's public poetry in the post-
Canto period, more than for their individual poetic quality, that these
four volumes merit a brief look.

In 1960, when *Chanson de Geste*[23] was published, the Cuban revolution was still young and full of energy. Neruda had seen Fidel
Castro in Caracas, and the experience had marked him strongly: "I
was one of the 200,000 people who stood listening to that long
speech without uttering a word," he recalls. "For me, and for many
others, Fidel's speeches have been a revelation. Hearing him address
the crowd, I realized that a new age had begun for Latin America."[24]
Chanson de Geste is a product of Neruda's militancy and of his solidarity with that new age.

A chanson de geste is an epic poem relating great deeds. The
word *geste* means "deed," and carries the "additional senses of 'history' and 'historical document.'" *Chanson* means "song," and these
epic works are literally a "singing of great deeds," celebrating "heroic
actions, historical or pseudo-historical" events or ideals.[25] Traditionally associated with Charlemagne or other feudal lords, the
chanson de geste flourished in France in the eleventh, twelfth, and
thirteenth centuries. The *Chanson de Roland* is the masterpiece of the
genre. The form was equally popular in medieval Spain and these

*See chapter 1.

songs exalting national heroes form an integral part of Spanish literature.

In his *Chanson de Geste,* Neruda remains faithful to the established purposes of this genre. He sings heroic deeds, only now the heroes are "the liberators of Cuba: Fidel Castro, his companions and the Cuban people."[26] As in *Canto General,* Neruda presents a poetic persona that speaks for an entire people and is conscious that his duty as a poet is a public one:

> I represent tribes that fell
> defending long beloved banners
> and nothing remained but silence and rain
> after the splendor of their battles,
> but I am here to carry on their actions . . .
>
> [*Chanson de Geste*]

The poet not only associates himself once more with America's indigenous heritage, using the word "tribes," but also defines his role as an activist: the poet here not only sings their deeds, but also carries on their actions. And it is the poet who will bring forth the "subterranean hopes" of the people:

> because of what use is a song,
> the gift of beauty and the word
> if it is not to inspire my people
> to fight together with me and to walk with me?
>
> [*Chanson de Geste*]

This definition of his poetic persona inevitably reminds us of *Canto General,* and the volume in its entirety clearly evokes certain portions of that earlier work. There is praise of the continent's liberators, as in section IV of the *Canto,* now with Fidel Castro added to the list; and there are the furious attacks against what Neruda considers South America's enemies, in particular imperialism from the north, as in section V of the *Canto.* Despite these similarities in attitude, in form, at times, in content, even in title (*canto* also means "song"), *Chanson de Geste,* is simply not on the same poetic level as *Canto General.* "Rhetoric, reiterations of other books, clichés in terms of subject and language that offer no major surprises," Camacho Guizado observes, "result in this book having a greater value as a political testimonial" than as poetry. One senses that Neruda wanted to honor his Cuban comrades by giving them the epic status of other heroes sung in the *Canto,* but the power of that earlier work is missing. The poet seems almost to be trying to imitate himself, to repeat what he had already done, and the impact of the original does not come forth in this volume. While Neruda himself would certainly deny it, we suspect that Camacho Guizado is not too far from the truth when he concludes that in this volume "the poet seems to have complied with an external obligation. . . . more than to have obeyed a genuine inspiration."[27]

If *Chanson de Geste* failed to become one of the most successful of Neruda's books, it seems to have failed as well in solidifying for very long a sense of fraternity between the poet and the leaders of the Cuban revolution. In 1956 Neruda accepted an invitation to attend a meeting of the P.E.N. Club in the United States. Despite his vigorous public defense of the Cuban revolution, the trip opened him up to attacks by the Cubans. A number of Cuban literary figures sent him a letter accusing him, as the poet recalls, "of little less than submission and treason."[28] While disillusioned with the Cubans' attitude, Neruda nonetheless stood by his *Chanson de Geste* to the end: "As for me," he wrote in his *Memoirs,* "I continue to be the same person who wrote *Canción de gesta* [*Chanson de Geste*]. It is a book I still like. I can't forget that with it I became the first poet to devote an entire book to praising the Cuban revolution. I understand, of course, that revolutions, and particularly those who take part in them, fall into error and injustice, from time to time. . . . I have continued to sing, love, and respect the Cuban revolution, its people, its noble protagonists." The poet's forgiveness is generous here, but it soon takes an ironic turn: "Everyone has his failings," Neruda adds, "I have many. For instance, I don't like to give up the pride I feel about my inflexible stand as a fighting revolutionary. Maybe that, or some other flaw in my insignificant self, has made me refuse until now, and I will go on refusing, to shake hands with any of those who knowingly or unknowingly signed that letter which still seems ignominious to me."[29] In concluding, we might just note a curious fact: *Chanson de Geste* is absent from the 1968 edition of Neruda's *Complete Works.* The omission is acknowledged only in a brief note in the Reference section at the end of the collection: "Reasons having nothing to do with the responsibility or wishes of Pablo Neruda impede the inclusion of *Chanson de Geste* in these volumes of his *Complete Works.*"[30] The "reasons," like the work itself, are not given.

In 1961 Neruda published *Ceremonial Songs,* which we will look at more closely in the next chapter. Here it will suffice to note that on occasion, in individual poems, the epic tone rings forth here also; this is true of "The Unburied Woman of Paita," for instance, an elegy to Simón Bolívar's lover, Manuela Sáenz. Yet this book contains much personal poetry as well, and it lacks the cohesive thrust of Neruda's more purely public volumes. Not until 1970 did Neruda again devote an entire volume to work that attempts to encompass universal dimensions beyond his own private world. That book is *The Flaming Sword,*[31] and while its history is an allegorical fantasy, its tone, its global range, and above all the poet's stance as prophet make it a book that needs to be considered in our discussion of Neruda's public poetry.

The Flaming Sword is one of Neruda's most unusual books. The title itself sets the book apart in the poet's work in that its reference is directly Biblical, naming the sword with which the angels protected the entrance to the Garden of Eden after the fall of Adam and Eve. Neruda cites the exact reference, Genesis 3:24, at the beginning of the book. The allusion is an apt one, since this book of poetry deals with a strange tale, rich in Biblical overtones. As Neruda explains in a brief preface: "In this fable, the story is told of a fugitive of the great destructions that put an end to mankind. He founded a kingdom situated in the spacious loneliness of South America and decided to become the last inhabitant of the world— until in his territory a maiden appeared who had escaped from the golden city of the Caesars. The destiny that brought them together lifts against them the ancient flaming sword in the new wild and lonely Garden of Eden. After the wrath of God, after the death of God, in a stage illuminated by a huge volcano, these Adam-like beings become conscious of their own divinity."[32]

A relatively long narrative-dramatic poem, *The Flaming Sword* reminds us occasionally of the Bible, and even at times of Tolkien's *The Lord of the Rings.* The story line, based on the legend of the "City of the Caesars," is rather simple: the world has ended, how we are never told explicitly, although we can guess that it is perhaps through nuclear war. After the devastation, a man and a woman find each other, love each other, and try to establish a new dynasty. Suddenly, however, the subject of guilt intervenes. Huge explosions in the sky and in the center of the world seem to signal the death of God, and at this point Neruda becomes not only philosophical and metaphysical, but also psychological. How, he asks, is it possible for guilt to reappear in the mind of the new man and the new woman once God is not present, the serpent no longer exists, and human solitude is now complete? Despite moments of intense gloom and anguish, the book ends on a positive note of joyous hope. Through their love, through the presence of natural beings, the birds and animals around them, the new man and woman will slowly learn that it is they who are in charge, that they are not accountable to anyone, that guilt belongs to the past and not to the new world order they are slowly creating.

Neruda's continued attraction to the Biblical and the mythological worlds that he touched on in *Canto General* may seem curious in an avowedly Marxist poet. Yet it should be remembered that mythology and the Bible, as well as the epic form, have proven to be extremely effective vehicles for awakening public faith and response, based as they are on simple emotions, allegory, and narrative-dramatic form. Aside from an artistic appreciation of the power of these works, it is possible that Neruda saw in them an effective propaganda vehicle for his public poetry. Fusing his ideological conception of the world into the popular and familiar forms of the Bible, the epic, or mythology could allow the poet to reach a large public and to awaken belief and stir emotions in the way these other forms have done.

In the case of *The Flaming Sword,* however, the formula did not work. The almost too facile nature of the allegory destined the volume to be largely disregarded by the critics and attacked as, in Camacho Guizado's words, "a religious book without belief, that encloses an allegory which is too simple yet uselessly complicated."[33] The harsh judgment of the critics could be tolerated if the book had, on the other hand, found its public and been warmly received by the masses of Neruda's countrymen. But for *The Flaming Sword,* critical disapproval has not to date meant popular acceptance, and despite the easy accessibility of the book's symbolism, this volume remains largely ignored by the majority of Chilean readers, who have never accorded it the accolade given to many of the poet's other works.

In 1973 Neruda published another book unusual for this period. This book is clearly political poetry. The title of the work leaves no doubt as to its blatantly, and exclusively, partisan orientation: *A Call for Nixonicide and Glory to the Chilean Revolution.*[34] We are dealing here with a political tract; *A Call for Nixonicide* is committed political poetry at its most virulent and passionate peak. Curiously, this book written to excite the indignation of an entire people was first published by a little-known publisher, Quimantú, which was unable to give the book a wide circulation. Today, the first edition cannot be found in most American libraries, and where it can be found, it is usually kept under lock and key as a rare book, hardly the fate Neruda would have wished for a pamphlet directed at the world at large.

In the Preface to this book, Neruda acknowledges that the goal of his writing is to provoke action: "These lines are an invitation, an incitation to an act never seen before. . . .This is a book whose goal is that ancient and modern poets place before the world a man who is a cold and delirious perpetrator of genocide. . . . History has proven the demolishing and explosive power of poetry—I am trying to prove it once more."[35]

We have already experienced in the *Canto* Neruda's wrath against those he deems betrayers of the public trust, particularly in sections v and xiii, where multinational corporations and contemporary politicians are bitingly attacked by the poet. Yet nowhere in that work does Neruda's rage reach the boiling intensity that surfaces in *A Call for Nixonicide*. Referring to the Vietnam war, for instance, the poet's condemnation of Nixon is absolute: "Nixon gathers to himself the sins of all those who came before him indulging in premeditated crimes. He came to the climax of his career: after having agreed to a cease fire, he ordered the cruelest bombings, the most destructive and cowardly bombings in the history of the world."[36]

In this political pamphlet, a broadside full of fire and fury, the poet makes use of simple images and rhymed verses that are easily understood and easily remembered. The choice of style is in accord with the rules of effective propaganda: appeal to the reader's emotions more than to his reason and give him "catch phrases," which can be repeated with ease. In effect, the short poems in this volume are elementary rhetoric that demand very little of the reader beyond a commitment to indignation.

The first poem invokes Walt Whitman, who is again, as earlier in the *Canto*, a symbol of all that is positive in the United States' past, the commitment to democracy, to the worker, to social justice. In appealing to Whitman, Neruda brings forth implicitly the memory of another American as well, Lincoln. The association is almost inevitable, given Whitman's fame as Lincoln's eulogizer in "O Captain, My Captain," and Neruda's own reference in the *Canto* to Lincoln and Whitman together as representatives of an heroic American past. The implicit recall, through Whitman, of Lincoln sets up once again a strong contrast between what America once was, with its idealistic commitment to freedom and equality, and what Neruda sees as a corrupted contemporary America under the leadership of a villainous President. In this sense, *A Call for Nixonicide* follows a structural pattern already established in the *Canto:* a beginning which recalls a period of positive action, no longer existent in the present, followed by an indictment of those guilty for this loss of innocence—in the *Canto*, the Spanish conquistadors, and in this volume, Richard Nixon.

Neruda appeals to Whitman as the bard of the United States, asking him to lend the Chilean his powerful vocabulary and rhetoric and his love of mankind. It is this love of mankind that must be the guiding force that will move our hands, our hearts, our minds. For Neruda, the goal is clear and inescapable, the death of a man who has become a menace for the world: Nixon. The message is recorded again and again in different keys and with slightly varying melodies, yet its essence can be summarized in two lines from Poem 39, "Warning Always": "My people, we are in an unsteady storm,/ We must close our fists and reject evil."

It is typical of this passionate and bitter book that Neruda renounces, for a while at least, some of the subjects dearest to his heart in order to return to what he sees as his duty as a public poet. Personal poetry, so dominant in these years, must now be abandoned for a time, he declares, and Neruda reluctantly puts private considerations aside and uses his poetry once more as a political weapon:

> Goodbye love, farewell kisses!
> My heart, you must cling to duty,
> because now I declare the court is in session.
>   ["I Say Farewell to Other Subjects"]

The public rejection of private subjects in order to respond to a political situation reminds us of Neruda's verses in "I Am Explaining a Few Things," from *Spain in My Heart*. There too, the poet anticipates being asked why he had abandoned his typical themes of Chile and his private dreams; he responds by citing the current national crisis before him: "Come and see the blood in the streets." In fact this is not the only reference to that earlier work; the Preface to *A Call for Nixonicide* bears the title "I Am Explaining a Few Things."

A Call for Nixonicide does not convey the same tone as *Spain in My Heart*, however. It is the most obsessed and direct political attack in all Neruda's poetry. Unlike the passionate and lyrical sense of tragedy of *Spain in My Heart* or the epic and global historical dimensions of *Canto General*, Neruda here directs all his energy to denouncing one single man, for him the incarnation of treachery. A book like this is hard for a critic to judge. If the critic fully shares the poet's system of values, he may be tempted to overlook anything that is simplistic, clumsy, or distorted in the poet's approach to history or in his poetic expression. An opposite and equally dangerous position is that of an unsympathetic reader who, again for political reasons, will not appreciate the moral quality of a poet who wants to stand up and be counted.

What can likely be said without risk of error is that Neruda's return to political poetry in this book was certainly consistent with what he deemed the obligations of a poet. If in the *Canto* Neruda adopted the *persona* of a prophet-spokesman, here he goes one step further and defines poetry as a direct call to arms. The concept behind this book is the might of the pen, and Neruda wields that pen like the deadliest of swords. For, virulent as the poet's attack on Nixon may seem, the historical context of the book must not be overlooked: we now know that the Nixon administration actively participated, in the very year *A Call for Nixonicide* was published, in the violent overthrow of the democratically elected Chilean government that Neruda supported. Given this acknowledged historical fact, Neruda, in *A Call for Nixonicide,* is once again reacting to a precise political circumstance and is certainly assuming for many readers the role of poet as national and moral spokesman. Like the medieval epics that sang praises of the king and denounced his enemies, *A Call for Nixonicide* captures the passionate feelings of a certain segment of the world's population. In its simplicity it expresses an outrage provoked by more complex political events, and it bers witness to an epoch tragic for millions of people on all sides of the political spectrum.

Synopsis

The books we have examined in this chapter amply demonstrate that from the publication of *Spain in My Heart* in 1937 until the poet's death thirty-six years later, political militancy was regularly a part of Neruda's poetry. Moreover, it defined a role for the poet as spokesman of a people, with an obligation to employ his art for public utility. Neruda did not shirk this responsibility; he alternated between his need for personal, lyrical expression and his sense of duty as a militant poet.

Political poetry that is artistically excellent is relatively rare. The sense of actual circumstances and concrete realities of the moment often invade the poetic atmosphere and interfere with the quality of the poetic expression. In poetry there is always a delicate balance between content and expressive form, and in political poetry there is the risk of disturbing this balance by giving too much weight to content. Far more than most other contemporary poets, Neruda was able to produce clearly political poetry where this balance remains intact. This is the case with much of *Spain in My Heart* and, of course, *Canto General.* In the *Canto,* Neruda reached his peak as a public poet. He produced an ideological work that largely transcended contemporary events and became an epic of an entire continent and its people. It is a monumental work, an extraordinary achievement; but it is also an uneven work and we see in this masterpiece the potential artistic dangers that plagued his later political poetry. Where Neruda remains historical, truly epic, and mythological in the *Canto,* the work is brilliant; where he allows contemporary political events to become the central focus, as in section v or xiii, for example, the poetic quality of his song suffers.

Unfortunately, beginning with *The Grapes and the Wind,* much of

Neruda's later public poetry follows the lead of the *Canto*'s weaker sections, rather than its most profound ones, and becomes primarily partisan or didactic poetry lacking the resonance of a poem such as "Heights of Macchu Picchu." Neruda's return to the epic form in *Chanson de Geste* or on occasion in *Ceremonial Songs* recalls certain parts of the *Canto;* the same is true for some of the Biblical overtones and cosmic vision in *The Flaming Sword,* and the political diatribes of *A Call for Nixonicide.* And in all these works Neruda adopts once more the stance of public bard, addressing himself to all mankind and to History. Neruda's definition of the poet's responsibility is evident in these works as it was in the *Canto,* and his sincerity is no less present here than in the earlier work. Yet none of these books rises to the level of the best portions of *Canto General.* The balance between content and poetic expression is not the same, and the richness, the depth, and the layers of meaning of the *Canto* are not repeated in these later works. We sense, rather, a weak echo of the original masterpiece. It is not in these works, but only in Neruda's treatment of Nature during the 1960s and 1970s, where the historical perspective and mythification of the *Canto* are at times replayed, that the profound essence touched in *Canto General* is once more revealed.

The *Canto* remains unchallenged as Neruda's outstanding accomplishment as a public poet. The vastness of its vision, tracing an entire continent from its genesis to its present reality, is virtually unique in contemporary poetry. We have insisted upon the fact that as a public poet, Neruda never ceases being at the same time a lyrical poet, expressing his own individual vision; the distinction between the two is a question of proportion, of stress, and not of mutual exclusion. Neruda's finest poems from the sixties and seventies are those where the lyrical carries the stress, those where the poet's personal "I," rather than a global public theme, is the primary focus. Neruda's commitment to public poetry was constant, and he took up his pen for public causes when he felt it was needed. Yet something seems forced in his public poetry of this period. It is as if Neruda the man, the militant, responded willingly to an external call to duty, but that the call came at a time when the urgent impulse of Neruda the poet was already moving toward contact with his own inner world. This is an observation, not a reproach. One can hardly fault Neruda for never duplicating the brillance of *Canto General* in his subsequent public poetry. Most poets never achieve what Neruda produced in this one single work.

4. The Personal Poet

Rodríguez Monegal has described the years from the late fifties to the early seventies as the "autumnal" period of Neruda's poetry.[1] It is certainly a prolific period: twenty works were published between 1958 and the poet's death in 1973. We have already discussed many of the books written during these years. *One Hundred Love Sonnets* (1959), and the love poetry in *Extravagaria* (1958) and *Barcarole* (1967) were examined in chapter 1; *Voyages and Homecomings* (1959), *The Stones of Chile* (1961), *The Art of Birds* (1966), *A House by the Shore* (1966), and *Sky Stones* (1970) in chapter 2; *Chanson de Geste* (1960), part of *Ceremonial Songs* (1961), *The Flaming Sword* (1970), and *A Call for Nixonicide and Glory to the Chilean Revolution* (1973) in chapter 3.

But much of the poetry from this period cannot be classified as love poetry or Nature poetry or public poetry. "Personal poetry" is a large term. There is no work of Neruda's that cannot be called "personal" to the degree that the poet's individual vision is presented, even where he adopts the role of public bard and addresses subjects of immediate social concern. And certainly all of Neruda's early poetry is personal, from the erotic love poems to the nightmarish perceptions of *Residence on Earth I* and *II*. Here we are using the term to designate the series of "I-oriented" works written during the late fifties, the sixties, and the early seventies. Their maturity of thought and reflective tone set them apart from Neruda's early intimate works, and their focus on the life, the private and existential concerns, of the poet distinguishes them clearly from his more public poetry. They are an eclectic group of books, with changing stresses and moods, yet unified by chronology and by Neruda's reemergence as a singer of his own private world. The vacillation, at times conflict, between Neruda's sense of public duty and his need for personal expression does not disappear during these years, but there is an unmistakable movement back in the direction of poetry centered around the poet himself. As Rodríguez Monegal notes, "the ever accentuating predominance of Neruda's autumnal spirit will lead the poet to the only possible exit: the contemplation of himself in the mirror of his life. . . ."[2] Self-contemplation and introspection link the diverse volumes we will now examine: *Extravagaria* (1958), *Ceremonial Songs* (1961), *Fully Empowered* (1962), *Notes from Isla Negra* (1964), *Barcarole* (1967), *The Hands of Day* (1968), *And Yet* (1969), *World's End* (1969), and *Barren Terrain* (1972).

Neruda plunged into personal, often autobiographical, poetry at a time when his public role had never been more in evidence. He was back in Chile, secure and successful. He had received the Stalin Prize, he had been celebrated by academies and critics, and he had been elected President of the Society of Chilean Writers. He was both a highly esteemed member of the establishment and a rebel poet, a paradox that could not have failed to delight him. He traveled constantly, making political speeches, and between trips he retreated to his splendid home at Isla Negra, whose ambiance so permeates the books written during these years. In the midst of this incessant public activity, while touring Chile during a Presidential campaign, Neruda drew into himself and wrote *Extravagaria*, the first of this series of personal volumes.

Extravagaria

This collection of poems, published in Buenos Aires by Losada in 1958, was born out of memories, out of immediate reactions to the present, and above all, out of a mind free from anguished obsessions. The poems in the volume are not easily defined as a unit. Ranging from irony to hymn, from wry comment to meditation, they represent what an adverse critic could call a "grab-bag." The title itself expresses the mixture of moods in the book, as Alastair Reid, the English translator, notes: "In Spanish, the original title, *Estravagario*, is nonsensical or rather, supersensical, being a mixture of the Spanish words *extravagante* [extravagant, eccentric], . . . *vagar* [to loiter], *extraviar* [to get lost, to wander off course] and *variar* [to change, be different]."[3] Yet in fact there is unity in the volume, a unity based on Neruda's mastery of style, on his newly acquired serenity, on his choice of personal concerns as subject matter, and even on the very label-defying nature of most of the poems in the collection.

Extravagaria is a book that seeks to do the unexpected. The opening poem, left untitled, sets the tone with its bold typography and unconventional word spacing:

```
        need    two wings
      you       a violin
    sky         and so many things. . .
      the
    to
  rise
to
want
you
If
```

The poem is a wholly original reworking of the beginning stanza of the traditional Mexican song "La Bamba," which Neruda must have heard thousands of times during his visits to Mexico. In chapter 2, in discussing the *Elemental Odes,* we noted that typography, as part of the message of a poem, had become a new dimension of style as far back as Mallarmé's "Un coup de dés" and had afterwards undergone the influence of Apollinaire and the Brazilian school of Concrete Poetry—Decio Pignatari, Haroldo de Campos, and their followers. Neruda had used the technique in the *Odes,* and now in *Extravagaria* we see him once again open to experimentation and to whatever cannot be predicted. "Play" is a key word for this volume; play with words, with structure, with syntax, with form is ever present. With that play comes humor, a humor Camacho Guizado describes as "smiling, not sarcastic . . . based on linguistic paradoxes and not on situations, that plays with words and images. . . . Paradoxes and oxymora stand out, deliberate syntactical incoherences, puns, colloquial language, lexigraphic inventions, breaks with the system, etc., and in the content, an ambiguous mixture of unconcern and seriousness, of laughter and melancholy."[4]

One of the themes treated with seriousness in *Extravagaria* is a new search for solitude, a radical departure from Neruda's terror of being alone in the *Residence on Earth* period and from his public solidarity in his political poetry. "I Ask for Silence" states the wish clearly:

> Now leave me in peace.
> Now grow used to my absence.
>
> I am going to close my eyes.

What we sense here is Neruda's fatigue with the ceaseless demands on his time and energy. Within the context of an exuberant love of

life, the two poles of his new vision are an awareness of fleeting time
and a consciousness of his own mortality. Neruda, the famous public
poet, is walking tall. But he knows that pride goeth before a fall and
that it is time to reassess his standing. Thus the title of another
poem, "Not Quite So Tall," in which he states: "From time to time
and at a distance/one has to bathe in one's own grave." The antidote
to public attention and demands is solitude and the infinite, desolate
yet beautiful horizon of the sea and shore. His retreat at Isla Negra,
later to be the focus of *Notes from Isla Negra,* begins to play a role
already in this volume. Isla Negra, facing the cold Chilean sea, is not
a tourist attraction, and it is the one place the poet can find refuge
from public demands. With the exception of the friends who come
to visit, Neruda prefers to be left alone there, with Matilde, with the
sea, the sand, the tides, the objects washed up on the shore. Once
again, Neruda, here in a somewhat defensive mood, expresses his
desire in the title of a poem: "Don't Pay Attention to Me." Let us
rather pay attention, he says, to the objects that the sea has crafted in
its eternal wisdom, in its endless effort:

> Among the things the sea throws up toward us
> let us look for the most calcinated,
> violet claws of crabs,
> little skulls of dead fish,
> smooth syllables of wood
> ....
> I know all the seaweeds,
> the white eyes of the sand,
> the tiny merchandise
> of the autumn tides
> and walk along them like a fat pelican

More and more the sea enters the poet's vision. Growing up in the
humid forests of southern Chile, Neruda had learned to live with the
rain as his constant companion. In *Canto General** he had dedicated
an entire section to the Pacific Ocean, and now, as a middle-aged
man living on the seashore, he is once more in constant contact with
water, that vast expanse which is both a homecoming and a refuge.
It is a leitmotiv that enters here and that will grow with the poet,
becoming, in his posthumous volumes, an all-pervasive presence.

Solitude and the sea go hand-in-hand with another recurring
theme in this multi-faceted volume: the poet's rejection of names
and classifications, of labels and agglomerations, of modern "civiliza-

---

*See chapters 1, 2, and 3.

tion" and man-made divisions that run in opposition to the unbroken flow of the sea. In "Too Many Names," for instance, the poet attacks the abundance and lack of meaning of names: Mondays are "meshed with Tuesdays/ and the week with the whole year." Time flows without interruption and it is impossible to label and organize neatly as man would so like to do. "Man cannot cut time/ with his exhausted scissors," and all the names of the day are washed out by the waters of the night. No one, Neruda says, should claim for himself the name Pedro; no woman is precisely and solely Rosa or María. We are all dust or sand, we are all rain under the rain. The poet has heard the names of countries, names such as "Paraguays" and "Chiles" but he does not understand what these names are about: "I know only the skin of the earth/ and I know it has no name" ("Too Many Names").

Neruda realizes that there is a vast philosophical problem hidden under his somewhat whimsical approach to the existence of names. It is the problem of Being and Becoming, of Essence and of Time:

> When I sleep every night,
> what am I called—or not called?
> And when I wake up, who am I?
>
> ["Too Many Names"]

Let us remember, he continues, that we have scarcely landed in life, we are as if newborn and it is too early to fill our mouths with faltering names and sad labels, with pompous letters and signatures. Neruda would like us to be still a part of the primeval confusion and pantheistic unity he described in *Canto General*. He wants to make us aware of the fundamental unity and indifferentiation of things:

> I would like to mix and confuse things,
> unite them, make them newborn,
> mix them up and undress them
> —until all the world's light
> has the oneness of the ocean,
> its generous, vast wholeness,
> its crackling, living fragrance.
>
> ["Too Many Names"]

In the same way that he rejects categories and searches for oneness, the poet rejects the arbitrary categories of "acceptable" and "unacceptable" social behavior. In the satirical poem "My Bad Manners," the poet recounts his endless gaffes in attempting to conform to society's rules and regulations of good conduct. Hopelessly inept in terms of polite behavior, the poet retreats into a kind of social non-being:

> That's why I don't go and I don't come,
> I don't dress and I don't walk naked,
> I threw away all the forks,
> the spoons and the knives.
> I only smile to myself alone,
> I don't ask indiscreet questions
> and when they come to get me,
> with great honor, to take me to banquets,
> I send my clothes, my shoes,
> my shirt with my hat,
> but even so they aren't happy:
> my suit went without a tie.

Whether the tone of a given poem is mocking or serious, it is possible on a certain level to see *Extravagaria* in its entirety as an attempt by Neruda to reject labels and clichés and categorization. The poet is breaking out of conventional structures, be they social or poetical. The book fits no easy classification; its tone is ambiguous—as Camacho Guizado puts it, somewhere between "humorous and melancholically mature."[5] It is Neruda's effort to get rid as well of the labels that critics have insisted on placing on his own work. This is precisely the interpretation that Ben Belitt gives to the book: "With the increasing polarization of his critics, Neruda has had to adopt increasingly Daedalian measures, inventing whole labyrinths, like the unplaceable *Book of Vagaries* [*Extravagaria*], from which there is no rational exit, to outwit his tidiers. In that extraordinary funhouse of metaphysical pratfalls, he has curved all the mirrors with illusions designed to dismay the gullible with parabolic distortions of their own meddlesome intrusions."[6]

Neruda, aware of being applauded by some critics and damned by others, claims that he prefers to stand alone, with Nature, and to leave the talking and the judging to others:

> . . . thus History passes in its carriage,
> collecting its shrouds and its medals,
> and passes, and all I feel is rivers.
> I stay alone with the spring.

> ["Pastoral"]

This attitude does not keep the poet from expressing in his prose *Memoirs*, however, his own unhesitating view of this very eclectic book: "Of all my books, *Estravagario* [*Extravagaria*] is not the one that sings most but the one that has the best leaps. Its leaping poems skip over distinction, respect, mutual protection, establishments, and obligations, to sponsor reverent irreverence. Because of its disrespect, it's my most personal book. Because of its range, it is one of the most important. For my taste, it's a terrific book, with the tang of salt that the truth always has."[7]

Ceremonial Songs

The three books published between *Extravagaria* and *Ceremonial Songs* (1961) had well-defined and unified themes: *Voyages and Homecomings* (1959) continued the cycle of the *Odes; A Hundred Love Sonnets* (1959) clearly fell into the category of love poetry; and *The Stones of Chile* (1961) had the unifying theme of the rock formations of Neruda's native land. This thematic unity does not carry over to *Ceremonial Songs*. No clear pattern can be discerned at first reading. The book is divided into nine principal sections, and the themes are varied. Some sections recall the epic tone of *Canto General:* "The Unburied Woman of Paita," an elegy dedicated to Manuela Sáenz, Simón Bolívar's lover; "Toro," an elegiac poem about Spain; "Cataclysm," about the devastating earthquake that shook southern Chile in 1960. Other sections are Nature poetry, and there is in addition a long poem dedicated to the French-Uruguayan poet Lautréamont. The absence of thematic unity within the book in itself in no way defines this collection of poems as less worthy than a more unified collection. Yet in fact, *Ceremonial Songs* is not one of Neruda's most memorable works in its entirety. As Rodríguez Monegal says: "In almost all the poems the pomp of the poetic material seems to dominate over the creative spontaneity."[8]

Three poems stand out in this otherwise unexciting volume: "Lautréamont Reconquered," "Cataclysm," and "Party's End," all of them characterized by an impending sense of doom and a perfume of death. In the first of these poems Neruda remembers one of the most mysterious figures of modern poetry, the poet Isidore Ducasse. Born of French parents in Uruguay in 1846, Ducasse adopted the pseudonym "Count of Lautréamont," a play on the French words for "the other world."[9] In France, where he was educated, Lautréamont wrote *Les Chants de Maldoror,* poems filled with the irrational, with violence, with ghosts from the unconscious, which were praised by André Breton for their celebration of dark forces. Lautréamont was found dead under mysterious circumstances when he was only twenty-four, yet he remained one of the precursors of twentieth-century poetry.

Neruda's aim in "Lautréamont Reconquered" is to reaffirm the poet's South American origins, to reclaim him from the Paris where he lived and died, constructing almost a "gaucho" fantasy origin for him: "You wrote on horseback, galloping/between the hard grass and the smell of the road," Neruda says to Lautréamont. In contrast with the open spaces and freedom in which Neruda fantasizes Lautréamont's years in South America, there is the urban oppression of Paris:

> The toad of Paris, the bland beast
> of the obscene city follows him step by step
> it waits for him and opens the doors of its snout:
> the tiny Ducasse has been devoured.
>
> ["Lautréamont Reconquered"]

Divided into six sections, the poem alternates between a vision of the young man in South America and this nocturnal vision of Lautréamont, the adult, in Paris, a vision filled with menacing atmospheres worthy of the darkest of Lautréamont's *Maldoror* verses, a vision that ends with the poet's death. It is a beautifully constructed poem, in which Neruda not only fantasizes a life for Lautréamont but also develops a dialogue with Lautréamont's verses, until the poet, his poems, Maldoror, his poetic personage, and Neruda's imagination mesh into one.

Death is a presence in "Lautréamont Reconquered"; in "Cataclysm" it is a fact of everyday life in the rugged terrain of southern Chile. "Cataclysm" is a long poem of shifting visions and sentences that seem to shake and explode. Neruda is once again returning to Nature poetry, but with a different perspective, for this is a poem in which human beings come to terms with the terror of Nature, with the chaos and destruction of earthquakes, volcanic explosions, and tidal waves. The subject is perhaps clearer to a Chilean reader than to an American, since in Chile these shudderings and death rattles of the natural world are much more common. The town where Matilde was born had been repeatedly ravaged by earthquakes and perhaps her childhood memories as told to Neruda formed the seed that gave birth to this poem:

> Now the great debt of life was paid with fear,
> it was overturned in the earth like a harvest
> from which everyone fled, praying, crying and dying,
> without understanding why we are born, nor why the earth

which waited so long for the wheat to mature
now, without patience, like a brusque widow
drunk and sputtering suddenly demanded to be paid
love and love, life and life, death and death.

["Cataclysm"]

Neruda's verses relive the age-old fears, the awesome experiences
of men and women faced with forces that no one can ever tame.
Rather than regarding Nature itself as an isolated external phenomenon, the poet looks at Nature here through man's eyes and recognizes the consequences of its force. The poet identifies with his
compatriots in their moments of anguish and impotence. He sings of
his "brothers in absence," reliving in his mind the powers of darkness: pain is a bitter cup of air descending from the sky, the earth
shakes and burns our hearts with a single thunderbolt, the very
churchyards where our ancestors sought peace are torn and
ploughed under by the tongues of fire of newly born volcanoes.
Coming to terms with the earth means finding out once and for all
that our life-giving fields and valleys may hide alien forces that ignore us and sooner or later may destroy us. This recognition of the
dark forces of Nature that we see in "Cataclysm" was already present
in some of Neruda's earliest poetry, but only in minor proportion
alongside the poet's exaltation of Nature. It is a theme that, with
variations, will appear strongly in the poet's posthumous works,
where, without focusing always on the destructive forces of Nature,
Neruda comes more and more to accept the feeble insignificance of
man confronted by the immense power of the natural world.

The last section of *Ceremonial Songs* is "Party's End," and here too
we see the poet coming to terms with the fact that life ends and that
hope has limits:

Party's end . . . Isla Negra shivers under the rains:
it rains on a chaotic emptiness, on the spray,
on the shimmering pole full of exploding salt.
Everything is frozen leaving only the glare of the ocean.
Where are we going? ask the masses of submerged beings.
What am I? the seaweed asks, silent till now,
and wave after wave after wave give their answer:
one single rhythm is born, destroys, and goes on:
truth is only a bitter mobility.

["Party's End"]

"Truth is only a bitter mobility." The line could sum up much of the
book. Here Neruda is primarily poet-philosopher, a moralist, de-

fining our always-menaced and precarious existence. This one single line denotes as well a recurring note in Neruda's *oeuvre* as a whole. Let us for a moment think back to the bittersweet experiences of the young Neruda in *Twenty Poems,** and his exploding anger and anguish in the *Residence* texts. Certainly his epic poetry in "Heights of Macchu Picchu" is also a testimonial to the passing of time and to the presence of the past in the minds and hearts of twentieth-century man. Even his loving descriptions of things, animals, and fleeting emotions in the *Elemental Odes* were perhaps an effort to slow down or counteract the bitter mobility of the passing of time, of decay and death. Truth and History can be said to be a part of the same bitter mobility that compels us to go on—yet, the poet hopes, without ever being unfaithful to our roots.

Fully Empowered

If the dominant mood of these poems from *Ceremonial Songs* is a dark one, there is still another more serene attitude in the poet's heart, and *Fully Empowered* (1962) expresses it. As Ben Belitt observes, a "redistillation of serenity clings to the whole of Neruda's *Plenos poderes* [*Fully Empowered*], ... imparting to each of the thirty-six poems that unmistakable "fullness of power" to which its title bears witness. Weary 'neither of being nor of nonbeing,' still 'puzzling over origins,' professing his old 'debts to minerality,' yet wavering 'as between two lost channels under water,' the poet 'forges keys,' 'looks for locks,' opens 'broken doors,' pierces 'windows out to living.'"[10]

Neruda uses diplomatic jargon for his title: "fully empowered" is the term used to designate an ambassador whose government has given him complete authority to negotiate a treaty or conclude delicate talks. The poet too is a kind of perpetual ambassador, fully empowered to deal with the important questions of mankind and the ever-changing relationship between man and Nature and man and History.

With power comes responsibility, and the introductory poem of this volume is entitled precisely "The Poet's Obligations." In it, Neruda defines what the poet can and must do, the private duties from which he cannot escape. He must listen to "the watery lament of my consciousness," he must feel the blows of hard rain, the rain of destiny, of conscious and unconscious reactions to destiny, and

*See chapters 1 and 2.

gather it back in "a cup of eternity" ("The Poet's Obligations"). In a word, the poet's first obligation is to pay attention and to register what others are too distracted to see and remember. The poet is ultimately the consciousness of mankind, or, as Heidegger puts it, "the shepherd of Being." He must try to see and hear everything and to preserve it in a meaningful way for all time. It is an awesome task, and one that calls for caution, but Neruda happily shoulders the monumental duty he has accepted: "I sing because I sing and because I sing," he says in the title poem, "Fully Empowered." His goal is to tell the truth in a way that will fuse the inner strength of the poet, ready to assume his responsibility, and the purity of Nature to which the poet is witness.

Poetry is not, however, a "miraculous" activity. It is something that dwells in each of us if we know how to nurture it. In order to make this clear, Neruda returns to the ode form in *Fully Empowered* and writes a poem entitled "In Praise of Ironing." Here, Neruda links the activity of the poet and the everyday act of ironing, using the latter as a metaphor for the former. Poetry, Neruda tells us, is white. It is something that comes out of water, covered with drops and then becomes all wrinkled in a heap. It is like the skin of a small planet, which has to be spread out:

> One has to spread out the skin of this planet,
> one must iron the sea from its whiteness
> and hands pass and pass,
> the sacred surfaces are smoothed out
> and that's how things are made:
>
> ["In Praise of Ironing"]

It is hands, our hands, that reshape the world every day, in the same fashion that we put our houses in order, cleaning, arranging furniture, ironing. It is in our hands and from our work of forging that "out of light a dove is born:/ and from sea foam once more comes chastity" ("In Praise of Ironing").

Notes from Isla Negra

The most ambitious book of this period is without doubt *Notes from Isla Negra* (1964), one of Neruda's longest works. In this volume the poet explores a world he knows well: that of his own life. It was not the first time that Neruda had written about himself. Aside from the childhood memories, his love life, his travels, his tastes and ideas that are continually present in all his poetry, Neruda had concluded

Canto General with a clearly autobiographical section, "I Am." He had also written a prose autobiography in the form of a series of articles published in 1962 in the Brazilian journal *O Cruzeiro Internacional*. This same material gave birth to *Notes from Isla Negra,* and finally to the second version of Neruda's prose autobiography that appeared posthumously as *Memoirs*.

Neruda's first prose memoirs bore a significant title, "The Lives of the Poet," and in fact each autobiographical version elaborates a slightly different aspect of the poet's experience. Comparing the two prose texts with the poetical self-portraits is a fascinating task, and an enormous one. Here we will content ourselves with a few general statements. Not unexpectedly, since Neruda was a poet and not a prose writer by profession, the self-portrait contained in Neruda's verses stands as a more personal, more forceful, and deeper statement. There are fewer anecdotes and jokes, the portrait is leaner, yet more intense, and the poet's pathos and self-realization come through more strongly. The prose memoirs reveal the mood of the times and the personality of Neruda's many friends. They are perhaps richer in conscious historical observation. Where the poetic memoirs are rich is in something else, in sensitivity, images, color, and rhythms. While we do not mean to disparage Neruda as a prose writer, there is no doubt that the essence of his powerful, yet subtle, personality is more easily captured in his poetry than in the many stories that dot his prose autobiography.

In the five books that make up *Notes from Isla Negra,* we find the basic Neruda, fully immersed in nostalgia and groping toward self-knowledge. The nostalgia is more acute when the place remembered has disappeared. As we have seen in "Cataclysm," Chile is a land where monuments and landmarks do disappear, wiped out by the explosions of Nature. In "Birth," the first poem of *Notes from Isla Negra,* Neruda tells us the fate of the house where he was born and the street where it stood. Both were obliterated when the mountain range "untethered its horses" and the slopes of mountains and hills came tumbling down in the stampede of an earthquake. The adobe walls, together with the dusty portraits nailed to them, sank back into dust. Neruda's mother, who had died of tuberculosis, was buried in the tormented soil of Parral. In the poem Neruda recalls a visit to the cemetery where he cried out to her, receiving silence as his only answer:

> and there she remained alone, without her son,
> elusive and evasive
> among the shadows.

And that is where I come from,
a quake-ridden soil, from Parral,
a land abundant in grapes
springing up
from the dead body of my mother

["Birth, "Where the Rain is Born"]

Only Nature, in the form of vineyards, continues living in this harsh terrain. In these last verses Neruda again touches on two themes that dominate the posthumous verses: the power of Nature in comparison with the weakness of man, so easily annihilated; and the regenerative patterns of the world. Death brings life, the disintegrating corpse fertilizes the earth, and from the earth new life, grapes, spring up. Man is weak and easily destroyed, and his dead body serves to feed the more powerful forces of the universe, Nature.

"Birth" quite appropriately introduces the first book of *Notes from Isla Negra,* "Where the Rain is Born," which deals with the poet's memories of childhood and adolescence; his discovery of Nature, love, sex, and the sea; his first travels; his own shyness. The second book is "Moon in the Labyrinth." It continues the chronicle of Neruda's adolescence, and his first passionate love affairs, as well as his moments of anguish and loneliness in the Orient. In "The Cruel Fire," the third book, poems about Neruda in Spain and the events of the Spanish Civil War are interspersed with poems harking back to Neruda's love affair in the Orient with Josie Bliss. Neruda, it would seem, did not want to give us a day-by-day account of his life, and soon we notice that the subjects become not only more varied, but also more ideological. Politics, war, commitment to the cause of the Left appear once again as sources of inspiration, as when the poet recalls his verses from *Spain in My Heart** and points the finger at present-day killers, new carriers of death in a Chile whose natural resources and workers are exploited:

I said: Yesterday the blood!
Come and see the blood of the war!
But here it was something else.
No guns sounded,
I didn't hear during the night
a river of soldiers
passing by,
flowing
toward death.

*See chapter 3.

> Here in the mountains it was something else,
> something grey that killed,
> smoke, dust from mines or cement,
> a dark army
> walking
> in a day without banners . . .
>
> ["My People," "The Cruel Fire"]

Books 4 and 5, while always focusing on the poet's personal vision, are less directly autobiographical than the first three, and there is no longer any attempt to describe life events or to follow a chronology. "Hunting for Roots," Book 4, is perhaps the finest of the volume in poetic quality, and its subject matter is once again the earth and Nature. In these first four books, there is a pattern, and Ben Belitt has noted that a case can be made for considering them a kind of odyssey through the four elements, since the titles refer respectively to water, air, fire and earth: "Water is cognate with the poet's Temucan childhood," Belitt explains, "Air with the erotic and the passional, Fire with revolutionary upheaval and world war, and Earth with the poet's return to his sources on the Chilean mainland: a thoroughly Blakean cosmology."[11] With the fifth book from *Notes from Isla Negra,* "Critical Sonata," this schema is broken, however. The perspective changes, and the themes include the poet's perception of art, literature in general, the role of the poet in the modern world, and the metaphysical and moral implications of living in a finite universe where imperfection and hope constantly mingle.

What we find in *Notes from Isla Negra* is a multiple vision, alternating between the lyric and the narrative, and juxtaposing the different, and occasionally conflicting, reconstructions of the poet's life and opinions. As Luis González Cruz points out, "many times the poet is no more than an 'observer,' a mere teller of anecdotes. At some points the poet reacts when confronted by the memories that his mind brings back to life and then he takes a stand, defines his moral, social or political position. Feelings which the poet lives again in his memory bring him to conclusions that had nothing to do with his past. The main thing is that Neruda is a poet with a newer and more mature understanding of the world and among anecdotes and memories, poems spring forth from his pen which define his existence in the present."[12] In a similar vein Ben Belitt comments that the "notebook" or "memorial" form that the work defines in its English and Spanish titles respectively is a "non-historical" form,

> in Coleridge's words . . . it 'emancipates [the poet] from the order of time and space . . . . *Notes from Isla Negra* is concerned with memory

rather than history. Into its five volumes there tumble a disorganized *recherche* of events, ruminations, obsessive images, words, doubts, allegiances, political mandates, and spiritual recoils in an *ordre du coeur* rather than an *ordre raisonné*. Their point of departure and their point of return are essentially the same: *time present,* in which the poet, brooding daily on the change and the permanence of things from a seacoast in Isla Negra, is induced to evoke an answering dialectic from within. The dialectic is not Marxian, but cosmological, and its polarizing genius is not History but Memory . . . .The scene, for all its flashbacks into the displacements of a lifetime, is Isla Negra, to whose sea-changes, cloudscapes, and seasonal immediacies the poet constantly returns for a 'residence on earth' fixed at last by the heart's choice and due process of mortality.[13]

We capture this sense of the past being seen from the present in a poem inspired by Neruda's father, that railroad man whom we've already encountered in *Canto General.* The locomotives' nocturnal lament is heard. The door starts trembling. The wind enters in gusts with his father:

> My poor brusque father,
> there on the axle of life,
> among virile friendships and overflowing cups.
> His life was a frenzied militia
> between daybreaks and road-bends,
> swift comings and goings.
> Then one day, when it was raining hardest,
> the conductor José del Carmen Reyes
> boarded the train of death
> and has not been seen since.
>   ["My Father," "Where the Rain is Born"]

The poet's attitude toward his father is, as it was in the *Canto,* ambivalent. Fear and admiration mix with nostalgia. Neruda is able to see not just the harsh side of his father, but the sadness of the man's life as well. The poem, almost narrative, is at the same time both warm and distant in tone. Using the adjective "poor," Neruda lets us sense the compassion he feels for this stern, hard-working man whose life consisted of boarding trains going nowhere, until that final train took him on a one-way eternal journey. We get, however, little sense of the man himself in Neruda's verses. Aside from the adjectives "poor" and "brusque," the father is not really described, and what we have is a rather sad, yet removed, image of his movements, but never of his inner being.

"The Father" illustrates a difference between Neruda's public poetry and his personal poetry. In the epic portions of *Canto General,*

Neruda's father appeared, but only as a name, "Reyes," and always dressed up as an historical personage within the epic. The poet's ambivalent feelings toward him could be deduced from the contradictory roles he assigned to "Reyes" in the epic, but the feelings were not stated as such. In the autobiographical section of the *Canto,* "I Am," and again in this period of explicitly personal poetry, Neruda treats the same subject, his father, in a very different fashion. Here he appears without the disguise of an historical context. He is presented directly as the poet's father and the ambivalence toward him is confessed frankly in the double adjective "poor brusque." The poem is, we suspect, an extremely accurate portrait of the father as seen by Neruda: the absence that we sense of inner knowledge of the father's private wants and feelings was probably the child's reality. We capture here what Neruda's father really was for the poet: a stern figure constantly on the move, always departing or arriving, the burdened reality of his work leaving little time for the kind of sentiment to which his son was sensitive. The mature Neruda, now looking back from the security of Isla Negra, understands the difficulties and spiritual poverty of his father's life, and thus the compassion. Yet he can paint no more sentiment than that into the picture, and the father remains a remote figure, coming and going in his child's life, like the provincial trains that were his life's work.

"Little Boy Lost" is an equally moving poem, evoking the change wrought by time on Neruda's naive vision of the world and of himself. The difficulty of attempting to speak from the present with the voice of the child that he once was runs throughout the verses:

> . . . and suddenly appeared in my face
> the face of a stranger,
> and yet it was also my face.
> It was I who was growing there
> and you are growing with me
> all of us one,
> everything changing,
> we no longer knew who lived there
> and sometimes we remember the one
> who lived within us,
> we ask something from him—that he
> remember us, perhaps—
> that he know, at least, that
> we were here and now speak with his tongue:
> but there from the rubble of worn-out time
> he looks at us and does not recognize us.
> ["Little Boy Lost," "Where the Rain is Born"]

The title of this poem is significant for it is not the only time in *Notes from Isla Negra* that the word "lost" appears. In fact, Belitt, referring to Neruda as "agonist of the Lost," notes that the word "lost," in various forms, is constantly present throughout the five books of the volume. This does not mean, however, that *Notes from Isla Negra* is the work of a beaten and despairing man. "On the contrary," Belitt insists, "Neruda's steadfast confrontation of the Lost, his avid immediacies and open-ended determination to live 'between the luminous and the desperate halves,' measure the strenuous vitalism of his position . . . reading the oceans and weathers of Black Island, construing interstices, gaps, collapses, losses, with a realism that dazzles the imagination, [Neruda] holds in his keeping the plenty and certainty of the world."[14]

In "Magnetic Art," from the fifth book, "Critical Sonata," Neruda returns to the question of what it means to be a poet. Living and poetry are once more linked in this poem, with Neruda asserting that it is only by fully plunging into the former that the latter can be born:

> It is from endless loving and walking that books come forth.
> And if they don't contain kisses and regions
> and if they don't contain man in abundance,
> if they don't have woman in every drop,
> hunger, desire, anger, roads,
> they will never serve as a shield nor as a bell.

All poetry is, in essence, autobiographical, Neruda suggests, perhaps in justification of this work. The poet's experiences in real life give him the material without which poetry becomes impossible. If the vibrancy of the poet's life is not there, his books are "eyeless and can't be opened,/ they will have the dead mouth of an administrative statute." And he concludes:

> I loved the intertwining branches of genitals
> and between blood and love I dug my verses,
> in hard earth I established a rose
> fought over by fire and dew.
>
> It is thus that I could walk along singing.
>   ["Magnetic Art," "Critical Sonata"]

Notes from Isla Negra is a major work, certainly Neruda's most important work of the sixties. Its autobiographical intent should not make us forget that it is above all a poetical reconstruction. Neruda comes through in these poetical portraits with all his intense feelings as a man, but he is not always a consistent and reliable witness of the concrete events of his own life. The poet himself acknowledges this fact:

> Many memories have vanished as I evoke them, have turned into dust like crystal irrevocably shattered. That's how things are. The memoirs written by professional writers are quite unlike the poet's memoirs. The average author of memoirs may well have lived less intensely, but he took many more snapshots and pleases us with an abundance of clear detail. The poet, on the other hand, gives us a gallery of ghosts shaken by the fire and darkness of his times. Perhaps I did not live with and through myself. Perhaps I have lived other peoples' lives. The pages of these memoirs of mine are like a forest in the fall, like vineyards in September, they give forth yellow leaves ready to die and grapes ready to live again in the sacred wine. This is a life made out of all other lives, for a poet always has many lives.[15]

Neruda wrote these words about his prose memoirs published in the Brazilian journal *O Cruzeiro,* and they serve equally well for *Notes from Isla Negra,* those five books in one that "turn around one sole axle: the life, the eyes, the mind, the sensitivity of Pablo Neruda."[16]

Barcarole

In 1966 *A House by the Shore* appeared. As we have already seen, it is a mixture both of prose and poetry, and of Nature poetry and personal poetry, focusing first and last on Nature—the sea, sand, rocks, and plants at Isla Negra—and in between on Neruda's very personal involvement in the building of his home there.

A year later, Neruda published another book, all poetry, *Barcarole* (1967). In it the reminiscences and the personal poetry of this period continue, but without the direct autobiographical intention of *Notes from Isla Negra.* Themes from Neruda's many earlier volumes of poetry come together again in *Barcarole,* and we have love poetry, Nature poetry, poetry about Chile, poetry about the poet's own role and obligations. The choice of title indicates the tone and atmosphere Neruda wants to create: a "barcarole," as we have previously noted, is a song sung by the gondoliers of Venice, and in his verses Neruda seeks to return to both the melodic qualities of this poetry and to its narrative functions. As he explains: "in this book there are episodes that not only sing, but that also narrate, because in another time it was thus, poetry sang and narrated, and I'm like that, from another time, and there's nothing to be done about it."[17]

Barcarole is a complex and composite book in which many ingredients, many moods, and many subjects have been combined. Neruda's technique verges on stream-of-consciousness; we jump from one theme to another without explicit transitions. The book is divided into multiple sections, some barely a page long. Many sections are entitled simply, "The Barcarole Goes On," that is to say, the song continues, at times without our knowing exactly where its melody will lead us. The poet is clearly in an introspective mood, but he seems unwilling to tell us what propels his mind from one subject to the next, from a memory of friendship or love, to one of doubt, anguish, or recrimination. As Camacho Guizado notes, the principal unifying characteristic of the book is the constant rhythm of its verses, a rhythm he classifies as "monotone."[18]

We are actually entering the poet's memory in *Barcarole,* and zigzagging through his past and his hopes for the future. As we have seen in chapter 1, the first memories are of love, and the opening poems, originally published in *Notes from Isla Negra,* are love poems dedicated to Matilde. Through a series of unconscious or partially conscious associations we enter into what is actually the second episode of *Barcarole,* although it is entitled "First Episode." The subtitle of this section is "Earthquake in Chile," and the association clarifies somewhat if we remember that Matilde was born in a province of Chile subject to frequent and devastating earthquakes. Here Neruda displays the same sense of solidarity with the victims of Chile's harsh landscape that he did earlier in "Cataclysm": "Whoever falls makes me fall too, the wounded wound me also, the dead also kill me" ("Earthquake in Chile").

After an interlude, "The Barcarole Goes On," in which the poet's thoughts fly back to the beauty and tenderness of Matilde, we enter the "Second Episode," subtitled "Paris Serenade":

> Beautiful is the rue de la Huchette, tiny like a pomegranate
> and opulent in our poor splendor, just like a ragged showcase;
> there, among the bearded beatniks in this year of sixty-five
> you and I, transmigrants from a star, lived happy and oblivious.

Reminiscences of Paris follow, as the poet relives the year he spent there with Matilde. The small, twisting streets of the Latin Quarter are recalled as Neruda mentally wanders through this city that "preserves in her twisted roofs the ancient eyes of time" ("Paris Serenade"). Other memories come back as well: accordion music; the French poet Louis Aragon and his wife Elsa; the Peruvian poet

César Vallejo drinking calvados and beer from a huge glass; St.-Louis, the island in the middle of the Seine; the Seine itself, laced with beautiful bridges.

It is with "Paris Serenade" that we begin to understand how *Barcarole* is organized. Hernán Loyola reports that the book was conceived as a conversation with Matilde in the intimacy of their home.[19] In effect we are in a zone of almost free association, where in a complex process of linkage, the poet extracts people, places, events from his mind; all are part of his life, or have been, all are haunting figures that emerge from the open doors of his memory. Further on in *Barcarole,* the coast land of Chile appears, the plain of Patagonia, crossed by wild horses, Neruda's close friend the Chilean writer Rubén Azócar, who had died in 1965. There are poems about the sound of bells under the rain, crowded streets full of drugstores and hardware stores, spring in Chile, the sound of bells in Russia, the memory of the poet Rubén Darío, Lord Cochrane, the Scottish sailor who became the first admiral of the Chilean navy, José Artigas who fought for and won the independence of Uruguay, the Brazilian port of Santos, a dreamlike encounter with an astronaut, and an encounter with a ship's figurehead.

In the midst of this welter of memories and associations, Neruda includes a narrative-dramatic poem entitled "Splendor and Death of Joaquín Murieta." The poem gives a fictionalized version of the life and death of a Robin Hood-style bandit, whom historians place as a Mexican who helped the Spanish-speaking inhabitants of California. Neruda, however, converts Murieta into a Chilean folk-hero, calling him "my compatriot, the honorable bandit/ Sir Joaquín Murieta":

> This is the long story of an inflamed man:
> Natural, valiant, his memory is a torch of war.
> It's time to shatter the peace, to open the tomb of the clear bandit
> and to break the rusty oblivion which now buries him.

In the verses that follow, Neruda recounts Murieta's departure for California—"and toward California death and gold called to him with ardent/voices which at last decided his black destiny"—and his meeting with Teresa, his great love. In the "Amorous Dialogue" between Murieta and Teresa, we see the immense tenderness of the man who was famous for his pride and his shiny knife:

Murieta's voice:

> Everything you've given me was already mine
> and to you I submit my free nature.

I am a man without bread or power:
I only have my knife and my frail person.

I grew up without a fixed direction, I was my own master
and I now begin to know that I have been yours
ever since I began this dream:
before I was nothing but a heap of pride.

This "Amorous Dialogue," together with another section entitled "The Head of Murieta Speaks," became central passages of Neruda's only play, *Splendor and Death of Joaquín Murieta,* which was presented in Santiago in 1967, under the direction of Pedro Orthous.

As the multiple themes—places, persons, the seed of a drama—indicate, *Barcarole* is one of Neruda's most chaotic works, a strange collage of images whirling faster and faster in the poet's memory, a subconscious combination of associations, united only by the poet's experience, his sensuality, his love of Matilde and of freedom. *Barcarole* is certainly not Neruda's best book of poetry; in fact, it is perhaps the most baffling and disorganized of his works, yet it offers the reader an introduction into the recesses and labyrinths of Neruda's mind and memory. It is fully the work of Neruda as personal poet, with a perspective not unlike that of *Notes from Isla Negra* at times, although without the explicit autobiographical intention and organization of that book. Perhaps even most important, *Barcarole* is the work of a poet still seeking to experiment, to change and to renovate his own style, here abandoning modern free verse to return to an "antiquated" form of poetry, to a poetry structured always in long, regularly metered verses, to a musical poetry that narrates as it sings. *Barcarole,* without being exclusively, or even primarily, love poetry, is clearly romantic—in the form of poetry Neruda chooses; in the memories, which float along like the gondolas of Venice; in the nostalgia that enters and reappears throughout the poet's song; and in the version he chooses to give of Joaquín Murieta's life.

The Later Works

Between 1968 and 1973, Neruda published still another series of works. Three of the books written during these years we have already discussed: *The Flaming Sword* (1970), *Sky Stones* (1970), and *A Call for Nixonicide* (1973). The others—*The Hands of Day* (1968), *Eating in Hungary* (1968),[20] a mainly prose work written with the Guatemalan writer Miguel Angel Asturias, *And Yet* (1969), *World's End* (1969), and *Barren Terrain* (1972) include some of Neruda's least discussed works. Squeezed between the production of the mid-1960s and the later posthumous works, these books constitute a kind of "lost generation" of Neruda's poetry, and, relatively speaking, are not widely read or known.

The reasons for this lack of attention are many. In part it may be due simply to the fact that the 1968 Losada edition of Neruda's *Complete Works*, the edition still owned by most libraries, does not include all of these books. A fourth edition, published in 1973, does include them, but by this time the posthumous books were already appearing in print, overshadowing these other works. Then too, it may be that Neruda's move toward largely personal poetry in this period reduced his active public; he was no longer dealing principally with themes of common concern—Nature, History—but more often with his own life and introspection. The result may well have been a loss of interest in these books from a general public that had already had enough of Neruda's personal reflection in the preceding works. Yet even literary critics have so far shown little interest in these volumes. A logistical consideration can perhaps explain this: in the ten years between 1963 and 1973, Neruda published thirteen works, including the immense *Notes from Isla Negra;* in 1973 and 1974, the eight posthumous volumes of poetry, as well as the prose *Memoirs,* appeared. Careful literary analysis takes time, and Neruda was, perhaps, too prolific for his critics, firing off a seemingly unending series of short books, leaving little time for absorption of one before the next appeared. The books published between 1968 and 1973 seem to have been caught in a time squeeze between the longer and more unusual *Barcarole* and the posthumous books, which immediately captured public and critical attention because they were the last ever written by Neruda. It should be recognized as well that none of the books published between 1968 and 1973 was a monumental work; two of the books, *The Hands of Day* and *And Yet,* contain much excellent poetry, but the others for the most part are not exceptional and there is no doubt that in terms of poetic quality several of the posthumous works outshine even the best of these. Nonetheless, *The Hands of Day, And Yet, World's End,* and *Barren Terrain* merit at least a brief examination, for no picture of Neruda's personal poetry can be complete without them.

The Hands of Day appeared in 1968. It is interesting for what it reveals about Neruda's ever-present conflict between his public identification with the working class and his reality as a highly cultured poet. A curious sense of guilt permeates this book, the guilt that the poet feels because he has only been able to work with words and has constructed nothing with his hands:

I declare myself guilty for not having
made, with these hands that they gave me,
a broom.

Why didn't I make a broom?

Why did they give me hands?

What good did they do me
if I only saw the murmur of the grain;
if I only had ears for the wind
and I didn't recognize the thread
of a broom,
still green in the earth

["The Guilty One"]

The poet concludes by asking how he could ever have aspired to greatness "if I was never capable/ of making/ a broom,/ not even one,/ one?"

The poems in this book are short and direct, a stylistic choice appropriate for a thematic return to the world of the common man, of concrete reality, of working people, of a poetry for a large public. The tone of the poems remains, however, one of introspection. Neruda is noting the passage of time and questioning whether that time has been well spent. In another poem from this volume, "The Blow," he despairs of the way he has spent his years, and we find in this poem some of the same rejection of language that we have already seen in *Extravagaria*. Speaking to the ink with which he has written his verses, Neruda says:

Perhaps it would have been better
to have poured over into a cup
all your essence, and to have thrown it
on only one page, staining it
with one single green star
and that stain alone
would have been everything
that I wrote throughout my life:
without alphabet or interpretations
one single dark blow
without words.

["The Blow"]

Implicit in Neruda's rejection of his own work with words is again the praise of manual labor and the guilt of an intellectual who has lived otherwise, who has in no way changed the natural world with his hands. It is the unifying theme that runs throughout this book:

Thus forgive me for the sadness
of my happy equivocations,
of my dark dreams,
forgive me, everyone, for all that's unnecessary:
I never succeeded in using my hands
in a carpenter's shop or in the forest.

["He Who Sang Will Sing"]

The poet's pain at his own lack of constructive physical contact is
real. Yet a problem of credibility at times colors *The Hands of Day*,
simply because Neruda's disparaging of his own contributions is not
always in accord with the reader's evaluation of his work. It is difficult on occasion to accept Neruda's cries of uselessness when he was
perhaps the greatest poet of his time. His moment of doubt is sin-
cere, but there is, we believe, a gap between his almost exclusive
exaltation of manual labor and the reader's own appreciation of
Neruda's intellectual labor. Neruda's vision, while genuine, can certainly be accused of being overly simplistic in *The Hands of Day*, and
should, perhaps, be best understood as the discomfort of a dedicated
Marxist who finds his creative activities isolated from the manual
creations of working men and women, and as the sadness of a Nature poet who has never physically transformed a natural element.
Nonetheless, the poet seems to recover from his despair at the end
of the book, and the final poem, only three lines long, "ends with an
exaltation of poetry, that is like a satisfaction which the poet offers
himself after the sort of prohibition which was put on it in certain
poems."[21]

Give a kiss of fire to your guitar,
hold it high, burning;
it is your banner.

["The Banner"]

A year after the publication of *The Hands of Day*, another book of
poetry appeared, *And Yet* (1969).[22] Bearing the shortest title of any of
Neruda's books—*Aún* in the Spanish—this book is a single long
poem of 433 verses, written in just two days in July, 1969. For
Robert Pring-Mill, the noted English critic, *And Yet* is "perhaps the
finest long poem [Neruda] has written in the past twenty years.
There are few tricks of style and no verbal pyrotechnics; the lines
flow with patterned rightness, swept along by the sad intensity of
feeling. Detached yet wholly involved, Neruda has never looked
quite so deeply into himself before, nor seen so clearly how the land
where he was born has always moved and steered him."[23]

The dominant theme of this long poem, personal like so many of the other works of this period, is the earth. Once again we have Neruda seeking contact with Nature and with his roots. Here, as is more and more often the case in the later books, especially in the posthumous ones, the natural world is for Neruda the one overwhelming reality of existence:

> Forgive me if when I want
> to tell my life
> it's soil that I recount.
> Such is the earth.
> When it grows in your blood
> you grow.
> If it dies in your blood
> you die.
>
> > [*And Yet*]

Neruda's identification with the earth is total here. If in other works we have repeatedly seen the earth portrayed as a life-giving and nourishing mother, here the earth takes on qualities almost resembling a primary divinity: it gives life and it takes away life; while its light glows within you, you live; when its light is extinguished, you die.

Camacho Guizado notes that throughout *And Yet* the "reflection on death leads to that telluric sentiment which now presents itself as a return, as a homecoming more than as a rebirth . . . [and] the earth becomes little less than an absolute in the work: 'let everyone know that at least in me/ the earth calls to me, it directs me, it seizes me!'"[24] Time, Neruda's own life, memories, Nature, the obligations of the poet reappear as themes in *And Yet,* just as they have in the other books of personal poetry of these years. But it is above all the earth, the land that dominates, and with it the original inhabitants of that land, the indigenous race that was once linked to the earth. We return to echoes of *Canto General* as the opposition between modern man and the earth is signaled in Neruda's verses, and the poet recalls the disappearance of the Araucanians as a race: "Their leaves were being taken away/ until they were only a skeleton/ of a race, or a tree already bared." They fought, proudly, but they were doomed, they ". . . felt the ground failing them/ the earth disappearing from under them" (*And Yet*). Once more we have the image of the earth as the force that gives or takes away life, and the disappearance of the ancient race is described in terms of their losing contact with the earth, of the earth slipping away from them, leading them to death:

"the reign of theft arrived," Neruda goes on, and now, no longer able to separate himself from the destructive forces of modern man as he did in the *Canto,* he feels guilty with the others: "the reign of theft arrived:/ and we were the thieves" (*And Yet*).

If *And Yet* anticipates some of the posthumous books by the dominating role it gives to Nature, it equally signals the new positive role that silence will play in those later books:

> And I was there all alone, looking for the reasons
> of the earth's being, the earth without men
> and without wings, yet all powerful,
> alone in its majesty, as if it had
> destroyed one by one every bit of life
> in order to establish its silence.
>
> [*And Yet*]

In this section of the poem, the poet finds himself alone in a strange, barren landscape and "silence comes charging at the poet like a revelation," Jaime Alazraki writes: "The first and ultimate reason of creation thus comes to be that great silence in which the poet once again finds his home, and into which he enters as if into a refuge of peace."[25] The poet's "refuge of peace" is now one of solitude, and one linked inexorably with the earth and its being. *And Yet,* in this sense, has set a tone that will continue in Neruda's poetry through the last verses he ever wrote.

In the same year as *And Yet,* Neruda published still another, very different, book of poetry, entitled *World's End* (1969).[26] If authorial intention were the sole definition of a work, *World's End* might well be classified with Neruda's public poetry, for its declared theme is a taking account of the world in the years during which the poet has lived. But this is a book of contradictions, and if Neruda does comment, often with sadness, on the state of the world in which he has existed, the poet himself, his "I," his *persona* end up being the true hub of this volume. Neruda himself recognizes this in a poem entitled "Always I":

> I who wanted to speak of our century
> within this twining,
> within my book still being born,
> everywhere I found myself
> while events escaped me.
> . . . .
> As tired as I might have been
> of my own acceptable person

I returned again and again to speak of myself
and what is worse
is that I painted myself
on top of each event.

These verses are in fact an accurate description of *World's End,* for if
this is a book which reflects the events of our times—the incessant
wars, the death of Che Guevara, the horrors of Vietnam, the invasion of Prague—it is, nonetheless, a very personal, "I"-oriented
book. The events are seen through the poet's own perspective, his
very real anguish over the disappointments and unrealized dreams
that have characterized the years in which he has lived. The mood of
this book is more reflective than declamatory, and it is this that
makes *World's End,* despite its largely political subject matter, more
closely related to Neruda's personal poetry of these years than to the
decidedly public poetry of *A Call for Nixonicide,* for instance.

In this work, Neruda is looking not only at the political world
around him, but at his own struggles and choices. The Russian invasion of Czechoslovakia, thus, is not described in any sort of objective
fashion as an event; rather it is seen within the context of the poet's
very personal reaction as someone forced to admit that militant
ideology can sometimes be blinding:

The hour of Prague fell
on my head like a stone.
My future looked unstable,
a moment of darkness
like the sudden gloom of going through a tunnel
and now forced to understand, yet
not able to comprehend anything:
. . . .
We suffered because we did not dare defend
a flower that was being amputated
in order to save the red tree
that also needed to grow.
. . . .
I ask forgiveness for this blind man
who saw and did not see.

["1967," *World's End*]

What we have in this poem, whose subject matter is clearly political,
is a tone quite different from Neruda's purely public poetry. There
is neither a forceful defense of the Soviet action, nor a vitriolic attack
on it. The event itself almost disappears into the poet's reflections on

his own role as a Party loyalist. The poem opens with the poet's "I"; we do not have a declaration concerning the event as an event, as we might have expected in Neruda's public poetry; we have instead a personal experience: "The hour of Prague fell/ on my head like a stone." Neruda is reliving a moment of sadness and shame, in the same way that he might have relived the death of a friend whom he failed to aid. The object of his lament is a public event; the tone of this poetry could not be more personal, nor further removed from the conscious oratory of his public poetry.

In all the books from 1968 on, we have seen Neruda apologizing, asking forgiveness not only for the things he has done, but primarily for the things he did not do; "forgive me" has been a refrain repeated in these books. We have also seen at times a sense of despair in the poet, such as in *The Hands of Day*. Nowhere, however, does this despair take on such global proportions as in *World's End*. Neruda's description of the twentieth century is constantly painted in the blackest of terms: "This is the age of ash," he declares in a poem entitled "Ash," "The ash of burned children," "the ash of eyes that cried." In another poem, "Epoch," he decries "the century of agony/ that taught us to kill." In still another poem, "It was the cold age of war/ the tranquil age of hatred" ("Let Them Know, Let Them Know It"). And in "The Bomb, 1" he writes: "But in these years was born/ the complete factory of death,/ the unchained atom/ and it wasn't enough for us to assassinate 100,000 sleeping Japanese . . ." Still later, in "Saddest Century," the poet defines our time as "the century of exiles."

The very personal perspective of this book is not the only thing that differentiates it from Neruda's public poetry. In *World's End*, Neruda demonstrates a subtlety of reflection which is not always characteristic of those other books. In *Spain in My Heart*, there was a right and a wrong, the Republicans being painted as heroes, the Phalangist forces as villains; in *Canto General*, the same facile division into "good" and "bad" existed, and once again in *A Call for Nixonicide*. In these books, designed as a sort of call to action, as ideological tracts, Neruda uses the clear-cut divisions of the propagandist, developing easy, compact formulas, and wielding his pen like a weapon. In *World's End*, by contrast, the mood is reflective and the poems are not constructed as calls to battle. The poet is taking his own personal accounting and the verses are less fiery: Neruda is not orating here, and in this quieter, more personal perspective, he finds that the lines are more blurred, the blacks and whites less clearly delineated. Remaining, of course, always a Marxist poet and a militant, Neruda now sees nonetheless that hands are bloodied on all sides of the political spectrum. There was not just Vietnam, but also Prague, not just Nixon, but also Stalin. "Even the enemy was sometimes right," Hernán Loyola notes, "without ever ceasing to be the enemy."[27] This is a softer, more gentle book than Neruda's purely political poetry, a more meditative one, and perhaps it is precisely because of its more personal nature that the poet can confess the doubts and despair that he preferred not to show in his public poetry.

While politics runs throughout this volume, *World's End* is not, however, exclusively political, and several of its eleven sections include almost no verses dealing with public events. There are poems dedicated to the wind, the sea, music, reminiscences of the poet's childhood, reflections on the art of poetry, on bees, on autumn; there is a bestiary, and portraits of cities and countries—Punta del Este, Rio de Janeiro, Venezuela—and of contemporary South American writers—Julio Cortázar, César Vallejo, Mario Vargas Llosa, and Gabriel García Márquez, among others. What we have in *World's End* is Neruda again looking around at every aspect of the world in which he has lived. The despair at what he sees is intense—the wars, the destruction, the unfulfilled dreams of revolution—and yet, a note of hope still comes through as the book ends:

> Once more, among the mortals
> I foretell without vacillation
> that despite this world's end
> man survives, infinite.

["Song"]

Three years later, having published *The Flaming Sword* and *Sky Stones* in the interim, Neruda published *Barren Terrain* (1972).[28] During these three years, Neruda had been actively engaged in Chilean politics. In 1969 he was the Communist Party candidate for the Presidency of Chile, until the various parties of the Left agreed to support Salvador Allende. During 1970, Neruda traveled throughout Chile campaigning for Allende, and when Allende won, Neruda was named Chile's Ambassador to France. "I had accepted the post without giving it much thought," Neruda recalls in his *Memoirs*, "once again letting myself be swept along by the current of life. I was pleased at the idea of representing a victorious popular government, after so many years of mediocre and lying ones. Perhaps, deep down, what appealed to me most was the thought of entering with new dignity the Chilean Embassy building where I had swallowed so many humiliations when I organized the immigration of the Spanish

Republicans into my country. Each of my predecessors had had a hand in my persecution, had helped to revile and hurt me. The persecuted would now sit in the persecutor's chair, eat at his table, sleep in his bed, and open the windows to let the new air of the world into the old Embassy."[29] Neruda's departure for Paris, Camacho Guizado notes, "gave rise to a new vital optimism, a new happiness, a sort of Renaissance. . . ."[30] But Neruda was already a sick man. Within months of his arrival in Paris, he had surgery for cancer, and from that time on he was never free of physical pain. *Barren Terrain* was begun in Chile and finished in France, and in it we see a mixture of optimism and an oncoming awareness of death. The optimism is perhaps related to public events, the excitement of finally having a leftist government in Chile, but the agony is personal, the inevitable reality of a man whose end is approaching.

Despite Neruda's active political engagement in these years, the poetry in *Barren Terrain* remains personal. As was already the case in *World's End,* this personal perspective produces a more mellow and reflective tone, and we don't find the simplistic divisions common in Neruda's public poetry. This is clear from the first moment, when in "The Sun," the opening poem of this volume, the poet declares:

> And I don't divide the world into two halves,
> into two black or yellow spheres
> but rather I keep it in full light
> like one lone grape of topaz.

Reading *Barren Terrain* today, one cannot help but be struck by how this volume anticipates some of the major themes of Neruda's posthumous works. There is, for instance, the contrast between the poet's observation of the regenerative cycle of Nature and the ebbing out of man's life:

> I go along without living, already mineralized,
> immobile, waiting for the agony,
> while the blue hills flower
> with the first fated signs of spring.
>
> ["The Coward"]

This theme of contrast between man and Nature has already been present in many of Neruda's earlier works, but more and more with *Barren Terrain* it takes on the added significance of the poet's anticipation and acceptance of his own death, while the natural world he leaves will go on flowering.

Another theme dominant in the posthumous works is also prefigured in this work: the theme of solitude. As Jaime Alazraki observes, ". . . in *Barren Terrain,* Neruda insists that his solitude is a point of arrival, a territory of foundations and buildings, a geography in which being and solitude become confused in a pure and continuous immutability, 'a place, / without anyone, with ocean and sand,/ lost, with my suit/ of solitude, looking/ without seeing, that which is furthest/ in the distance that erases the flowers/ *there I am,* continuous,/ as if time had frozen/ in the distance my photography/ impassioned in its fixedness.'"[31] We see in these verses not just the positive attitude toward solitude, but also the ever-present theme of time. Neruda is comforted by the fixedness of a photographic image, much like those stopped images that he produced in his late Nature poetry, by the illusion of halting for a moment the onward flow of time. Of course this theme is not new in Neruda's poetry, but it takes on another dimension when we realize that the poet is watching his own time running out, that the march of time is quickly bringing him toward death. Because of the reemergence of these themes, because of the time period in which it was published, *Barren Terrain* forms a bridge between the works of the late 1950s through the early 1970s, and the posthumous volumes. It closes the "autumnal" cycle of Neruda's poetry and anticipates the "winter" cycle, the eight books published after the poet's death. As Robert Pring-Mill notes, the fact that Neruda chose to entitle one of the major works of the posthumous volumes *Winter Garden* shows that he himself was fully aware of the change, of the end of one cycle with *Barren Terrain,* and the opening of another cycle, the final cycle, with the works that would follow.[32]

Synopsis

The late 1950s, the 1960s, and the early 1970s were clearly for Neruda an enormously prolific period and a period of astounding variety as well. During these years he published some of the finest love poetry in *One Hundred Love Sonnets* and parts of *Extravagaria* and *Barcarole;* he produced Nature poetry that continued the movement toward close examination, almost still shots of every aspect of the external world, in the odes of *Voyages and Homecomings,* in *The Stones of Chile,* in *The Art of Birds,* in *A House by the Shore,* and in *Sky Stones.* He continued as well his role as public poet in *Chanson de Geste,* in parts of *Ceremonial Songs,* in the mythical *The Flaming Sword,* and the angry *A Call for Nixonicide and Glory to the Chilean Revolution.*

In addition to these works, which were discussed in previous chapters, Neruda put forth as well an important collection of deeply personal poetry whose themes encompass virtually every subject and whose only unity can be found in their singular focus on the mind, memories, thoughts, and life of Pablo Neruda. Throughout most of Neruda's career the movement between the two poles of public and private poetry has been evident, and the period between the late 1950s and the 1970s is no exception. What is exceptional in this period is the number of works produced in which the poet's "I" dominates in a conscious fashion, in which the poet is openly recounting his life or concentrating on his own private metaphysical concerns. As Alazraki observes, with *Extravagaria* Neruda begins the "thawing out of his 'I,'" and it is a process which will continue throughout the rest of his published poems.[33] Public works continue to appear during these years, as we have seen, but their poetic quality is decidedly inferior to that of the personal works and they are far outnumbered by them as well. Most of the books of this period are invariably to some degree "Neruda on Neruda." In them we can see the poet's "will to return to the 'I,' the vindication of solitude and mystery as inalienable voices in his song."[34] It is not always an easy road for Neruda. As we have seen in more than one book of this period, the poet experiences at times a despair over language, a guilt over his intellectual work, he apologizes more than once for the continued intrusion of his self into his poetry: and yet the presence of that self undeniably continues to dominate the works of these years, and to define them as a unity.

What is remarkable in these works—*Extravagaria, Ceremonial Songs, Fully Empowered, Notes from Isla Negra, Barcarole, The Hands of Day, And Yet, World's End* and *Barren Terrain*—is that within the unifying context of being very personal books of poetry, the variety among them is immense. Thematically, the books cover a staggering range, moving from the irreverent and playful satire of parts of *Extravagaria* to the autobiographical *Notes from Isla Negra* to the romantic nostalgia of *Barcarole* to the lament on his lack of manual labor in *The Hands of Day* to the focus on the events of this century in *World's End*. Stylistically as well, Neruda shows constant versatility in these books: the long verses and musical quality of *Barcarole* convey the tenderness and romanticism of that book; the 433 lines of *And Yet* are mainly short verses; the view of the twentieth century in *World's End* is communicated in a harsh rhythm of nine syllables that accords with the dark picture of the contemporary world which the poet paints. In the books of this period we see Neruda exploring not only diverse regions of his memory and of the world around him, but finding as well the poetic rhythm and style appropriate to each vision. The quality of a number of the books written during the sixties and early seventies is not always as high as Neruda's best; yet it is generally good, and the books are rich above all in what they tell us about the man himself, about Neruda inquiring into every aspect of his own being, delving into autobiographical introspection and metaphysical reflection. As Robert Pring-Mill observes, "Neruda grew earthwards till he reached the roots, and those roots proved to be his own."[35] As we look back from the present, we see that it is these roots that Neruda excavates and exposes, making them the central core of his poetry in this autumnal period of his life and his work.

5. The Posthumous Poetry

B y 1972 Pablo Neruda had been sick with cancer for several years, and his failing health forced him to resign his post as Chile's Ambassador to France and return to Chile. Nonetheless, his death on September 23, 1973, in Santiago, came unexpectedly. "What brought about his sudden collapse," Robert Pring-Mill writes, "was the shock of the coup and of Allende's death. Salvador Allende had been a close friend, and his end in the Palacio de la Moneda hit Neruda as hard as Lorca's murder at the outbreak of the Spanish civil war; but where that earlier sequence of events had driven him into political commitment, at the age of thirty-two, when a parallel situation arose later his failing health gave way. His funeral, protected by the presence of foreign journalists and cameramen, was the only time dissenting voices could be raised in Chile in defiance of the new regime."[1]

Neruda had been working on eight books of poetry, which he had planned to publish on his seventieth birthday, July 12, 1974. According to Losada, which first published the works, they were written almost simultaneously, yet with a specific order in mind. Had that order been carried out, the works would have appeared in the following sequence: *The Separate Rose, Winter Garden, 2000, The Yellow Heart, The Book of Riddles, Elegy, The Sea and the Bells,* and *Selected Failings.* It was not, however, and in 1973 *The Sea and the Bells* was the first to appear in print. In this chapter we follow the chronological order designated by Neruda for these eight volumes, considering it a more accurate reflection of the poet's artistic cycle than the order chosen by Losada after Neruda's death.

This small detail of publication dates illustrates the more fundamental problem of analyzing posthumous works in general. One is confronted with a body of work that the poet himself did not mold into its final form. These poems were salvaged despite the ransacking of Neruda's homes. Neruda had nearly finished work on these books, but we have no way of knowing whether the poet, had he lived, would have chosen in fact to publish all of these poems, or in what order, or with what alterations. Despite the final version that these eight books appear to represent, the poems must really be considered a kind of unfinished symphony. We are left with the broad strokes of the composition on which the poet was working, but we have no idea what kind of fine adjustments or tuning he might have added had he lived to oversee the publication of these books. As a result, these volumes must, to a certain extent, be looked at differently from Neruda's other poems; we can observe what is there, but we cannot make definitive judgments, simply because the poems themselves are not necessarily in the definitive form Neruda might have chosen.

While the eight books vary in content, mood, and quality, certain general observations can be made about them as a group. To begin with, they contain, for the most part, short poems, and nowhere is there the suggestion of building a monumental work along the lines of *Canto General** or even the *Residence** poems or *Notes from Isla Negra.** Whether this was a result of a deliberate poetic choice or only of physical circumstance, or a combination of both, we cannot know. What can be stated as fact is only that Neruda in his last years was seriously ill and knew that his life was ending. Under such conditions, it would not be surprising to find him writing short poems, rather than embarking upon a monumental work he might not live to finish.

A second general observation on these posthumous books is that their style clearly continues Neruda's march toward clarity. The poems are easy to read, the vocabulary simple, the images accessible. This is particularly true of *The Book of Riddles,* which has almost a childlike quality in its constant questions about the material world. As is usually the case with Neruda, however, simplicity of form and language does not mean simplicity of content—often a complex intellectual vision of the world is embodied in the most elementary form of expression.

Still another element common to these books is that the movement toward personal poetry, begun in the 1950s and the 1960s, reaches its climax here. These volumes often touch deeply private realms of the poet's existence, an existence that he contemplates in solitude and silence.

Within these private domains, the poet's great companion is Nature. There are, of course, love poems and even political poems in the posthumous works; the erotic poet and the public poet are still in evidence. But overwhelmingly the finest of these volumes belong most of all to Neruda as personal poet and as Nature poet. "I"-

---

*This book is discussed in earlier chapters. See Contents page.

oriented poems abound in these volumes; a constant dialogue plays between the persona of the poet and the world of Nature. Metaphysical at times, existential at others, Neruda now seeks above all to renew his contact with Nature and to meditate on his own life and on man's relationship with the natural forces that predate him and outlast him.

Finally, there is a certain unity of mood in several of the posthumous volumes. The poet is almost always alone, a solitary figure, and volumes such as *Winter Garden, The Sea and the Bells,* and *Elegy* are often characterized by nostalgic meditation. *The Sea and the Bells* and *Winter Garden,* moreover, are clearly books written by a man aware that he is dying; the taking account, the reflection on life and death, the nostalgia for Nature and the past, and the anticipation of a coming end can be sensed everywhere. There is no panic, no intense or anguished desire to live in the face of oncoming death; rather we perceive an acceptance of what is to come, a calm, a tranquility, a mood of reflection. These are not sad books. They are, more accurately, the works of a man who knows the near future holds only death, but a man also at peace with life and with himself. There is no struggle against death, nor is there any morbid exaltation of it. What we find in these books is a vision of the poet slowly, almost serenely, moving, with acceptance, toward the sea that will absorb him and carry him into infinity. In that vision, and to a degree that is notable, refrains of much of Neruda's earlier poetry are replayed and reworked. Whether it was the poet's intention or not, these eight posthumous volumes together form an extraordinary grande finale in which notes from virtually Neruda's entire opus resound with clarity.

The Separate Rose

One center unites this fine volume of poetry—Easter Island—and in *The Separate Rose* (1973)[2] the island becomes a symbol of a primordial, primitive world, still fierce, still savage, still proud. Neruda had long been fascinated by Easter Island and its huge stone statues and had included several poems on the subject in his *Canto General.* This particular book grew out of a trip Neruda made to the island in 1971 as part of a team working on a television documentary.

The rapport with the *Canto* is evident in this volume, and the island represents for the poet one last vestige of the ancient order, the world as Neruda had described it in the opening of his epic poem, the universe before the "wig and frockcoat" ("Love America"), before the invasion of civilized man with his sadness, his weakness, his pathetic coverings, and his false ways.

But there are men on Easter Island, and Neruda's book alternates between poems entitled "The Men" and those entitled "The Island." We see the opposition clearly in comparing Poem IV, "The Men," and Poem V, "The Island":

> All of us who walk around are clumsy people. Our elbows get in the
>   way,
> our feet, our trousers, our suitcases,
> we get off the train, the jet plane, the ship, we come down
> with our wrinkled suits and our sinister hats.
> We are all guilty, we are all sinners,
> we arrive from somnolent hotels or from industrial peace,
> that is perhaps our last clean shirt,
> we have misplaced our tie,
> yet even so, going out of our minds, impressive and pompous,
> sons of a whore moving in the best circles
> or silent men who don't owe anything to anybody,
> we are the same, the same thing when facing time
> when facing solitude: we are poor devils
> who earned a living and a death by working
> in a bureaucratic or normal fashion,
> sitting down or heaped together in subway stations, jails,
> Universities, breweries,
> (under our clothes the same thirsty skin,
> the hair, the same hair; only with different colors).
>
> [Poem IV, "The Men"]

The description of man reminds us of "Ritual of My Legs" from *Residence on Earth;* yet here there is a solidarity not present in that earlier poem. The unity of men that Neruda now perceives is a unity based on man's lamentable state. All professions are in the end equally pitiful, professor or aristocrat, miner or bureaucrat, the same "thirsty skin" breathes underneath whatever garments, all are one and the same, united in their sad condition, all equally guilty, all subject to time, all equally and absurdly enveloped in clothes and encumbered with suitcases. In radical opposition to this pathetic portrait of men arriving is the portrait, in the following poem, of the island.

> All the islands in the ocean were built by the wind.
> But it is here that the High One, the living wind, the first wind,
> established his home, folded his wings, dwelled:

it is from this small Rapa Nui that he organized his Empire,
he blew, he inundated, he showered us with gifts
toward the West, toward the East, toward the smoothest space
until the purest buds appeared,
until roots were born.

[Poem V, "The Island"]

We notice immediately the sharp difference in vocabulary between the two poems. Men are "clumsy," covered in "trousers," encumbered by "suitcases," traveling on artificial industrialized convoys such as a "train," a "jet plane," a "ship," covered in sad casings, "wrinkled suits," "sinister hats," they are "guilty," "sinners." In contrast, everything in the island is vital, pure, and energetic: the "living wind," "wings," "space," "the purest buds," "roots." The opposition continues throughout the entire volume, repeating in structure at least the kind of alternation we have seen in the "Marisol" and "Marisombra" poems of *Twenty Poems*.* Where men appear, they are equalized, despite their different social conditions, by the march of time, by death, by a sense of encumberment, oppression, suffocation, and fatigue that sometimes reminds us of the *Residence* cycle. Where the island appears we feel, in contrast, a sense of space, purity, birth, freedom, energy, and life that recalls the opening of *Canto General*.

The treatment of Nature in this volume is in fact very close to that in the *Canto* and *The Stones of Chile*.** As in those earlier works, Neruda here personifies Nature, attributes a history to Nature, and creates an entire mythology around Nature as it existed before modern man. The only men who seem at home in Neruda's verses are prehistoric men, like the *Canto*'s men of clay and stone, men still intimately linked to Nature. In his description of the enormous stone statues that dot Easter Island, Neruda returns to the time of these prehistoric men, to a mythical "before" when the work of man and the work of Nature were indistinguishable:

When giants multiplied
and walked tall and straight
until the whole island was full of huge stone noses
and, busy, they kept going on: the sons
of wind and lava, the grandsons
of air and ashes went up and down the island
treading it with their enormous feet.

*See chapters 1 and 2.
**See chapter 2.

Never had the breeze
kept her hands so busy,
the typhoon and his murders
roared without pause,

. . . .

and the great creatures sleeping on the horizon
are the stone larvae of mystery:
left here by the wind when the wind fled the earth
and no longer begot children of lava.

[Poem VII, "The Island"]

Man and Nature are perfectly intertwined here. The wind has sons, the air and ash grandsons running along the island, the breeze works with its hands, the wind flees. The poet's imagination carries us once more into a realm of almost mythological existence, a state of vitality and creation that once existed, but is no more. In *The Separate Rose* Neruda does not treat the external world of matter primarily as an expression of his own state as he did in *Twenty Poems* or in the *Residence* cycle. He also abandons the pure contemplation of matter of the *Odes*,* and plunges fully into the mythification so characteristic of the *Canto*. The difference lies in the end, more so than in the means: in the *Canto* a pure external world was mythified in order to make a political commentary, to contrast the beauty and force of this world and its men to the imperialistic invasion of clothed and bewigged conquerers who would come later. Here, the commentary is more general and directed toward the modern human condition in its totality. Nature alone, or in harmony with prehistoric man, is opposed to the sad condition of modern man, beaten down by trappings and oppression, regardless of country of origin or political ideology.

In this finely chiseled work of metaphysical and mythological travels through Easter Island, a good number of the currents of Neruda's entire poetic production thus come together: the contrast of city man versus Nature, the recurring theme of modern man burdened by trappings that separate him from Nature, the personal and mythological conception of Nature as a purer force, once in close harmony with man, but now separated from modern man, the concept of a lost past, a mystery once known and now forgotten. All these themes, present in varying form and degree in *Twenty Poems*, in *Residence on Earth*, in *Canto General*, and in *The Stones of Chile*, come together here, still throbbing with life, still expressed in a collection

*See chapter 2.

of moving metaphors, in texts which are at the same time social, existential, and historical poetry.

Yet there is a difference, and it is a significant one. In *Canto General,* above all in "Heights of Macchu Picchu," Neruda was able to achieve a total identification with his "ancestors," with those primitive men who once lived in close union with Nature. Now, in *The Separate Rose,* Neruda is no longer able to penetrate to the same degree the stone before him and his identification is with the "guilty" tourists, with modern man, in the same way that in *And Yet** the poet included himself in saying "and we were the thieves." As Robert Pring-Mill notes, "There is no way of getting through to the long-forgotten race which carved the statues, whose blank eyes shut [Neruda] out. Forced to recognize how closely he resembles the other tourists who arrive . . . he ends up having to withdraw like them, equally baffled . . . the end of this sequence contrasts sharply with the triumphant mood in which he returned from the heights of Macchu Picchu, glorying in the new role of spokesman that enabled him to vanquish solitude through solidarity."[3] In *The Separate Rose,* Neruda documents a despair over the condition of modern man that is not new. But now there is a note of compassion for man's pitiful state and the poet seems less and less able to separate himself from the sad men around him. Perhaps it is this which leads him finally to choose solitude in so many of the posthumous books; perhaps it is only in solitude that the poet sees the possibility of recapturing a profound tie to his roots.

Winter Garden

The title suggests the tone of this book.[4] We are no longer in the regenerative abundance of spring, but at the end of a cycle and of a life. One of the leitmotivs of this book is precisely the poet's consciousness of the life and death cycle as it unfolds in Nature:

> This is the hour
> of fallen leaves, crumbled and crumpled
> on the earth, when
> to be and to not be return to the depths
> leaving behind the gold and the greenery
> until they are roots once again
> and once again, torn down and being born,
> they move up to know the springtime.
>
> ["The Egoist"]

*See chapter 4.

As in his earlier Nature poetry, death here is seen as part of life. We are reminded of Neruda's use of the tree in *Canto General* as a symbol of the ongoing life of the Latin American peoples, despite the death of individual leaves. The passing of one leaf is not an end, but only the necessary movement to open up the place for the birth of a new leaf. This same movement of death turning into new life, of winter opening up into spring is present in "With Quevedo, in Springtime," and again in the title poem of this volume:

> . . . give me for today the sleep of nocturnal
> leaves, the night in which we come face to face
> with the dead, the metals, the roots,
> and so many extinguished springtimes
> that awaken in each springtime.
> > ["With Quevedo, in Springtime"]

> I knew the rose had to fall
> and the pit of the passing peach
> would sleep and germinate once more
> . . . .
> the earth's pure death inspires
> my will to germinate once again.
> > ["Winter Garden"]

What is notable in these two poems, and throughout the volume, is that neither death nor the winter season is portrayed as a negative or threatening force. The key to this vision is perspective. Neruda doesn't focus either on death or on winter in isolation. Rather, he places both within the broader vision of the movements of Nature at large. It is within this context that both lose their menacing force and become simply one momentary part of Nature and man's life cycle. Neruda's essential optimism rests with this ability to see the total picture. He can accept without fear death and winter because he sees at the same time the regenerative forces of youth and springtime that will follow.

The association of man's life cycle with Nature's is not, of course, a new concept or one unique to Neruda. What is perhaps more crucial in examining the development of his poetry is the imagery with which the Chilean expresses this classical philosophy. Once again, Neruda has recourse to Nature to express man: leaves, roots, seasons, the rose, the peach, the earth. In these final poems, as in his earliest, and throughout his career, Nature is for Neruda the overwhelming universal force, and it is man who fits into Nature's cycle, not vice versa. In the books he wrote during the fifties and sixties,

Neruda portrayed the immense force of Nature in poems such as "Cataclysm." Now, more and more in these posthumous volumes, the forces of Nature—the source of the poet's imagery—take on titanic proportions that dwarf men.

Within this context of Nature looming ever larger before the poet, solitude, equally a condition of the barren season of winter, takes on a dominant role. As it had already begun to do in his personal poetry, solitude here assumes a positive value. It is the poet's refuge from man-made institutions and crowded societies, it is his necessary companion for the return to Nature and to his own inner being:

> No one is missing from this garden, yet
> no one is here, only a green and black winter,
> a day pale as a ghost,
> a white phantom wearing its cold garments
> up the stairs of a castle. It is the time
> when no one should arrive. Just a few drops
> of chilly dew keep falling
> from the bare branches of winter,
> just you and I in this circle of solitude,
> invincible, alone, waiting
> for no one to arrive, no, no one should come
> with a smile or a medal or a budget
> no one should talk to us or ask for anything.
>
> ["The Egoist"]

The solitude he fled, panic-stricken, in *Residence I,* Neruda now invites in this opening poem of *Winter Garden.* As Jaime Alazraki notes, solitude is no longer "a hairy spider" here, or "a dung-heap fly," as it was in the "Ode to Solitude." Now the poet "coincides with a sentiment that has been the refrain of modern literature from the romantics to Beckett: solitude is the great companion of modern man . . . solitude here is not a punishment, but rather a cause for enjoyment and celebration."[5]

We have seen that this attraction to solitude had its precedents in Neruda's work of the fifties and sixties. In the *Odes,* Neruda was alone in his contemplation of Nature, as he was in *The Stones of Chile, Sky Stones,* * and *The Art of Birds**; and in both *Extravagaria*** and *Barren Terrain,*** Neruda approached Nature with a positive perspective. The difference lies in degree: what in the late 1950s and the 1960s was a tentative and circumstantial glance at solitude, has in

*See chapter 2.
**See chapter 4.

the posthumous books become a firm and unhesitating embrace.
The poet, nearing death, looking into himself, seeks to reflect on his
own life and the fate that soon awaits him; for this task, he now
needs solitude as his companion. Neruda is not, however, always
comfortable with this need. Again the conflict between his desire for
solitude and his sense of duty as a public poet, as a political poet who
had pledged himself to make poetry a weapon to be used daily,
troubles him and Neruda still feels the need to anticipate his critics
and to justify his right to produce intimate poetry centered around
his "I":

> . . . and there is a smell of sharp solitude,
> of humidity, of water, of being born again:
> what can I do if I breathe without anyone,
> why am I going to feel myself wounded to death?
>
> ["The Egoist"]

Here too the imagery chosen by Neruda tells us much. If it is traditional, even a cliché, to describe man's life cycle in terms of Nature, it
is far more revealing of Neruda's bond with natural forces that he
describes solitude—a state of being with no necessary link to
Nature—in terms of Nature. Solitude has a "smell," it is compared to
"humidity," to "water," and its odor is that of rebirth.

Water, constantly present throughout Neruda's poetry, is—in the
form of the sea—perhaps the single most recurrent image in these
posthumous volumes:

> Two homecomings comforted my life
> and the daily sea at my feet:
> . . . .
> a journey home
> that I accepted serenely, without fuss,
> it was my will, and here I shall remain:
> now the main truth is for me my homecoming.
>
> I felt it as a blow,
> like a crystal nut
> breaking on a boulder.
> . . . .
> And this time among temptations
> I feared to touch the sand, the splendor
> of this wounded and scattered sea,
> but accepting my injustice
> my decision fell with the sound
> of a glass fruit that shatters

> and in this resounding blow I glimpsed life,
> the earth wrapped in shadows and sparks,
> and the cup of the sea below my lips.
>
> ["Homecomings"]

In this poem Neruda dives into his own being as if he were diving into the sea, Alazraki notes, and all the imagery relates to marine life. The poet captures a unity in his life, and "From that unity a peace filters through. . . . For Neruda, it is a peace which leaves him facing a dark well. The well might be death, but that no longer matters. Life and the world have now been incorporated with the being that breaks itself like a crystal nut on the rock; and in the blow, as in a flash of lightning, life glimmers in its incommensurable unity. . . . It is a return to the poet's being, but also a return to the universal consciousness represented by the sea, a blow which, like a luminous revelation, puts the poet in front of the totality of life, quintessentially contained in a cup."[6]

Neruda's selection of imagery here recalls another period in his poetry and suggests a specific cyclic pattern at work in the poet. A "weapon of moist crystal" opened *Canto General,* an arm upon which "the initials of the earth were/written" ("Love America"). Now, two decades later, we are back with another object of crystal, once again in an unusual juxtaposition of images, since we do not usually think of a weapon or a nut or a fruit as being made of crystal, and in this case the crystal is also related to a type of illumination in which all of life and history are gathered in a moment of cosmic transparency and unity. This essential repetition at the end of his life of a concept first annunciated much earlier is striking and suggests that the cyclic patterns to which Neruda is so sensitive in Nature also exist in his poetic work.

Nor is this the only echo of *Canto General* in this posthumous book. In "For All to Know," Neruda returns to the Whitmanesque style so characteristic of much of the *Canto:*

> . . . .
> it was my duty to understand everybody, I had to be
> delirious, weak, tenacious, compromised, heroic, vile,
> loving people until I cried—yet an ingrate at times,
> a saviour entangled in his own chains,
> all dressed in black yet toasting to Joy.
>
> Why describe your truth, your wisdom,
> if I lived with every one of them,
> I am Everybody and Everytime,
> my name has always been also your name.

The concept of the poet here is similar to that in the *Canto* and in Whitman's poetry: he is again a spokesman, the person obligated to sing everyman's story, the poet is everyman. Neruda equally returns in these verses to the Whitmanesque style of chaotic enumeration with "weak, tenacious, compromised, heroic, vile." What has changed, perhaps, is that the quasi-pantheistic vision of the *Canto,* the desire for continuity with everyone and everything, here takes on a different value. Facing his own death, Neruda's approach toward continuity can be seen more in the sense that the French writer Georges Bataille has defined it: continuity is death, it is the disintegration of the individual, discontinuous person.[7] It is this that Neruda is facing, a cosmic continuity in which the individualized Neruda will become part of the vast sea of unindividualized existence.

Winter Garden is a volume exceptionally unified in tone and theme. One poem, however, stands out and differs from the others because it centers on a political reality, rather than on the poet's inner reality alone. Called "Autumn," it is a poem about the last days of Salvador Allende's government in Chile. They were also the last days of Neruda's life:

> Day after day the grating clashing noises
> of an undeclared civil war.
> Men and women, screams and challenges,
> while in the hostile city,
> on the now deserted beaches,
> to the ever-faithful foams and waves,
> Autumn, dressed like a soldier,
> its head is grey, its march slow:
> the invading Autumn covers the earth.

"War," 'screams," "challenges," "hostile," "deserted," "Autumn," once again the image taken from Nature, "dressed like a soldier," "grey," "invading," this is a poem of violence and of death, and the images could not be clearer. Chile and the Allende government, like Neruda himself, would fall in September, but here they are symbolized as a tree, still hanging on to life, "still green-leafed, hesitating/ before losing its leaves and falling down/ dressed first in gold, then in rags." Yet the die is cast, and Neruda senses that for both himself and the government he supported, death approaches this autumn:

> I fly to the sea all wrapped up in sky,
> the silence between one wave and the next
> creates anguish and suspense,

life ebbs out, blood stops flowing
until the new wave crashes on
and we hear the booming voice of infinity.

In these verses, as in "Heights of Macchu Picchu," the poet's persona becomes identified with a larger destiny. He is returning to the sea, going toward death, and so is the Allende government; his life is running out, "life ebbs out," that of the government as well as his own. Neruda's sadness is manifest here in a way that is not the case where he deals exclusively with his own life and impending death. But the Nature imagery, above all the sea—that constant when he speaks of his own death—is present here too, its unending movement washing away one life, until in a new movement another life is brought forth.

2000

While still reflecting the stance of a man taking account before death, *2000* (1974)[8] is very different from *Winter Garden,* and in many ways not as successful. Here Neruda leaves behind the lyrical meditations of *Winter Garden* and contemplates contemporary reality and the future. The style is less meditative and more proclamatory than that in his earlier volume *World's End,** and in *2000* Neruda surfaces again as a public poet. He remains always a poet of matter in terms of observing the external world around him, but here it is a man-made world of violence and commercialism, juxtaposed and contrasted with the benevolent and generous world of Nature.

In discussing Neruda as a public poet, we observed that he can rise to great heights when he writes about the everyday modern world; he can, however, also rest on a more pedestrian level. The poems collected in *2000* amply demonstrate the uneven poetic quality that often accompanies Neruda's "oratory" in the consideration of not inherently poetical subjects. As earlier with "Chronicle of 1948," from *Canto General,* Neruda here constructs a series of poems that together constitute a commentary on the state of the world, this time as he imagines it will be in the year 2000. The mood is mixed, revealing sadness where man's past and present failures are recognized, and at the same time, a desire to keep an optimistic outlook for the future. On occasion, as in "The Earth," the optimism achieved is due less to man than to Nature:

*See chapter 4.

Let us praise the old excrement-hued earth,
her cavities, her holy ovaries,
her cellars of wisdom that enclosed
copper, oil, magnets, hardwares, purity,
the lightning that seemed to come down from hell
was treasured by the ancient mother of roots
and every day bread would come out to greet us
ignoring the blood and death that we men always wear,
we who are both the accursed race and the light of the world.

This "ode" to the earth which, despite the violence that man wreaks on it and on himself, keeps reproducing and providing nourishment recalls many of the images used in Neruda's earlier Nature poetry. Earth is again personified as female, as mother; it is the source of natural riches ("copper, oil"), of "roots," the source of life, of nourishment ("bread"), and reproduction ("ovaries"). The verses exemplify the prevailing vision of this book: despair over the condition of man—his continued wars and destruction—and, simultaneously, a confidence in the continued cycle of life, in Nature, and, in spite of all, also in man who is "the light of the world." The verses are as well indicative of the poetic quality of the book. There are no new or exceptional images, the use of words and metaphors is more expected than surprising. It is, in some ways, poetry more like the work of Neruda's imitators than like the master's best.

The Yellow Heart

Avoiding for the most part the serious, contemplative mood of *The Separate Rose* or *Winter Garden, The Yellow Heart* (1974)[9] offers a tone that is irreverent, playful, even nonsensical at times, yet always with a point to be made. The themes are often social satire, with strange and amusing anecdotes to illustrate the absurdity of social customs. A case in point is "An Untenable Situation," centered around the extravagant personages who make up the Ostrogodo family. So much of the Ostrogodos' daily conversation revolved around dead relatives and everything that no longer lives, that one day, Neruda tells us, something unusual happened:

To that mansion of dark courtyards and orange trees,
to that drawing-room with its black piano,
to the tomb-like corridors,
many ghosts came to stay,
feeling perfectly at home.

The invasion is progressive until the family is forced to take refuge in the garden. But the Ostrogodos never complain, "so pure was their respect/ for the diverse faces of death." And finally, the inevitable:

> Until after so many deaths
> they joined the others
> becoming silent, passing away
> in that house of death.
> One day no one was left,
> no doors, no house, no light,
> no orange trees, and no ghosts.

The playful, hyperbolic tone of this poem is representative of the volume as a whole. Yet is would seem reasonable to ask if Neruda was not also recounting in this apparently irreverent poem, the implacable march of death invading his own home and body.

Curiously, just where Neruda chooses to be irreverent in content, his form becomes traditional and the poems in this book are written in carefully regularized meter. They are also as a rule longer than the poems in some of the other posthumous books. The length of the poems can be explained perhaps by the anecdotal nature of the content. Yet at times this extended length undermines the effect and weakens the volume as a whole. Irreverent humor is difficult to sustain in any work. While in certain poems, such as "An Untenable Situation," space is needed to develop the hyperbole that creates a humor of the absurd, in others the subject matter is simply too light to easily endure long treatment. Too often in *The Yellow Heart* what might have been effective as a short poem becomes tiresome when drawn out into a long one. The same problem exists in terms of the book as a collection. The flippant attitude, the satire, the exaggeration, and the absurdity certainly function as humor. But they are techniques more effective in small doses, and *The Yellow Heart* suffers from the repeated use of attitudes and techniques that finally become too predictable.

This is an amusing volume, and an interesting one to the extent that it shows Neruda's versatility as a poet and testifies that even close to death, he could produce humorous, satirical poetry as well as more meditative works. But the interest of this volume, we believe, stops there. Camacho Guizado calls *The Yellow Heart* a "delicious book"[10] and it can be. It is not a substantial book, however, nor an essential one, and the poetry is more often pleasant than remarkable. It certainly cannot be compared in our mind with the equally irreverent *Extravagaria*. *The Yellow Heart* is a book which Neruda, already established as a great poet, could produce; by itself it would not have established Neruda's reputation as a great poet.

The Book of Riddles

In contrast stands *The Book of Riddles* (1974),[11] perhaps the simplest and yet the most complex of the eight posthumous volumes, and certainly one of the most delightful to read. The book is literally a book of questions: every verse ends in a question mark. There are only questions. No statements here, except, of course, for those implicit in the questions themselves, which together add up to a declaration of the poet's way of seeing the world. Neruda returns in this volume to the clear observations of the *Odes* and once more we have Nature poetry, with the poet examining and questioning every aspect of the world around him.

While there are individual poems with a common theme (dreams, for instance, in poem XLIII or reflections on Hitler's fate in poem LXX), for the most part each poem is simply made up of a series of questions that have no apparent necessary link to the other questions within the same poem. We see this in poem IV:

How many churches does Heaven hold?
Why don't the sharks attack
the serene mermaids?

Does the smoke talk to the clouds?
Is it true that hope
must be watered with dew?

The questions appear to be random, and yet the poem achieves unity. Some natural element—the sky, then the sea, then the sky again, and finally the dew—appears in each verse, linking the whole. A still more profound unity is found in the tone of each question and in the repeated interrogatory form. Unlike its effect in *The Yellow Heart,* where satire was the goal, the repetition here of the same technique and tone produces a tremendously forceful cumulative effect, and the unrelenting questions intensify, rather than weaken, the whole.

In each verse of *The Book of Riddles* we are dealing with the unanswerable questions of life, the "whys" a child might ask on every conceivable subject. Neruda observes Nature in the same way that when a child asks "Why is the sky blue?" it shows that he has noticed the color of the sky. What is brilliant in this work is precisely this: the master poet has protected his childlike innocence and imagination in looking at Nature, and he remains open to seeing and wondering about everything. There is a perfect blend of the newly born observer of the world, full of whys and wonder, and the man close to death, still asking. The form of the interrogation is childlike, the questions themselves contain the complexity and openness of a sophisticated poetic mind that refuses to avoid the "absurd" questions of life:

> Is it always the same Spring
> repeating a well-learned lesson?
>
> > [Poem LXXII]
>
> If we run out of yellow
> how are we going to make bread?
>
> > [II]
>
> Why do trees always hide
> the splendor of their roots?
>
> > [III]
>
> How many bees does a day have?
>
> > [VI]
>
> What angers volcanoes so much
> that they spit fire and fury?
>
> > [VIII]
>
> Where is the center of the sea?
> Why don't the waves travel to it?
>
> > [XXI]
>
> If water is sweet in every river
> why is it salty in every ocean?
>
> How do the seasons find out
> when they should change their shirt?
>
> > [LXXII]

In many ways this apparently simple book is also an excellent summary of various facets of Neruda as a poet. He asked questions like these in his first published book, *Crepusculario:** there, speaking of afternoon coming on, the poet asks "Who gave it for this journey/ the wings of a bird?" ("The Afternoon Over the Roofs"). There is as well the exuberant celebration of everyday material life that formed the fundamental basis of the *Odes;* and the eruption of the unexpected or even the absurd in many of the questions replays refrains

---

*See chapter 2.

from the *Extravagaria* period. It is not surprising that we find these recurrent strains of different moments of Neruda's work in this slender volume, since in *The Book of Riddles* Neruda returns to a primary function of a poet: the observation and interrogation of the world around him.

While there are individual poems (XXXVI-XL and LXII, for instance) where the theme of death enters, in general this is a marvelously happy and vibrant book. It is also a generous book. Neruda has returned to the concept of poetry as a gift. Here he lends us for a moment his eyes, his ears, his ability to ask the questions that "one doesn't ask," and he opens up our minds and senses to perceiving the world differently. In showing us that it is not absurd to ask, for example, "Why are there so many wrinkles/and so many holes in a stone?" (L), Neruda frees the reader, he lifts the censorship of logic and social convention and offers the reader the joy of interrogating his surroundings. In this way, in its tone and impact on the reader, this book is very close to the *Odes*. If the *Odes* prompted in the reader a new awareness and appreciation of the everyday material things that make up our world, this book does the same and more. *The Book of Riddles* is a wonderful legacy. Neruda, close to death, leaves us his way of seeing the world. We inherit from him an exceptionally "living" book, the unanswered and unanswerable questions of the poet's accumulated years of observing the world in which he has lived.

Elegy

Elegy (1974)[12] is Neruda's last look at Soviet Russia. Neruda had already written extensively on Russia, beginning with his "Song to Stalingrad" in *The Third Residence*. Now, in a final reflection, Neruda contemplates the country that for forty years had been the center of his political ideology and commitment. *Elegy* is a sentimental journey through that country, which for Neruda represented the projection of an ideal.

Walking through Moscow, the poet recalls both the dream and his fellow dreamers, with elegies to Mayakovsky, Pushkin, and Nazim Hikmet. In these short, almost sketched poems, distant Russia re-emerges, the Russia of the days when this country was expected to revolutionize the world. The dream and the reality mix in Neruda's mind as he mentally wanders the streets of Moscow:

> Moscow, city of huge wings,
> albatross of the steppes,
> with your gilt nest the Kremlin,

and St. Basil's, a huge toy,
city also with a rectangular soul,
with infinitely grey suburbs,
cubes just out of the factory
and snaking like a loving arm
the river
around the fortress' waist . . .

[Poem v]

Immediately the vision of Moscow is ambivalent, and Russia is both visionary symbol and ominous reality. The soaring poetic imagery of the old Russia—Moscow like an albatross spreading its wings, the Kremlin like a "gilt nest"—sharply contrasts with the new, post-revolutionary Moscow, where everything is regimented, where the fantasy element of the toylike St. Basil's no longer dominates. Now the city's soul is rectangular, her neighborhoods are infinitely grey, pre-fabricated cubes just out of the factory. The mixed and ambivalent imagery reappears in the last verses, where the river carries both the unpleasant image of a snake coiling and the soothing image of being a "loving arm," where "waist," a soft image which gives a decidedly feminine touch to the city, is followed by the harsh word "fortress." What we have in this opening stanza are two faces of Russia: its permanent features, what existed before and after the revolution, the fantasy-inspiring facet of the great bird and the playful St. Basil's, the river as a "loving arm," the "waist"; but there is also contemporary Russia, with its "rectangular soul," its grey atmosphere, its pre-fabricated cubes, the city like a "fortress."

The poet's mixed feelings about this city, the symbol of everything Russia has stood for and still does stand for in his idealistic revolutionary mind, continue throughout the poem. There are references to "Tsar Ivan and Stalin the Terrible," to "temples dark as jail cells." But the fascination and the mystique reappear as well, and the poem ends with a powerful image of strength and magnetism, the realization of the impossible: Moscow has "an ardent and silent energy/ like a fire underneath the sea."

What we see in *Elegy* is above all a sense of revolutionary nostalgia. As Camacho Guizado observes: "*Elegy* is a Soviet book that exudes the melancholy of the old and glorious epoch of anti-Fascist struggle, of the people and of the cities which were already legendary in Neruda's years of Internationale militancy. In comparison with *The Grapes and the Wind,** a book of joyous discovery of socialist solidar-

*See chapters 1 and 3.

ity, *Elegy*, resulting from the poet's last visit to the Soviet Union, contemplates and laments the passage of time for the same places that he wandered about twenty or thirty years earlier."[13]

The book is both personal and political. Neruda is the ideologue speaking of a political dream in which he participated for most of his life, and an individual looking back, remembering his youth, his comrades, the places, the struggle. Although *Elegy*'s political orientation could make one think of Neruda's earlier public poetry, or even of *2000*, the book is in reality closer to the tone of the very personal *Winter Garden*. The age of the poet and the sense of farewell are everywhere apparent in its pages. The biting satirical humor of *The Yellow Heart,* or the childlike exuberance of *The Book of Riddles* are not to be found. As the title indicates, this is a book about things past, friends who have died, places that have changed, and the excitement of a revolutionary struggle that is now but a memory. It is a compelling volume in what it tells us about Neruda looking back over a lifetime of political struggle and the choices he made as a young man. It is certainly an important book in an autobiographical context, more so, perhaps, than in a strictly poetical one.

The Sea and the Bells

In *The Sea and the Bells* (1973),[14] we find many of the same thematic concerns as in *Winter Garden*. We are again with the poet taking account of his life, dealing with the great themes of man's existence, and of his own being. Also like *Winter Garden,* this is a book of intimately personal poetry, the poet turning in toward himself, and it is a book whose title makes use also of external elements to describe the poet's internal state. Here those elements are the sea, an aspect of Nature always important in Neruda's poetry, and the bells, which "constitute the communication with Nature, a kind of last-minute religious contact, of comfort, of security."[15]

These two elements, the sea and the bells, carry the mood of the poetry in this volume. Both are images that connote at once a life force and a death force. The sea has always been for Neruda one of the most vibrant forces of life and mystery, and bells can ring out for joy; but now, the sea is also a symbol of death, of the poet's final immersion into the continuity of being, and the bells will soon toll his death knell. The bells and the sea are connected, moreover, in a fashion particularly appropriate to the mood of this book: at sea, the passing of time is recorded by ship's bells. The bells and the sea also share a rhythm that once more recalls the life-cycle symbolism of the

sea discussed in connection with *Winter Garden:* as the dying out of
one wave brings on the next, so the echo created as one bell dies out
serves to usher in the clear ring of the next bell. For Neruda the
association is so automatic that he uses bells as the image to mark the
movement of the sea: he realizes

> . . . that I am a part
> of winter,
> of the flat expanse that is repeated
> from bell to bell in endless waves,
> a particle of silence like a woman's hair,
> a silence of seaweeds, a submerged song.
>
> ["Forgive Me If through My Eyes . . ."]

In this one poem, Jaime Alazraki notes, "all the central motifs of
Neruda's posthumous poetry converge: solitude as inalienable sov-
ereignty, the sea as a double of the poet's secret being, death as a
conquered unity, as a 'submerged song' that integrates itself into the
total song of the great ocean. From these three motifs, a fourth de-
rives, one which is already present in his late poems, but only enters
fully in his posthumous books: silence."[16] Silence is the predominant
theme in this volume, sought after and cultivated by the poet, just as
silence's companion, solitude, was invoked in *Winter Garden.*

The silence Neruda seeks in *The Sea and the Bells* is intimately related to the sounds named in the title. He yearns to escape from the
useless noise, the verbosity of meaningless discourse; he yearns for
the silence needed to get back into contact with his innermost being,
the silence to contemplate, to hear the rush of the sea and the
chimes of the bells. It is a silence that will be achieved when the
empty chatter of convention is eliminated and we return to the essentials of life. The concept is put forth directly in "Pedro is the
When . . .":

> Pedro is the When and the How
> Clara means perhaps Of Course,
> Roberto means However:
> they all walk with the help of prepositions,
> adverbs and nouns
> which pile up in stores,
> corporations and streets,
> and the weight of each man weighs on me,
> with his connecting word,
> like an old hat:
> where are they going?, I ask myself.

Where are we going
with our carefully chosen merchandise,
all wrapped up in little words,
dressed up in nets of words?

Neruda had already attacked meaningless words in works such as *Extravagaria* and *The Hands of Day** and here we find that words are given the same negative value that was assigned to clothing in Poem IV from *The Separate Rose,* for instance, or years earlier in "Ritual of My Legs." Words are "carefully chosen merchandise," we are "wrapped up in little words." In the earlier poems clothing kept us from contact with what is real, with our own nakedness and with Nature; in these verses it is everyday words that have become meaningless appendages covering up what is true; they have now become the barrier. "Neruda despairs of that so-called 'language of communication' which has ended up destroying communication," Alazraki observes, "a language of alienation with which 'we understand each other' without ever coming to comprehend each other . . . . In contrast to these signs and countersigns that take us everywhere without taking us anywhere, Neruda proposes a language which finds its answer in silence and whose fulfillment is the negation of language: 'we must hear what has no voice,/ we must see those things that do not exist. . . .'"[17] "Gold or sugar, real beings,/ happiness,/ all these things are not spoken," Neruda tells us ("Pedro is the When . . ."). This same characterization of words as useless adornments, as "merchandise," reappears in "I Want to Know," where the poet invites us to come with him "to not walk and not talk," to "finally . . . see the pure air," and "not to have anything to interchange: at last, not to introduce merchandise:/ as was done by the colonizers/ who traded baubles for silence."

Attacks on conventional language are certainly one of the cornerstones of modern literature, and Latin American literature is no exception. Examples abound, in prose and poetry alike: Horacio Oliveira's diatribes on language and experiments with nonconventional forms such as "glíglico" in Julio Cortázar's *Hopscotch,* for instance; or Octavio Paz's rejection of everyday language in his search for original, pure language, for what he calls the Word. Jorge Luis Borges too, while not directly rejecting everyday language, searches for a return to magical language, to the mythological powers of words, where to say "Thor" was to invoke thunder. His interest in the ancient practices of the Jewish mystics, or Kabbalists, is at least in part due to their belief in the power of the word to create, and not

*See chapter 4.

simply describe, a reality, in a universe where the word and the thing are one and the same.

For these and other modern writers, the negative value assigned to conventional language has at times almost a mystical or metaphysical aspect to it. It is often tied up with the concept of the impossibility of expressing certain extreme experiences in conventional words, at other times with the loss of the once magical power of words, or with the idea of a once-existent and now shattered primordial unity. The idea is not new. In fact most religions and mythologies depict totality as a state preceding individualization. Unity and continuity are the pure original states; individuality and discontinuity come afterward and, above all, come to acquire importance in western bourgeois society with its emphasis on the individual. We have seen Neruda touch this concept already in the opening poems of *Canto General*. "Love America," for example, presents a confusion of natural elements suggesting an essential unity prior to the divisive invasion of man-made names and classifications. As in modern literature in general, Neruda's rejection of language is a rejection only of disunified, meaningless, cliché-ridden language, where words are spoken that no longer have significance, and where the original power and unity have been lost. It is essentially a mystical and mythological rejection of language insofar as it presupposes the prior existence of a unified state that has disappeared, a world before the "fall." As noted by Alazraki, Octavio Paz puts it well in his poem "A Fable":

> All things were everybody's
>   All the human beings were the Whole
> There was only one immense word without wrong side
> A word like a sun
> One day it broke into small fragments
> These are the words of the language we now speak
> Fragments that will never come together
> Broken mirrors where a broken world is reflected.[18]

Paz's vocabulary again recalls Neruda's in "Love America." The words written on the hilt of man's sword were once impregnated with meaning, Neruda tells us in that poem; but they have since been forgotten:

> No one could recall them afterwards: the wind
> forgot them, the water's language
> was buried, the keys were lost
> or were overrun by silence or blood.

> ["Love America," *Canto General*]

It is to recapture that lost meaning, to recover contact with what is essential in life, uncluttered by false and useless gibberish, that Neruda in *The Sea and the Bells* asks for silence. The request is a difficult one, and an ironic one. The poet, says Alazraki, "seeks to transcend words, but he is condemned to use words, he seeks to reveal signifieds that are not in the words, but he has to avail himself of them. His nonsensical undertaking consists of finding recourse in language in order to annul language, of utilizing words to define silences that express signifieds inexpressible in words."[19] As with Mallarmé, René Char, Paz, and other modern poets, Neruda's wish for silence is in reality a search to strengthen the power of poetry, to allow meanings to reveal themselves through the magic of true language. Neruda is "speaking . . . of a silence that rejects names and forms, interpretations and explanations in order to find its fulfillment in an absence which, nonetheless, includes all presences."[20]

These metaphysical explanations of Neruda's wish for silence are, we believe, justified. Yet they do not exclude asking at the same time whether this wish—already apparent in *The Hands of Day,* but certainly more developed in *The Sea and the Bells*—doesn't reveal a more purely personal despair with the state of the world and a hint of fatigue and disappointment. The poet who in *Spain in My Heart** saw poetry as a vital political weapon, who in *Canto General* wanted to sing America's story, who in *A Call for Nixonicide** defined words as action, is now seeking silence. We can call his attitude in *The Sea and the Bells* a new maturity, but perhaps it is also the weariness of someone who has battled with the only weapon he has and who sees the battle, after so many years, no closer to being won. He needs the space to reflect. The poet wonders, after so many words, if it is not now the time to halt the flow of words and to listen to the sounds of Nature and of his own inner being. Perhaps there, a new, pure language will emerge, more powerful, more capable of changing the world than before.

The simple beauty of *The Sea and the Bells* is the silence that surrounds the poet. In this silence we hear the sounds he hears and we share the thoughts of his solitude:

> Long ago in my journeys
> I discovered a river.
> It was no more than a small child, a dog or a bird,
> that newly-born river
>
> . . . .

*See chapter 3.

it murmured and moaned
among the stones
of the iron-stained sierra:
it begged for life
among the solitudes of sky and snow,
far away, far above.

["Long Ago"]

We listen to the river with the poet, we see it jump and grow, "sing-ing with a clear voice," a river which "cried at birth/ and that was growing/ before my eyes." The poet, in the silence of Nature, hears the sounds of creation: "a heartbeat, a sound among the stones/ was being born."

In another poem, "A Small Animal," the same silence of solitude, away from the noise of civilization, allows the poet to hear the cries of a small wounded animal. It is once more this silence in "It Rains" that lets us listen, with Neruda, to the drops of water on the sand, on the roof. In this sense, Neruda's desire for silence is also a desire for a return to Nature, the theme that has consistently run through his poetry. The images have changed, but only slightly: the bustle and wild passion of the city present in the "Marisombra" verses of *Twenty Poems* were contrasted with the pure, open beauty of the country, of "Marisol," of Nature. Here, the meaningless gestures of everyday reality are painted as words, as empty noises and are contrasted with the silence of introspection, the silence that allows us to hear Nature, for Neruda the truest of languages.

Before leaving *The Sea and the Bells,* it should be noted that this splendid book of gentle reflection also contains political poetry ("Yes, Comrade") and love poetry, including the last poem Neruda ever wrote "The End." It is because of this poem, dedicated to Matilde, that the book was rushed to press before the other posthumous vol-umes. In it Neruda is now clearly a sick man, a dying man: "Matilde, years or days/ asleep, with fever" in "beds in clinics, with alien win-dows." When the poet speaks, it is for a moment already in the past tense, in recognition that his life is, in reality, over:

It was such a joy to be alive
when you were alive!

The world is bluer, more earthy
at night, when I sleep,
enormous, within your small hands.

["The End"]

Thus the long cycle of Neruda's love poetry closes. As Camacho Guizado states, "That adolescent who searched sadly or desperately

for a love that would reveal the 'other,' an intimate solidarity, a refuge, a maternal warmth, is now an old sick man who has found this
protective haven."[21]

Selected Failings

In speaking earlier about the difficulties of judging posthumous
poetry in general, we noted that we can never be sure whether the
poet, had he lived, would have finally decided to publish certain
works in the form we have received them. Nowhere in Neruda's
posthumous work does this question loom larger than in contemplating the nineteen poems that make up *Selected Failings* (1974).[22]

One concrete example illustrates the problem: the end of one
poem of *Selected Failings*, "The Other," strangely repeats, word for
word, the end of the preceding poem, "Antoine Courage." Looking
at the text published by Losada, the reader might conclude that
Neruda had chosen to relate these two poems by a shockingly out-
of-context repetition. Yet Neruda never made such a choice. The
repetition is quite simply a printing error, a fact made evident by
consulting the French edition in which the repetition does not occur.[23] Even in the case of a book rushed to press, as occurred with
much of Neruda's posthumous poetry, it is difficult to imagine that
an error as glaring as the substitution of the end of one poem for
another would not be picked up either by the editors or Neruda's
family. It would at least seem reasonable to venture that such an
error would never have occurred if Neruda himself had controlled
the final publication of this work.

Sadly, this "failing" is not the only one in *Selected Failings*. Most of
the poems are without great interest or importance, whether judged
from a literary, a thematic, or a biographical point of view. Mainly
centered around little known individuals of whom Neruda paints,
for the most part, unflattering portraits, the verses are simply prosaic and the imagery bland. Every great poet, especially one as prolific as Neruda, has written unexceptional poetry, and it is easy to
imagine the poems in *Selected Failings* as pieces that Neruda dashed
off and later, making closer judgment, might well have decided not
to publish in their present form. But death intervened and we will
never know whether the poet himself would have released all the
poems in this volume. In our judgment, it is unfortunate that this
book stands as the last published work of Pablo Neruda.

As tempting as it is to attribute the weaknesses of this volume to
the circumstances which denied the poet the possibility of a final
revision of the book, we recognize also that there are clear examples

in Neruda's earlier works of the deliberate publication of poems that in the opinion of many critics hold little literary interest. Most of the earlier poems that fall into this category are, like those in *Selected Failings,* poems where Neruda directs his attention to criticizing rather insignificant political figures. *Canto General* offers examples in parts of sections v and xiii, where a number of poems are given over to local political figures in Chile or elsewhere who are of small historic consequence and who are known today only because Neruda immortalized them in his verses. Minor men are sketched in rather ordinary poetry, and these sections constitute the weakest link in what is otherwise one of the most splendid achievements of Neruda's career. From this precedent, one can postulate that Neruda had, perhaps, the weakness of a touch of vindictiveness in regard to his political enemies, and the vanity of assuming that his views on anyone or any subject, no matter how petty, were of public concern. What these sections of the *Canto* and the later groupings of *Selected Failings* reveal is the fallacy of the belief "that any poem written by a great poet is poetry."[24] *Selected Failings* is not great poetry in general; it is, as its title, intentionally or not, indicates, the selected failings of a great poet.

Two poems in this book, however, stand exempt from our general comments: "Oregano" and "Another Castle." Happily, both are worthy of Neruda at his best:

> When slowly, very slowly, I learned
> to speak
> I think I also learned how to be incoherent:
> no one understood my words, not even myself,
> and I hated those words
> that always made me come back
> to the same pit,
> to the pit of my still dark being,
> still recovering from being born.
> Until one day I found on a railroad track
> or perhaps it was a newly sown field
> a word: *oregano.*
> This word made me unwind,
> as if guiding me out of a labyrinth.
>
> ["Oregano"]

What follows is an ode, as fine as any of the *Elemental Odes.* Only this time there is a difference: the object of the poet's praise is not the thing in itself, but a name, a word which for him becomes the passport out of the claustrophobic world of himself. "I refused to learn any more words," the poet affirms. He burns dictionaries and everywhere he goes, "I went on chewing up my word, *oregano*/ the word was like a dove/that was set free from among ignorant men. . ." As if it were the Aleph or the primal Word, the single unity containing all else, *oregano* becomes the center of the poet's existence: "night is full of *oregano*/ and at times it became like a pistol/ it went with me to walk among wild beasts:/ this word protected my poems." Faced with the danger of wild animals, the poet draws his word out of his pocket and cries, "Oregano":

> A miracle happened. The frightened beasts
> asked my forgiveness and
> humbly asked for *oregano*.

The word is "like a priestly presence . . . that helped me avoid talking to others,/ and that shed light on my destiny/ I renounced rhetoric and speeches/ I had my secret language, the language of oregano."

Here Neruda recaptures, and even surpasses, the exuberant imagination present in the *Odes*. Taking the surprising absurdity of a commonplace word, the poet develops it almost into a philosophical and metaphysical system. He rejects common cliché language, as he did in *The Sea and the Bells*. But here he constructs an alternate system, one that reaches the nonsensical yet is a clear affirmation of a language that has real meaning for the poet, a language of incommunication that allows him to avoid banal discourse with others, to speak in a way that he comprehends, that Nature's beasts comprehend, but which remains secret from civilized man. "Oregano," the poet's protection against the frivolous conversation of his peers, "oregano," a secret code with Nature's language, "oregano," the shield that protects the poet and his verses, "oregano," the silence which frees the poet to clarify his destiny. With "Oregano" we find Neruda in full form.

"Another Castle" is the other exceptional poem in *Selected Failings*. In it, the poet declares, "I am not made of fire . . .":

> I am made out of clothes, arthritis,
> torn papers, forgotten quotations
> poor traces and signs on the walls
> of what were once proud stones.

Where has the "castle of rain" gone, he asks, adolescence with its sad dreams and open-ended propositions, the grand aspirations of an extended bird, an eagle, heraldic fire? In contrast with the dramatic images of a "ray of blue fire, thrust like a spear/ into any heart without bitterness" and "a starry blow," the poet sizes up man's mediocre reality: life is none of these miraculous things, but only "a wasting away inside our clothes,/ a shoe a thousand times repeated,/ a medal slowly getting rusty/ inside a dark, dark box." Salt and wind erase man's writing and the human soul "is now a silent drum/ by a river bank, by that river that was there and will be there forever more."

Once again, man in comparison with Nature loses in the match. The dashing images of man's dreams are all made up of elements taken from Nature: "a ray of blue fire," "a starry blow." Man's banal reality consists of things that separate him from Nature: clothes, shoes, physical maladies, torn papers. In the end, not even man's writing remains—it is eroded by the stronger forces of Nature, salt and wind; and man's soul is but a "silent drum" next to the unending flow of the natural world, which preceded man and which will continue to flourish long after his feeble life on this planet has ended.

In discussing his Nature poetry we noted that more and more Neruda would see in Nature a permanence that escapes the fleeting life of man: "Another Castle" offers clear evidence of that attitude in Neruda's posthumous works. In the midst of this volume dominated by "portraits of unknown and unimportant people," of "tourist visits" and banal reflections, "Another Castle" stands out as "a model of melancholic self-reflection, of concision, of expressive precision and last emotion," Camacho Guizado concludes. "It is a naked confession, a final balance of the poor condition of man in the midst of durable Nature."[25] It is, together with "Oregano" and perhaps one or two other poems, the singular achievement in this book of *Selected Failings*.

Synopsis

As if offering us a final summary of Neruda's poetic life, the eight volumes of posthumous works constitute almost a microcosm, recalling aspects of virtually all his books. In these eight volumes we find love poetry and Nature poetry, we observe Neruda as public poet and as a deeply personal poet. We encounter him still in contact with Nature and still using Nature as his primary source of imagery. The simple questions of *The Book of Riddles,* for instance, remind us of certain aspects of *Crepusculario* or of the *Odes.* The contrast between civilized, urban, modern man and pure Nature in several of the posthumous volumes recalls the contrasts made in *Twenty Poems* and in *Canto General*. The mythification of Nature and of a pure past, of a time when man and Nature were in harmony and not separated by the useless trappings of clothing, language, or other "merchandise" evokes the *Canto* also, and at times *The Stones of Chile* or *Sky Stones*. The oppressive description of modern man reminds us of moments of the *Residence* poems, although Neruda never repeats either the anguish or the complex imagery to the same degree. The poet, adopting the role of public spokesman and prophet, uniting his persona with the destiny of a nation, as in "Autumn" or with all mankind in "For All to Know" from *Winter Garden*, echoes once again the *Canto*, as do the political portraits of *Selected Failings* or the observation of the "state of the world" in *2000*. The very personal aspects of much of the poetry continue the focus apparent in the books published during the fifties and sixties. Even specific images, such as crystal as a container of knowledge and illumination, are repeated here in a context similar to their earlier appearance in Neruda's works. We see Neruda demonstrating once more his poetic greatness in works such as *The Separate Rose, Winter Garden, The Book of Riddles,* and *The Sea and the Bells,* and we see him repeating some of the weaknesses of his earlier works in volumes such as *2000* and *Selected Failings*. All the recurrent themes of fifty years of poetry are here, and all the variations of poetic quality as well.

The extent to which the posthumous books vividly evoke the gamut of Neruda's poetry is striking; yet these volumes are no mere repetition of the past. The emphasis has changed notably, and the mood is different. Silence and solitude were present in earlier poetry, but nowhere were they embraced as fully and unhesitatingly as in *Winter Garden* and *The Sea and the Bells*. The contemplative mood, the reflection on the life cycle and man's place in the world were present in much of Neruda's personal poetry of the fifties, six-ties, and early seventies; but they are given a new power in the post-humous books within the context of the poet openly facing his own death. While themes are repeated, the change in perspective, the shift in degree and intensity define a tone which marks these vol-umes as unique in the course of Neruda's poetry. And two elements above all reverberate most strongly and define these works by their dominance: Neruda as Nature poet and as personal poet, and in the best of these volumes the two facets merge completely.

We have stressed throughout our discussion of Neruda's poetry that simple divisions are not always accurate and that when we speak of Neruda as "public poet" or as "personal poet" we are pointing to a difference in stress, and not a mutual exclusion, since Neruda's personal vision is present even in his most apparently public poetry. In looking at the eight posthumous volumes, we can distinguish such a difference in stress. *Elegy* is at once personal and social poetry, but the remaining seven volumes are divided almost evenly between personal poetry and public poetry. It is not an equal division in terms of poetic quality, however. In the four volumes where the personal element dominates—*The Separate Rose, Winter Garden, The Book of Riddles, The Sea and the Bells*—the poetry is superbly executed and we find "the mastery and personal imprint of a man who to the last moment was a great poet."[26] In the three volumes where the personal aspect is mixed with public or ideological considerations or with social satire—*2000, The Yellow Heart, Selected Failings*—the poetic level is less consistent. In these more "socially oriented" volumes Neruda's poetry can be excellent, yet none of the volumes in its entirety can rival, on a poetic level, the volumes of more purely personal poetry. In part this may be due simply to the difficulty of incorporating public themes into a poetic format. We suspect, however, that another factor is equally responsible. As throughout most of his career, in the 1970s the pendulum continued to swing for Neruda between private poetry and a call to public duty. In fact, though, as we have noted earlier, from the late 1950s on, Neruda seemed to feel more and more at home in the solitude of Nature and personal introspection. He performed his public duty, he was a good soldier, but we sense that his overwhelming need in this period was for private meditation, and this is reflected in the superior quality of the personal poetry produced during these years.

In the posthumous works we find a Neruda who knows that he is dying as he writes, and he turns in to himself and to Nature, singing to the end in tones of the earth. He regards the fact of his own approaching death with serenity and acceptance, taking comfort in the regenerative cycle of life and death that he observes in Nature. We find him sensing that perhaps the true reality of life is found in what endures beyond man, in Nature. He wants one last contact with Nature, and he asks for silence and solitude to encounter that force into which he will soon blend in the unending continuity of death. Thus closes the cycle of Pablo Neruda's poetry, and of his life:

> . . . and now, nothing more, I want to be alone
> with the primary sea and with the bells.
> I want to not speak for a very long time,
> silence, I want to learn still,
> I want to know if I exist.
> ["Is That Where the Sea Is?," *The Sea and the Bells*]

Selected Bibliography

The bibliography of Neruda's life and works is very copious. Most of the books and essays on Neruda are, of course, written in Spanish and many of them are unavailable to the North American reader and scholar—they were published in specialized South American magazines or journals to which few North American libraries subscribe or are, for other reasons, impossible to find in the U.S. We have listed items that seem to us most relevant to the North American reader and scholar. An asterisk indicates an especially valuable book or article.

Books about Neruda's Life and Poetry

*Alazraki, Jaime. *Poética y poesía de Pablo Neruda*. New York: Las Américas, 1965.
*Alonso, Amado. *Poesía y estilo de Pablo Neruda: interpretación de una poesía hermética*. Buenos Aires: Losada, 1940.
*Aguirre, Margarita. *Las vidas de Pablo Neruda*. 2d ed. revised. Buenos Aires and Barcelona: Grijalbo, 1973.
Aragon, Louis. *Élegie à Pablo Neruda*. Paris: Gallimard, 1966.
Bellini, Giuseppe. *Pablo Neruda e altri saggi sulla poesia latinoamericana*. Milan: La Goliardica, 1966.
———. *La poesia di Pablo Neruda da "Estravagario" a "Memorial de Isla Negra."* Padua: Liviana Editrice, 1966.
———. *Quevedo y la poesía hispanoamericana del siglo XX*. New York: Elíseo Torres and Sons, 1973.
*Camacho Guizado, Eduardo. *Pablo Neruda: Naturaleza, historia y poética*. Madrid: Sociedad General Española de Librería, 1978.
Carson, Morris E. *Pablo Neruda: Regresó el caminante*. New York: Ediciones Plaza Mayor, 1971.
Concha, Jaime. *Neruda, 1904–1936*. Letras de América. Santiago: Editorial Universitaria, 1972.
*———. *Tres estudios sobre Pablo Neruda*. Hispanic Studies (University of South Carolina), vol. 1. Palma de Mallorca: Mosén Alcover, 1974.
*Costa, René de. *The Poetry of Pablo Neruda*. Cambridge: Harvard University Press, 1979.
Flores, Angel. *Aproximaciones a Pablo Neruda*. Barcelona: Llibres de Sinera, 1974.
Gatell, Angelina. *Neruda*. Madrid: EPESA, 1971.

*González-Cruz, Luis F. *Memorial de Isla Negra: Integración de la visión poética de Pablo Neruda*. Miami: Ediciones Universal, 1972.

Hamilton, Carlos D. *El nuevo lenguaje poético: de Silva a Neruda*. Bogotá: Publications of the Instituto Caro y Cuervo, 1965. (See chapter "Pablo Neruda," pp. 147–85.)

————. *Pablo Neruda, poeta chileno universal*. Santiago: Lord Cochrane, 1972.

*Loyola, Hernán. *Ser y morir en Pablo Neruda, 1918–1945*. Santiago: Editorial Santiago, 1967.

————, editor. *Pablo Neruda: Antología esencial*. Buenos Aires: Losada, 1971.

Lozada, Alfredo. *El monismo agónico de Pablo Neruda. Estructura, significado y filiación de Residencia en la tierra*. México: B. Costa-Amic, 1971.

*Marcenac, Jean. *Pablo Neruda*. 3d ed. Poètes d'aujourd'hui, vol. 40. Paris: Séghers, 1971.

Melís, Antonio. *Neruda*. Il Castoro, vol. 39. Florence: La Nuova Italia, 1970.

Montes, Hugo. *Poesía actual de Chile y España*. Barcelona: Saymá, 1963.

————. *Macchu Picchu en la poesía*. Santiago: Ed. Nueva Universidad, 1972.

Neruda, Pablo. *Elementary Odes*. Introduction by F. Alegría. Translated by C. Lozano. New York: G. Massa, 1961.

————. *Extravagaria*. Translated by Alastair Reid. New York: Farrar, Straus and Giroux, 1974.

————. *Five Decades: A Selection. Poems, 1925–1970*. Edited and translated by Ben Belitt. New York: Grove Press, 1974.

————. *Fully Empowered*. Translated by Alastair Reid. New York: Farrar, Straus and Giroux, 1975.

————. *The Heights of Macchu Picchu*. Translated by Nathaniel Tarn. London: Jonathan Cape, 1966. 2d ed. New York: Farrar, Straus and Giroux, 1968. (See introduction by Robert Pring-Mill.)

————. *Let the Rail Splitter Awake and Other Poems*. New York: Masses and Mainstream, 1950.

*————. *Memoirs*. Translated by Hardie St. Martin. New York: Farrar, Straus and Giroux, 1977.

*————. *A New Decade. Poems, 1958–1967*. Edited with an introduction by Ben Belitt. Translated by Ben Belitt and Alastair Reid. New York: Grove Press, 1969. (See introduction by Belitt.)

*————. *New Poems (1968–1970)*. Edited and translated with an introduction by Ben Belitt. New York: Grove Press, 1972.

*————. *Pablo Neruda: A Basic Anthology*. Selection and introduction by Robert Pring-Mill. Oxford: Dolphin Books Co., 1975.

————. *Pablo Neruda: The Early Poems*. Translated by David Ossman and Carlos Hagen. New York: New Rivers Press, 1969. (See introduction by Ossman.)

*————. *Residence on Earth*. Translated by Donald Walsh. New York: New Directions, 1973. (See preface by Walsh.)

————. *Selected Poems*. Edited by Nathaniel Tarn and Anthony Kerrigan. London: Jonathan Cape, 1970. (See introduction by Tarn.)

————. *Songs of Protest by Pablo Neruda*. Translated and with an introduction by Miguel Algarín. New York: Morrow, 1976.

————. *Splendor and Death of Joaquín Murieta*. Translated by Ben Belitt. New York: Farrar, Straus and Giroux, 1972. (See preface by Belitt.)

————. *Twenty Poems*. Translated by James Wright and Robert Bly. Madison, Minn.: Sixties Press, 1967. (See "The Lamb and the Pine Cone: An Interview with Pablo Neruda in New York," pp. 102–10.)

*————. *Twenty Poems and a Song of Despair*. Translated by W. S. Merwin. London: Cape, 1969.

————. *We Are Many*. Translated by Alastair Reid. New York: Grossman, 1968.

*Neruda, Pablo, and Vallejo, César. *Neruda and Vallejo: Selected Poems*. Edited by Robert Bly. Translated by Robert Bly, John Knoepfle, and James Wright. Boston: Beacon Press, 1971. (See preface and introduction by Bly, "Refusing to Be Theocritus.")

Osorio, Nelson, and Moreno, Fernando. *Claves de Pablo Neruda*. Valparaíso: Ediciones Universitarias de Valparaíso, 1971.

Paseyro, Ricardo. *Le Mythe Neruda*. 2d ed. Paris: L'Herne, 1971.

Pérez, Galo René. *La poesía de Pablo Neruda*. Montevideo: Centro de Estudios de Literatura Latinoamericana, 1968.

*Riess, J. Frank. *The Word and the Stone: Language and Imagery in Neruda's "Canto general."* London and New York: Oxford University Press, 1972.

*Rodman, Selden. *South America of the Poets*. Illustrated by Bill Negrón. New York: Hawthorn Books, 1970. (See "Pablo Neruda's Chile," pp. 228–56.)

*Rodríguez Monegal, Emir. *El viajero inmóvil: introducción a Pablo Neruda*. Buenos Aires: Losada, 1966.

————. *Neruda, le voyageur immobile*. Translated from the Spanish by Bernard Lelong. Les Essais, vol. 184. Paris: Gallimard, 1973. (Revised edition of *El viajero inmóvil*, 1966.)

Schwartzmann, Félix. *Teoría de la expresión*. Santiago: Ediciones de la Universidad de Chile, 1967. (See "Silencio y palabra en la poesía de Neruda," pp. 47–49.)

Siefer, Elisabeth. *Epische Stilelemente im "Canto General" bei Pablo Neruda*. Munich: Wilhem Fink, 1970.

Solar Silva, Miguel Angel. *Palabra de juventud y palabra de poeta*. Santiago: Departamento de la Vicerrectoría de la Universidad de Chile, 1969.

Sarmiento, Alvaro. *Neruda: entierro y testamento* (with pictures by Fina Torres). Las Palmas: Inventarios Provisionales, 1975.

*Suárez Rivero, Eliana. *El gran amor de Pablo Neruda: estudio crítico de su poesía*. Madrid: Ediciones Plaza Mayor, 1971.

Willard, Nancy. *Testimony of the Invisible Man: William Carlos Williams, Francis Ponge, Rainer Maria Rilke, Pablo Neruda*. Columbia, Mo.: University of Missouri Press, 1969. (See pp. 83–115.)

*Yurkievich, Saúl. *Fundadores de la nueva poesía latinoamericana: Vallejo, Huidobro, Borges, Neruda, Paz*. Barcelona: Barral Editores, 1971. (The second edition, published in 1973, has a chapter on Oliverio Girondo; pages 163–249 in the second edition constitute the chapter on Neruda.)

Zagury, Eliane. *Traduçao e leitura de Pablo Neruda*. Río de Janeiro: Sabiá, 1968.

Articles

Aguirre, Margarita. "Entrevista con Pablo Neruda." *Crisis* (Buenos Aires, August 1973.) (Reproduced by José María Carranza in *Hispania* 57, no. 2 (March 1974):367–69.)

————. "Pablo Neruda íntimo." *Mundo Nuevo* 17 (1967):80–81.

Alazraki, Jaime. "Pablo Neruda, the Chronicler of All Things." *Books Abroad* 46 (1972):49–54.

————. "Poética de la penumbra en la poesía más reciente de P. Neruda." *Revista Iberoamericana.*

*————. "El Surrealismo de *Tentativa del hombre infinito* de Pablo Neruda." *Hispanic Review* 40 (1972):31–39. (See summary in 1972 *MLA Abstracts* 2 (1974):42.

————. "Observaciones sobre la estructura de la oda elemental." *Mester* 4, no. 2 (April 1974):94–102.

————. "Music as Silence in Neruda's Eight Posthumous Books of Poetry." *Books Abroad* 50 (1976):40–45.

————. "Punto de vista y recodificación en los poemas de autoexégesis de Pablo Neruda." *Symposium* 32 (1978):184–97.

Albizúrez Palma, Francisco. "La muerte en un poema de Pablo Neruda." *Comunidad* (Univ. Iberoamericana) 10 (1975): 270–75. (In "La muerte.")

Alegría, Fernando. "Las preguntas de Neruda." *The American Hispanist* 2, no. 12 (1976):3–5.

————. "Las preguntas de Neruda." *Nova* (Lisbon) (Fall 1976):69–75.

Aligher, Margarita. "Don Pablo at Home." *Soviet Literature* 11 (1977):88–100.

Alone (pseud. of Hernán Díaz Arrieta). "*Las vidas de Pablo Neruda,* por Margarita Aguirre." *El Mercurio* (Santiago de Chile), 5 May 1968.

————. "*Las manos del día,* por Pablo Neruda." *El Mercurio,* 12 January 1969.

————. "*Aún,* poemas de Pablo Neruda." *El Mercurio,* 27 July 1969.

————. "Pablo Neruda y Lord Cochrane." *El Mercurio,* 8 February 1970.

————. "*La espada encendida,* por Pablo Neruda." *El Mercurio,* 1 November 1970.

————. "Pablo Neruda, Premio Nobel." *El Mercurio,* 24 October 1971.

————. "Confieso que he vivido." *El Mercurio,* 21 July 1974.

————. "Algo más sobre las *Memorias* de Pablo Neruda." *El Mercurio,* 28 July 1974.

"Alone y Neruda." *El Siglo* (Santiago de Chile), 25 July 1968.

*Alonso, J. M. "Neftalí Ricardo Reyes Invents Pablo Neruda." *Review* 72 (Winter-Spring 1972):33–38.

Araya, Guillermo. "Les *Mémoires* de Neruda." *Europe* 561–62 (1976):199–210. [Rev. art.]

Armand, Octavio, "'La United Fruit Co.,' de Neruda como estructura alegórica." *Mester* 5:73–78.

Arrieta, Hernán Díaz. See Alone.

Arrouye, Jean, "Pablo Neruda: Attention du poète portée aux éléments. . . ." *Ecole des lettres,* 63d year, no. 9 (January 1972):3–6.

*Barnstone, Willis. "Hispanic Chronicle." *Poetry,* no. 111 (October 1967):46–55.

*Bary, David. "Sobre la 'Oda a Juan Tarrea.'" *Cuadernos Americanos* 159 (1968):197–214.

Beckett, Bonnie. "Entrevista con Margarita Aguirre." *The American Hispanist* 1, no. 8 (1976):3–4.

————. "The Reception of Pablo Neruda's Works in the German Democratic Republic." *Dissertation Abstracts International* 38 (1978):6711A.

*Belitt, Ben. "The Mourning Neruda." *Mundas Artium* 1 (1967):14–23. (Spanish translation in *Mundo Nuevo* 24 (June 1968): 86–91.)

*————. "The Burning Sarcophagus: A Revaluation of Pablo Neruda." *The Southern Review,* no. 4, Summer (June 1968):598–615.

————. *Adam's Dream: A Preface to Translation*. New York: Grove Press, 1976. [Prev. pub. essays & prets., esp. on Neruda.]

Bellini, Giuseppe. "La Francia nell 'opera di Pablo Neruda." *Studi Revel* 75:101–12.

Benavides, José D. "Cómo murió Neruda (Interview with Matilde Urrutia, his Widow)." *Imagen*, nos. 92–93 (15 April 1974):8–9.

Bennett, John M. "Estructuras antitéticas en 'Galope muerto' de Pablo Neruda." *Revista Hispánica Moderna: Columbia University Hispanic Studies* 38 (1974–75):103–14.

Bergen, Carol Janson. "Pablo Neruda's Poetry of Quest." *Dissertation Abstracts International* 38 (1977):298A.

"Bibliografía Pablo Neruda." *Taller de Letras* (Universidad Católica, Santiago de Chile), no. 3 (1973):139–44. (Enlargement of critical bibliography, which appears in *Taller de Letras*, no. 2.)

Bly, Robert. "On Pablo Neruda." *London Magazine* 8, no. 5 (1968):24–25.

Bosch, Rafael. "El 'Canto General' y el poeta como historiador." *Revista de crítica literatura latinoamericana* 1 (1975):61–72.

Brines, Francisco. "La imitación como itensificación poética (Neruda y García Lorca." *Insula* 368–69 (1977):3, 38.

Camurati, Mireya. "Significación del *Canto General* en la obra de Pablo Neruda." *Revista Interamericana* 2, no. 2 (1972):210–22.

Cano, José Luis. "Pablo Neruda: *Una casa en la arena*." *Insula* 22, no. 245 (1967):8–9.

*Cano Ballesta, Juan. "Miguel Hernández y su amistad con Pablo Neruda." *La Torre* 60 (1968):101–41.

*————. "Pablo Neruda and the Renewal of Spanish Poetry During the Thirties." In *Spanish Writers of 1936*, edited by Jaime Ferrán and Daniel P. Testa, pp. 94–106. Crisis and Commitment in the Poetry of the Thirties and Forties. London: Tamesis Books, 1973.

*————. "La renovación poética de los años treinta y Miguel Hernández." *Symposium* 22 (Summer, 1968):123–31.

Cardoza y Aragón, Luis. "Neruda." *Eco* 26, no. 156 (1973):373–75.

Carrera Andrade, Jorge. "Trayectoria de la poesía hispanoamericana." *Cuadernos Americanos* 30, no. 6 (1971):182–97.

Carrillo, Gastón. "La lengua poética de Pablo Neruda." *Boletín del Instituto de Filología de la Universidad de Chile* 19 (1967):133–64.

————. "La lengua poética de Pablo Neruda: Análisis de *Alturas de Macchu Picchu*." *Boletín del Instituto de Filología de la Universidad de Chile* 21 (1970):293–332.

Carvajal, Antonio. "Pablo Neruda: Confieso que he vivido (memorias)." *Camp de l'Arpa: Revista de Literatura* 14 (1974):20–21. [Rev. art.]

Catri, Liana. "Neruda e l'uomo." *La Prova* 9, no. 1 (1968):22–24.

Celaya, Gabriel. "Pablo Neruda: Poeta del tercer día de la Creación." *Revista de Occidente* 36 (1972):95–101.

Christ, Ronald. "Poet Who Is Too Big for the Nobel Prize." *Commonweal*, 26 December 1969, pp. 388–94.

————. "Review of *A New Decade (Poems: 1958–1967)*, tr. Ben Belitt and Alastair Reid." In *Review 69*, edited with an introductory note by Alexander Coleman, pp. 99–101. New York: Center for Inter-American Relations, 1970. (See same vol. reviews by Victor Howes, pp. 102–4; Violette Newton, pp. 104–6; and Selden Rodman, pp. 106–8.)

Clements, R. J. "Neruda Laureate." *Saturday Review,* 3 November 1971, pp. 50–51.

Colinas, Antonio. "Entrevista con Pablo Neruda." *Revista de Occidente* 37 (1972):255–66.

Concha, Jaime. "*La Barcarola* de Pablo Neruda." *El Siglo* (Santiago de Chile), 20 October 1968, reproduced in *Atenea,* no. 420 (April-June 1968):388–91.

———. "El *Canto General* de Pablo Neruda." *El Sur* (Concepción, Chile), 21 November 1971.

———. "Neruda: La tierra se llama Pablo." *Nova* (Lisbon) (Fall 1976): 114–19.

* ———. "Los orígenes (la primera infancia de Neruda)." *Revista Iberoamericana* 36 (1971):389–406.

Contino, Ferdinand Vito. "La Poesía de Pablo Neruda entre 1958 y 1971." *Dissertation Abstracts International* 37 (1977):6526A.

*Cortázar, Julio. "Neruda entre nosotros." *Plural* 30 (1974):38–41.

Cortinez, Carlos. "Commentario critico de los diez primeros poemas, de Residencia en la tierra." *Dissertation Abstracts International* 36 (1974):2239A–4OA.

———. "Emir Rodríguez Monegal, 'de vacaciones.'" *Revista de Bellas Artes* 31 (January-February 1970):28–38.

———. "Fidelidad de Neruda a su visión residenciaria." *Tláloc* (SUNY, Stony Brook) 5, no. 8 (October-December 1974).

———. "Introducción a la muerte en Residencia en la tierra: 'Ausencia de Joaquín'." *Explicacion de Textos Literarios* 7, no. 1 (1978):93–99.

———. "Un autorretrato espiritual del joven Neruda." *Dialogos* 81 (1978):4–9.

Costa, René de. "Pablo Neruda's Tentativa del hombre infinito: Notes for a Reappraisal." *Modern Philology* 73 (1974):136–47.

Couffon, Claude. "Pablo Neruda, premio Nobel." *Papeles de Son Armadans* 64 (1972):287–301.

Dantas, Lívio. "Neruda, um Nobel merecido há quarenta años." *Jornal de Letras* 255, no. 2 (1971):1.

*Debicki, Andrew. "La realidad concreta en algunos poemas de Pablo Neruda." In *Estudios de literatura hispanoamericana en honor a José J. Arrom,* edited by Andrew Debicki and Enrique Pupo-Walker, pp. 179–92. Chapel Hill: University of North Carolina Press, 1975.

De Cesare, Giovanni Battista. "Une Influence d'Asturias sur Neruda." *Europe* 553–54 (1974):193–96. (Tr. Armand Monjo)

Descola, J. "La literatura latino-americana." *Revue des Deux Mondes* (November 1972), pp. 283–88.

Díaz, Ramón. "Pasos entre las dos Residencias de Neruda." *Papeles de Son Armadans* 54 (1969):229–42.

Díez, Luis A. "Grandeza telúrica y aliento épico del *Canto General,*" *Sin Nombre* 4, no. 2 (1973):9–22.

D'Ors, M. "Una perla y una estrella (sobre una narración de John Steinbeck y un poema de Pablo Neruda)." In *Anales de Literatura Hispanoamericana,* vol. 1. Madrid: Chair of Spanish American Literature, Faculty of Philosophy and Letters, 1972.

*Durán, Manuel. "Pablo Neruda y la tradición romántica y simbólica." *Cuadernos Americanos* 3 (1980):187–99.

* ———. "Sobre la poesía de Neruda, la tradición simbolista y la desintegracíon del yo." *Simposio Pablo Neruda, Actas* (1974):123–44.

*Durán, Manuel, and Durán, Gloria. "Notas sobre Neruda, Brecht, el teatro épico y 'El signo del Zorro'." *Insula* (Madrid) 29, no. 330 (1974):1–14.

Droguett, Iván. "Apuntes sobre *Fulgor y muerte de Joaquín Murieta* de Pablo Neruda." *Latin American Theatre Review* 2, no. 1 (1968):39–48.

Ehrmann, Hans. "Neruda's Western." *New Statesman*, 15 December 1967, p. 857.

*Ellis, Keith. "Change and Constancy in Pablo Neruda's Poetic Practice." *Romanische Forschungen* 84 (1972):1–17.

* ———. "'Poema veinte': A Structural Approach." *Romance Notes* 11 (1969–70):507–17.

Engler, Kay. "Image and Structure in Neruda's *Las Alturas de Macchu Picchu*." *Symposium* 27, no. 2 (1974):130–45.

Eshleman, Clayton. "Neruda: An Elemental Response." *TriQuarterly* 15 (Spring 1969):228–37.

Evtushenko, Evgeni. "The Feast of Justice." *Soviet Literature* xi (1977):104–9.

Faraggi, Claude. "Évolution de la poésie de Neruda du début jusqu'à ses oeuvres récentes." *Nouvelle Revue Française* 212 (August 1970):83.

*Felstiner, John. "A Feminist Reading of Neruda." *Parnassus* 3, no. 2 (1974):90–112.

———. "Neruda in Translation." *Yale Review* 61 (1972):226–51.

———. "Nobel Prize at Isla Negra." *The New Republic*, 25 December 1971, pp. 29–30.

———. "Pablo Neruda, 1904–1973." *The New Republic*, 13 October 1973, p. 27.

———. "Translating Pablo Neruda's 'Galope muerto'." *PMLA* 93 (1978):185–95.

Fossey, Jean Michel. "Habla Neruda." *Imagen*, no. 21, 6–13 November 1971, p. 16. [Interview]

Foster, Merlin H. "Pablo Neruda and the Avant-Garde." *Symposium* 32 (1978):208–20.

Foti, F. "La poesia d'amore di Pablo Neruda." *Ausonia* 20, no. 2 (1965):56–58.

Foxley, Carmen. "La impertinencia predicativa. Una figura del lenguaje de *Residencia en la tierra*." *Taller de Letras*, Catholic University, Santiago de Chile, no. 4, 1975.

Friedmann, Florinda. "Neruda. Canta el reciente viajero." *Sur* 313 (July-August 1968):57–61.

Garrido, Manuel S. "Praxis poética y reflexión política." *Plural* 78 (1978):28–37.

Gatell, Angelina. "Neruda, Premio Nobel 1971." *El Urogallo*, nòs. 11–12, September-December 1971, pp. 10–12.

Gaucheron, Jacques. "Neruda, charpentier d'amour." *Europe*, nos. 447–48 (1966):207–12.

Gee, Maria Carolina. "El 'consensus omnium' al artista Neruda." *P.E.C.* (Santiago de Chile), no. 425, 29 October 1971, p. 13.

Giordano, Jaime. "Dialéctica de la libertad en *Plenos Poderes* de Pablo Neruda." *Razón y Fe* 17:22–38.

186 **Bibliography**

*González-Cruz, Luis F. "El viaje transcendente de Pablo Neruda: Una lectura de Tentativa del hombre infinito." *Symposium* 32 (1978):197–208.

Gottlieb, Marlene. "La Guerra Civil española en la poesía de Pablo Neruda y César Vallejo." *Cuadernos Americanos* 54 (1967):189–200.

———. "Pablo Neruda, poeta del amor." *Cuadernos Americanos* 149 (1966):211–21.

Guerra-Cunningham, Lucía. "El habitante y sue esperanza de Pablo Neruda: Primer exponente vanguardista en la novela chilena." *Hispania* 60 (1977):470–77.

*Guibert, Rita. "Pablo Neruda: The Art of Poetry XIV." *Paris Review* 51 (Winter 1971):149–75. [Interview with Pablo Neruda appeared in *Seven Voices*. New York: Alfred A. Knopf, 1973.]

*Gullón, Agnes. "Pablo Neruda at Macchu Picchu." *Chicago Review* 27, ii (1974):138–45.

*Gullón, Ricardo. "Relaciones Pablo Neruda-Juan Ramón Jiménez." *Hispanic Review* 39 (1971):141–66.

*Himelblau, Jack. "Poesía de Pablo Neruda, un canto de desolación: 'Sólo la muerte.'" *La Torre* 64 (1969):93–100.

———. "Pablo Neruda's 'Ausencia de Joaquín': An Analysis." *Norte* 14, no. 1 (January-February 1973):9–13.

Hochman, Sandra. Review of *The Heights of Macchu Picchu*. Tr. Nathaniel Tarn. In *Review 68*. New York: Center for Inter-American Relations, 1969. [See in the same volume other reviews by M. L. Rosenthal, pp. 23–25; Dudley Fitts, pp. 25–27; and James Wright, pp. 27–30.]

Holzinger, Walter. "Poetic Subject and Form in the *Odas elementales*." *Revista Hispánica Moderna* 36, nos. 1–2 (1970–71):41–49.

Honig, Edwin. "Kaleidoscopic Entertainment." *Review* 72 (Winter):70–72.

Jara, René. "La crítica ante Neruda." *Chasqui: Revista de Literatura Latinoamericana* 7, no. i (1978):56–62.

Juin, Hubert. "A la rencontre de Pablo Neruda." *Nouvelles Littéraires*, 29 January 1972, p. 7.

*Karsen, Sonja. "Neruda's Canto general in Historical Context." *Symposium* 32 (1978):220–35.

Lagos, Belén. "Temor y destrucción en la erótica de Neruda." (1974)

Lajoie, Jacques. "'Significa sombras,' de Pablo Neruda." *Reflexión* 2, no. 3, year 2 (February 1970):38–45.

Le Clec'H, Guy. "Neruda, le poète diplomate." *Le Figaro Littéraire*, no. 1.290, February 1971, pp. 8–9.

*Lerner, Vivianne. "Réalité profane, réalité sacrée dans les *Odas Elementales* de Pablo Neruda." *Bulletin de la Faculté des Lettres de Strasbourg* 44 (1966):759–76.

———. "Les grand prix nationaux." *Nouvelles Littéraires*, 10–16 December 1971, pp. 4–5.

Levčev, Ljubomir, "Mestožitelstvo v bezsmartieto: 70 godini ot roždenieto ne Pablo Neruda." *Literaturen Front: Organ na Sajuza na Balgarskite Pisateli* (Sofia) 30, no. 26 (1974): 1, 7.

Ley, Charles D. "Influencia de Pablo Neruda y de otros poetas hispanoamericanos en la moderna poesía de España." In *Actas del Tercer Congreso Internacional de Hispanistas*, edited by Carlos H. Magis, pp. 543–52. México: El Colegio de México por la Asociación Internacional de Hispanistas, 1970.

Lichtblau, Myron I., ed. "Pablo Neruda." *Symposium* 32, no. 3 (1978). [Special issue.]

Lihn, Enrique. "El surrealismo en Chile." *Atenea* 423 (1970):91–96.

———. "Residencia de Neruda en la palabra poética." *Mensaje* 22, nos. 224–25 (November-December 1973):552–56.

Lora Risco, Alejandro. "Las teoría lingüísticas de Amado Alonso subyacentes a su crítica de *Residencia en la tierra.*" *Cuadernos Americanos* 195, no. 4 (July-August 1974):106–13.

Lorenzo-Rivero, Luis. "Neruda y Alberti: amistad y poesía." *Cuadernos Americanos* 31, no. 182 (August-September 1972):204–26.

———. "Similaridades estilístico-temáticas entre Alberti y Neruda." *Reflexión* (2ₐ época) 2, nos. 2–4 (January-December 1973):65–74.

Loveluck, Juan. "Neruda, colaborador de *La Nación,* 1927–1929." *Sin Nombre* 3, no. 2 (1972):21–37. [Also reproduced in "Estudios sobre Pablo Neruda." *Anales de la Universidad de Chile* 129, nos. 157–60.]

———. "Pablo Neruda en Oriente: Un texto desconocido." *Sin Nombre* 8, no. 1 (1977):52–56.

———. "Tributo y despedida, Pablo Neruda (1904–1973): Más sobre Neruda en Oriente." *Hispania* 57, no. 4 (December 1974):976–78. [Article by Neruda, "Oriente y Oriente," published originally in *La Nación* in 1929.]

Loyola, Hernán. "Dánai canta a Neruda." *El Siglo* (Santiago de Chile), 28 June 1970.

*——. "Itinerario de una poesía." Prologue to *Antología esencial de Pablo Neruda.* Buenos Aires: Editorial Losada, 1971, pp. 7–37.

———. "Itinerario de una poética (1919–1969)." *Aisthesis* (Santiago) 5 (1970):225–47.

———. "Mi deber es vivir, morir, vivir." *El Siglo* (Santiago de Chile) 28 December 1969. [About *Fin de mundo.*]

———. "Neruda: antología general." *El Siglo* (Santiago de Chile), 13 September 1970.

———. "Neruda y América Latina." *Cuadernos Americanos* 218 (1978): 175–97.

———. "Pablo Neruda: el amor y la vocación poética." *Mensaje* 184 (November 1969):539.

———. "Pablo Neruda: *Las Manos del día.*" *El Siglo* (Santiago de Chile), 30 March 1969.

———. "Presencia de la U.R.S.S. en la obra de Neruda." *El Siglo* (Santiago de Chile), 9 November 1969.

———. "Tentativa del hombre infinito: 50 años después." *Acta Linguistica Academiae scientarum Hungararicae (Budapest)* 17 (1974):111–23.

———. "*Veinte poemas de amor,* los inmarchitables." *El Siglo* (Santiago de Chile), 12 April 1970.

Lozada, Alfredo. "La interpretación socio-política de *Residencia en la tierra.*" *Journal of Inter-American Studies* 8 (April 1966):268–78.

———. Neruda y Schopenhauer." *Revista Hispánica Moderna* 32 (1966):217–30.

———. "Rodeada está de ausencia: La amada crepuscular de *Veinte poemas de amor y una canción desesperada.*" In *El ensayo y la crítica literaria en Iberoamérica* (Memoirs of the 14th International Congress of Iberoamerican Literature, University of Toronto, Toronto, Canada,

24–28 August 1969), edited by Kurt L. Levy and Keith Ellis, pp. 239–48. Toronto: University of Toronto Press, 1970.

———. "Pablo Neruda: Cartas a una amada ausente." *Symposium* 32 (1978):235–53.

[MacShane, Frank.] "Neruda in New York." *The New York Times Book Review,* 13 March 1977, pp. 3, 20.

Maya, Hamid. "Pablo Neruda: A l'écoute d'une mémoire collective." *Afrique-Asie* 155 (1978):46–47.

*Mejía Sánchez, Ernesto. "Tríptico de Pablo." *Cuadernos Americanos* 32, no. 192 (January-February 1974):201–3.

*Monguió, Luis. "Kingdom of This Earth: The Poetry of Pablo Neruda." *Latin American Literary Review* 1, no. 1 (Fall 1972):13–24.

Montes, Hugo. "Las estapas de Neruda." *Norte* 8, nos. 2–3 (1967):35–39.

Morales, Leónidas. "Estructura mítica de *Alturas de Macchu Picchu.*" In *Homenaje a Eleazar Huerta, Estudios Filológicos,* vol. 1, pp. 302–16. Valdivia: Universidad Austral de Chile, 1965.

Morales Toro, Leónidas. "Fundaciones y destrucciones: Pablo Neruda y Nicanor Parra." *Revista Iberoamericana* 36 (1970):407–23.

Mundt, Tito. "Neruda Speaking." *Atlas,* 15 January 1968, p. 55.

Murray, P. "Comment." *Poetry* 120 (August 1972):309–12.

*Neruda, Pablo. "Lives of a Poet: In the Far East: A Memoir." *Salmagundi* 19 (1972):3–17. (Translated by Ben Belitt.)

———. "Palabras de Pablo Neruda." *Congreso Latino-americano de Escritores* (Caracas), bulletin no. 9, 1970, pp. 21–22.

Nuez, Sebastián de la. "Arrebatos de amor y furia en la poesía de Neruda." *Papeles de Son Armadans* 66 (1972):257–59.

Ortega, José. "Pablo Neruda: the making of a Political Poet." *Perspectives on Contemporary Literature* 2 (1976):3–11.

Osorio, Nelson. "Apuntes para un análisis marxista de la obra de Neruda." *Apuntes* (Santiago) 2 (1972):16–23.

Otaño, Rafael. "Neruda América." *Mensaje* 22, no. 223 (October 1973):472–73.

*Oviedo, José Miguel. "Neruda: Las vidas de un poeta." *Plural* 38 (1974):67–69.

Oyarzún, Martha J. K. "Life Symbolism in the Works of Pablo Neruda: The Composite Image." *Dissertation Abstracts International* 32 (1971):971A. (Doctoral dissertation, University of Illinois.)

"Pablo Neruda: entrevista exclusiva para *El Siglo.*" *El Siglo* (Santiago de Chile), 28 October 1971.

Padrón, Justo J. "Viaje a través de Pablo Neruda." *Insula* 26 (November-December 1971):13–15.

Paseyro, Ricardo. "The Dead Word of Pablo Neruda." *TriQuarterly* 5 (1969):203–7.

Pazos de Balbes, Carmen. "La fuerza de la naturaleza en Neruda." *Imagen* 15 (25 September - 2 October 1971):15.

Peniche Vallado, Leopoldo. "Mexico en las memorias de Pablo Neruda." *Cuadernos Americanos* 200 (1974):101–8.

———. "Pablo Neruda: Claridad de una poesía hermética." *Cuadernos Americanos* year 33, no. 191 (January-February 1974):204–12.

Peralta, Jaime. "España en tres poetas hispanoamericanos: Neruda, Guillén, Vallejo." *Atenea,* nos. 421–22, July-December 1968, pp. 37–49. Reproduced from *Boletín Cultural y Bibliográfico* 9, no. 10 (1966):37–51. Bogotá: Biblioteca L. A. Arango.

Pérez, Galo René. "Neruda." *Américas* 24 (January 1972):9–11.

"Política y poesía." *Razón y Fe*, no. 183, (1972):114–18.

*Pring-Mill, Robert. "Both in Sorrow and in Anger: Spanish American Protest Poetry." *Cambridge Review*, 20 February 1970, pp. 112–17.

*————. "La elaboración de la cebolla." In *Actas del Tercer Congreso Internacional de Hispanistas*, edited by Carlos H. Magis, pp. 739–51. México: Mexico por la Asociación Internacional de Hispanistas, 1970.

*[Pring-Mill, Robert.] "A Poet and His Roots." *Times Literary Supplement*, 16 April 1970, pp. 397–99.

*[Pring-Mill, Robert.] "The Winter of Pablo Neruda." *Times Literary Supplement*, 3 October 1975.

*Reid, Alastair. "The Chilean Poet Pablo Neruda, 1904–1973." *Listener* 90 (4 October 1973):437–39.

Rey, Tomás. "Apuntes sobre el para-surrealismo y el surrealismo en Chile." *Zona Franca*, year 2, Segunda Epoca, no. 11 (February 1972):39–49.

Reyes Baena, J. F. "'A su paso por París.'" *Cultura Universitaria de la Universidad Central de Venezuela* 88 (1965):18–27. (About Borges, Guillén, Asturias, and Neruda in Paris.)

Rinaldi, Angelo. "Neruda: Le Souffle de l'optimisme." *L'Express* 22–28 (1975): Sept. 58–59.

Rivero, Eliana. "Análisis de perspectivas y significación de *La rosa separada* de Neruda." *Revista Iberoamericana* 42 (1976):459–72.

*Rodríguez Monegal, Emir. "Darío y Neruda: Un paralelo imposible." In "Homenaje a Rubén Darío." *La Torre* 55–56 (1967):15–25.

————. "Introducción al método del Sr. Concha." *Revista Iberoamericana* 37 (1971):349–56.

*Rodman, Selden. "A Day with Pablo Neruda." *Saturday Review*, 9 July 1966, pp. 6–18.

Rojas Herazo, Héctor. "Esquela para Neruda." *Eco* 26/6, no. 156 (1973):376–78.

Rosenthal, M. L. "Journey Toward Rebirth." *Saturday Review*, 2 September 1967, p. 25.

Rudd, Margaret. "Neruda-Mistral dialogue." *Américas* 24 (May 1972):14–17.

Ruperto, Roberto. "A Isla Negra con Pablo Neruda." *Ponte* 20 (1970):1686–1706.

Saalman, Dieter. "Die Konzeption des 'hombre invisible' bei Pablo Neruda und Rainer Maria Rilke." *Romanistisches Jahrbuch* 24 (1973):381–99.

*————. "The Role of Time in Pablo Neruda's *Alturas de Macchu Picchu*." *Romance Notes* (University of North Carolina) 18 (1977):169–77.

Salmon, Russell, and Lesage, Julia. "Stones and Birds: Consistency and Change in the Poetry of Pablo Neruda." *Hispania* 60, no. 2, May 1977.

*Salomon, Noel. "Un Evénement poétique: Le Canto general de Pablo Neruda." *Bulletin Hispanique* 76 (1974):92–124.

Santi, Enrico Mario. "Canto general: The Politics of the Book." *Symposium* 32 (1978):254–75.

*————. "Neruda: La modalidad apocalíptica." *Hispanic Review* 46 (1978):365–84.

*————. "Somber system: Modes of Prophecy in the Poetry of Pablo Neruda." *Dissertation Abstracts International* 38 (1977):301A–2A.

Sarduy, Severo. "Los métodos del crítico. Severo Sarduy entrevista a Emir Rodríguez Monegal." *Imagen,* supplementary number 30 (1–15 August 1968), pp. 9–16. (References to *El Viajero Inmóvil.*)

Selva, Mauricio de la. "Mínima rememoración: Pablo Neruda." *Cuadernos Americanos* 33, no. 1 (January-February 1974):213–42.

*Sicard, Alain. "Neruda, ou la question sans réponse." *La Quinzaine Littéraire,* no. 129, 16 November 1971, pp. 13–14.

Silva, Ribeiro da. "Pablo Neruda: Memorias." *Broteria* 104 (1977):192–208.

Simonis, Ferdinand. "Pablo Nerudas frühe Lyrik und die *Residencias:* Wege der Wandlung." *Neophilologus* (Grónigen) 51 (1967):15–31.

Stackelberg, Jürgen von. "Neruda deutsch." *Romanistisches Jahrbuch* 19 (1968):286–93. (Spanish version in *Taller de Letras* [Santiago], no. 2, 1972.)

Suarès, Guy. "Lettre ouverte à Pablo Neruda: Cher Pablo." *Nouvelles Littéraires,* no. 29, October 1971, p. 17. (On the occasion of the Nobel Prize.)

*Suárez Rivero, Eliana. "Fantasía y mito en la obra de Pablo Neruda: *La espada encendida."* In *Otros mundos otros fuegos: Fantasía y realismo mágico en Iberoamérica* (Memoria del XVI congreso internacional de Literatura Iberoamericana), edited by Donald A. Yates. East Lansing: Michigan State University, Latin American Studies Center, 1977.

*———. "Simbolismo tematico y titular en *Las Manos del día."* *Mester* 4, no. 2 (1974):75–81.

*Sucre, Guillermo. "Neruda y el tiempo recobrado." *Imagen,* no. 12 (1–15 November 1967), pp. 4–5. (About *El Viajero Inmóvil.*)

*Terracini, Lore. "Il 'Sumario' di Neruda e la poesia della memoria." *Paragone* 6, no. 186 (1965):37–56.

*Tolman, John M. "Death and Alien Environment in Pablo Neruda's *Residencia en la tierra."* *Hispania* 5 (1968):79–85.

———. "Morte e alienaçao na poesia de Pablo Neruda." *Minas Gerais, Suplemento literario,* 13 September 1971, pp. 2–3.

Tomás, Angel C. "Neruda y Pushkin." *Camp de l'Arpa: Revista de Literatura* 23–24 (1975):24–25.

Toro-Garland, Fernando, "Las Cartas de amor de Pablo Neruda a Albertina Rosa." *Festschriften* 139 (1978):857–64.

Valdivieso, Jaime. "Neruda: misión y poesía." *Atenea* 170, nos. 421–22 (July-December 1968):21–36.

Vasile, George, tr. "XXVIII,' 'VII. Ceilalti oameni,' 'Grâdinâ de iarnâ,'" *Steaua* 25, no. 7 (1974):38.

Villegas, Juan. "La aventura maravillosa: 'Oda a un albatros viajero' de Pablo Neruda." *Hispania* 60 (1977):242–49.

Walter, Monika. "Zwischen Protest und Parteilichkeit: Zu Pablo Nerudas Residencia en la tierra." *Weimarer Beitrage: Zeitschrift f ür Literaturwissenschaft, Asthetick und Kulturtheoric* 24, no. 12 (1978):165–71.

Whitman, Alden. "Walt Whitman, votre ançêtre, est un bon ami à moi . . . ." *Intellectual Digest,* March 1972, p. 49.

*Wood, Michael. "The Poetry of Neruda." *The New York Review of Books,* 3 October 1974, pp. 8–10.

———. "Latin American Poetry: Excavations of El Dorado (Borges, Neruda, Vallejo, Mistral, Parra)." *Parnassus,* Fall/Winter 1972, pp. 25–35. (Reviews three books of Neruda in translation.)

*Yglesias, José. "Pablo Neruda: The Poet in New York." *The Nation,* 11 July 1966, pp. 52–55.

[Yglesias, José.] Review of *Memoirs* by Pablo Neruda. *The New York Times Book Review,* 13 March 1977, pp. 3, 18, 20.

———. "Report from Chile: The Left Prepares for an Election." *The New York Times Magazine,* 11 January 1970, pp. 24–25.

Zampa, Giorgio. "Il *Murieta* di Neruda e il Toller di Dorst." *Drama* 46 (1970):58–64.

Special Magazine Issues on Neruda

1. *Anales de Literatura Hispanoamericana,* "Homenaje a Pablo Neruda y Miguel Angel Asturias." Madrid, vol. II, nos. 2–3, 1973–1974.

  Loveluck, Juan. "Neruda ante la poesía hispanoamericana." pp. 13–24. (Contains prose texts by Neruda: "Introducción a la poética de Angel Cruchaga Santa María," "Silva en la sombra," "Ramón López Velarde.")

  Sáinz de Medrano, Luis. "Sobre Neruda y los clásicos españoles." pp. 25–50.

2. *Anales de la Universidad de Chile,* "Estudios sobre Pablo Neruda" (Santiago de Chile), yr. CXXIX, nos. 157–160, Jan.-Dec. 1971. (Appeared in 1973.)

  Loyola, Hernán. "Itinerario de Pablo Neruda y esquema bibliográfico." pp. 9–28.

Texts by Neruda
"Discurso de Estocolmo." pp. 31–38.
"Discurso pronunciado por Pablo Neruda en el PEN Club de N.Y., en abril de 1972." pp. 39–44.
"Album Teresa, 1923" (unpublished early texts by Neruda, presented by Hernán Loyola), pp. 45–55.
"Neruda en *La Nación* (1927–1929): prosa olvidada" (ten texts collected and introduced by Juan Loveluck), pp. 57–78.
"Mariano Latorre, Pedro Prado y mi propia sombra" (speech given for the Faculty of Philosophy and Education of the University of Chile, read March 30, 1962), pp. 79–88.

Articles
Santander, Carlos, "Amor y temporalidad en *Veinte poemas de amor y una canción desesperada,*" pp. 91–106.
Sicard, Alain, "La eternidad en el instante: un análisis de *Tentativa del hombre infinito,*" pp. 107–16.
Shopf, Federico, "Análisis de 'El fantasma del Buque de Carga,'" pp. 117–28.
*Puccini, Darío, "Dos notas sobre Pablo Neruda (un poema de 'Tercera Residencia' y 'Neruda, tranductor de Joyce')," pp. 129–38.
Villegas, Juan, "Héroes y antihéroes en el *Canto general,*" pp. 138–52.

*Goić, Cedomil, "Alturas de Macchu Picchu: la torre y el abismo," pp. 153–66.

*Cros, Edmond, "Análisis del poema IX del Canto II del *Canto general*," pp. 167–76.

*Felstiner, John, "La danza inmóvil, el vendaval sostenido: *Four Quartets* de T. S. Eliot y *Alturas de Macchu Picchu*," pp. 176–96.

Sanhueza, Jorge, "Neruda 1949," pp. 197–208.

Concha, Jaime, "Sobre algunos poemas de *Canción de gesta*," pp. 209–16.

Rodríguez Fernández, Mario, "La búsqueda del espacio feliz: la imagen de la casa en la poesía de Pablo Neruda," pp. 217–28.

*Lerner, Vivianne, "Función del símbolo en la poesía de Pablo Neruda," pp. 229–33.

Loyola, Hernán, "El ciclo nerudiano 1958–1967: tres aspectos," pp. 235–54.

Reviews

Finlayson, Clarence, "Pablo Neruda en 'Tres cantos materiales,'" pp. 257–62. (Reproduced from *Poetas y poemas*, Santiago, Ediciones Revista Universitaria, 1938.)

Cantón, Wilberto, "Pablo Neruda (1940–1943)," pp. 263–69. (Reproduced from *Posiciones*, México, 1950.)

Testimonials

Aragon, Louis, "Una casa barajada como un juego de cartas," pp. 273–74. (Poem translated from the French by Altenor Guerrero and Jorge Teiller.)

Calderón, Alfonso, "Nosotros, los de entonces," pp. 275–76.

Castellano, Hernán, "El Neruda que nos trajo al mundo," pp. 277–78.

Domínguez, Delia, "Semana Santa del Poeta," pp. 279–83.

Rojas, Waldo, "El retablo de las maravillas," pp. 284–86.

Teitelboim, Volodia, "Neruda siempre," pp. 287–96.

Valdés, Hernán, "Navegación con Neruda y conflictos de la admiración," pp. 297–302.

3. *Crisis* (Cuadernos de) (Buenos Aires), no. 2, Nov. 1973.

Presentation by Federico García Lorca, p. 5.

Textos de Pablo Neruda

"La copa de sangre," p. 7; "Conducta y poesía," p. 11; "Sobre una poesía sin pureza," p. 12; "¿Nosotros los poetas? Sí, nosotros los pueblos," p. 13.

*Aguirre, Margarita, "Sólo tengo cuarteles de primavera (El último reportaje a Pablo Neruda)," pp. 15–21.

Diez Poemas de Pablo Neruda

"Integraciones," p. 25; "Animal de luz," p. 26; "Triste canción para aburrir a cualquiera," p. 27; "Orégano," p. 29; "Las preguntas," p. 30; "El héroe," p. 31; "La situación insostenible," p. 32; "Rechaza los relámpagos," p. 33; "El gran orinador," p. 34; "Canción de amor," p. 35.

Neruda, Pablo, "La poesía no habrá cantado en vano" (Nobel Prize acceptance address), pp. 37–43.

"El camino del poeta" (Biographical synthesis of Pablo Neruda), pp. 45–58.

"Pablo Neruda en la Argentina," pp. 59–62.

Neruda, Pablo, "La última convocatoria," p. 63.

4. *Insula* (Madrid), year XXIX, no. 330, May 1974.

*Durán, Manuel and Gloria, "Notas sobre Neruda, Brecht, el teatro épico y 'El signo del Zorro,'" pp. 1, 14.
Earle, Peter, "Neruda: la experiencia compartida," pp. 1, 15.
Colinas, Antonio, "Cosmogonías del *Canto general*," p. 3.
*Miró, Emilio, "Poesía de la esperanza: de *Tercera Residencia* a *Canto General*," p. 4.
Ifach, María de Gracia, "Pablo Neruda y Miguel Hernández," p. 5.
Fuentes, Victor, "*Nixonicidio:* Ultimo testamento poético de Pablo Neruda," p. 6.
Carmona, Darío, "Ultima residencia," p. 7.

5. *Modern Poetry Studies,* "Pablo Neruda, 1904–1973" (Buffalo, N.Y.), vol. 5, no. 1 (Spring 1974).

Neruda, Pablo, "Four Poems," pp. 1–5.
*Belitt, Ben, "Pablo Neruda: Splendor and Death," pp. 6–14.
*Neale-Silva, Eduardo, "Neruda's Poetic Beginnings," pp. 15–22.
*Rodman, Selden, "Pablo Neruda," pp. 23–40.
*Alegría, Fernando, "Neruda: Reminiscences and Critical Reflections," pp. 41–50.
Jaimes-Freyre, Mireya, "The Revolutionary Poetry of Pablo Neruda," pp. 51–55.
Gugelberg, Georg M., "Pablo Neruda's Socialist Epic," pp. 56–63.
*Barnstone, Willis, "Pablo's Bestiary," pp. 64–70.

6. *Review '74,* "Focus/Residence on Earth," (New York, Center for Inter-American Relations), Spring.

*Rodríguez Monegal, Emir, "The Biographical Background," pp. 6–15.
*Alonso, Amado, "From Melancholy to Anguish," tr. by Enrique Sacerio Garí, pp. 15–19.
Walsh, Donald D., "Some Thoughts on Translation," pp. 20–22.
Belitt, Ben, "The Translator as Nobody in Particular," pp. 23–29.
Rosenthal, M. L., "Voyage into Neruda," pp. 30–32.
Coleman, Alexander, "Neruda: Vox Dei," pp. 33–37.
Gallagher, David, "Review of *The Word and the Stone: Language and Imagery in Neruda's 'Canto general'* by Frank Reiss," pp. 68–69.

7. *Revista Iberoamericana,* vol. XXXIX, nos. 82–83, Jan.-June, 1973.

Testimonials
"Discurso del Embajador Pablo Neruda ante el PEN Club de N.Y.," pp. 9–14.
Asturias, Miguel Angel, "Un mano a mano de Nobel a Nobel," pp. 15–20.
*Cortázar, Julio, "Carta abierta a Pablo Neruda," pp. 21–26.
Sánchez, Luis Alberto, "Comentarios extemporáneos: Neruda y el Premio Nobel," pp. 27–40.

Articles
*Rodríguez Monegal, Emir, "Pablo Neruda: El sistema del poeta," pp. 41–72.

*Alegría, Fernando, "*La Barcarola:* Barca de la vida," pp. 73–98.

Sicard, Alain, "La objetivación del fenómeno en la génesis de la noción de materia en *Residencia en la tierra*," pp. 99–110.

Yurkievich, Saúl, "Mito e historia: Dos generadores del *Canto General*," pp. 111–35.

Concha, Jaime, "Sexo y pobreza," pp. 135–58.

Cortínez, Carlos, "Interpretación de *El habitante y su esperanza* de Pablo Neruda," pp. 159–74.

Loveluck, Juan, "*Alturas de Macchu Picchu:* Cantos I-V," pp. 175–88.

*Paley de Francescato, Martha, "La circularidad en la poesía de Pablo Neruda," pp. 189–204.

De Ferraresi, Alicia C., "La relación yo-tú en la poesía de Pablo Neruda: Del autoerotismo al panerotismo," pp. 205–26.

Bratosevich, Nicolás, "Análisis rítmico de "Oda con un lamento," pp. 226–46.

González-Cruz, Luis F., "Pablo Neruda: Soledad, incommunicación e individualismo en *Memorial de Isla Negra*," pp. 245–62.

*Alazraki, Jaime, "Poética de la penumbra en la poesía más reciente de Pablo Neruda," pp. 262–92.

Bellini, Giuseppe, "*Fin de mundo:* Neruda, entre la angustia y la esperanza," pp. 293–300.

Figuerosa, Esperanza, "Pablo Neruda en inglés," pp. 301–48.

Volek, Emil, "Neruda y algunos países socialistas de Europa," pp. 349–68.

Marelli, Gabriele, "Bibliografía de Neruda en Italia," pp. 369–71.

8. *Simposio Pablo Neruda. Actas.* University of South Carolina-Las Américas. I.J. Lévy, J. Loveluck, editors. L.A. Publishing Co., Inc., 1975. Long Island City, N.Y.

Testimonials
Vicente Aleixandre
Matilde Neruda
Jorge Amado
Laura Reyes

Articles
*J. Alazraki, "Para una poética de la poesía póstuma de Pablo Neruda," pp. 41–78.

*Suárez Rivero, Eliana, "La estética esencial en una oda nerudiana," pp. 79–96.

Cortínez, Carlos, "Lectura de 'Madrigal escrito en invierno,'" pp. 97–106.

*Concha, Jaime, "Observaciones sobre algunas imágenes de *Residencia en la tierra*," pp. 107–22.

*Durán, Manuel, "Sobre la poesía de Neruda, la tradición simbolista y la desintegración del yo," pp. 123–44.

Sicard, Alain, "Soledad, muerte, y conciencia histórica en la poesía reciente de Pablo Neruda," pp. 145–70.

Osorio, Nelson, "El problema del hablante poético en *Canto General*," pp. 171–88.

*Rodríguez Monegal, Emir, "Pablo Neruda: las *Memorias* y las vidas del poeta," pp. 189–208.

Lima, Robert, Selected poems by Neruda, translated by R. Lima, pp. 209–16.

*Loveluck, Juan, "El navío de Eros: *Veinte poemas de amor* . . . número nueve," pp. 217–32.

Yates, Donald A., "Neruda and Borges," pp. 233–42.

Roggiano, Alfredo A., "Ser y poesía en Pablo Neruda," pp. 243–66.

*Franco, Jean, "Orfeo en Utopía: el poeta y la colectividad en *Canto General,*" pp. 267–90.

*Anderson-Imbert, Enrique, "La prosa vanguardista de Neruda," pp. 291–300.

*Alegría, Fernando, "Neruda: reflexiones y reminiscencias," pp. 301–14.

*Felstiner, John, "A Feminist Reading of Neruda," pp. 315–38.

Loyola, Hernán, "Lectura de *Veinte poemas de amor* . . ." pp. 339–54.

*Santí, Enrico-Mario, "Fuentes para el conocimiento de Pablo Neruda, 1967–1974," pp. 355–82.

Yurkievich, Saúl, "El génesis oceánico," pp. 383–401.

Notes

The Man: A Biographical Outline

1. Pablo Neruda, *Memoirs,* trans. Hardie St. Martin (New York: Farrar, Straus and Giroux, 1977).
2. José Yglesias, Review of *Memoirs* by Pablo Neruda, *New York Times Book Review,* 13 March 1977, p. 3.
3. Hernán Loyola, "Pablo Neruda: Itinerario de una poesía," *Pablo Neruda: Antología esencial,* 3d ed. (Buenos Aires: Losada, 1978), p. 7.
4. Neruda, "Infancia y poesía," *Obras Completas,* vol. 1, 3d ed. (Buenos Aires: Losada, 1967), p. 31.
5. Neruda, *Memoirs,* p. 21.
6. Ibid., p. 29.
7. Loyola, p. 21.
8. Ibid., p. 25.
9. Ibid., p. 26.
10. *Memoirs,* p. 364.
11. Fernando Alegría, "Neruda: Reminiscences and Critical Reflections," trans. Deborah S. Bundy, *Modern Poetry Studies* 5, no. 1 (Spring 1974):47.

Chapter 1. The Erotic Poet

1. Quoted by Emir Rodríguez Monegal, *El viajero inmóvil* (Buenos Aires: Losada, 1966), p. 41.
2. Quoted by Margarita Aguirre, *Las vidas de Pablo Neruda* (Buenos Aires: Grijalbo, 1973), p. 113.
3. Julio Cortázar, "Neruda entre nosotros," *Plural,* No. 30, March 1974, p. 58.
4. Letter to *La Nación,* Santiago de Chile, 20 August 1924, p. 4.
5. Robert Bly, "Refusing to be Theocritus," Introduction to *Neruda and Vallejo: Selected Poems,* ed. Robert Bly and trans. Robert Bly, John Knoepfle, and James Wright (Boston: Beacon Press, 1971), p. 3.
6. Unpublished lecture quoted by Margarita Aguirre, p. 113.
7. Robert Bly, pp. 14–15.
8. *Memoirs,* p. 10.
9. Maurice Nadeau, *Histoire du Surréalisme* (Paris: Editions du Seuil, 1945), p. 71.
10. *Memoirs,* p. 51.
11. Preface to *El habitante y su esperanza* (Santiago: Nascimento, 1926), p. 4.
12. Quoted by Rodríguez Monegal, p. 55.
13. *Memoirs,* p. 91. For more detailed accounts of this period in Neruda's life, see Aguirre and Rodríguez Monegal.

14. *Memoirs,* p. 87.

15. John Felstiner, "A Feminist Reading of Neruda," in *Simposio Pablo Neruda* (Long Island City, New York: Las Américas, 1975), p. 327.

16. Ibid., p. 332.

17. Ibid., p. 327.

18. *Memoirs,* pp. 274–75.

19. Ibid., p. 275.

20. Luis Monguió, "Kingdom of this Earth: The Poetry of Pablo Neruda," *Latin American Literary Review* 1, 1 (1972): 14.

21. Monguió, p. 13.

Chapter 2. The Nature Poet

1. Quoted by Rodríguez Monegal, p. 39.

2. Monguió, p. 15.

3. Quoted by Juan Larrea in *Del Surrealismo a Macchu Picchu* (México: Joaquín Mortiz, 1967), p. 59.

4. Quoted by Nadeau, p. 320.

5. Quoted by Alfredo Cardona Peña in *Pablo Neruda y otras ensayos* (México: Ediciones de Andrea, 1955), p. 20.

6. Jaime Alazraki, *Poética y poesía de Pablo Neruda* (New York: Las Américas, 1965), p. 142.

7. Juan Ramón Jiménez, *Españoles de tres mundos* (Madrid: Aguado, 1960), p. 218.

8. Neruda, *Caballo Verde para la Poesía* (Madrid), no. 1, October 1935, pp. 1–3.

9. Amado Alonso, *Poesía y estilo de Pablo Neruda: interpretación de una poesía hermética* (Buenos Aires: Editorial Sudamericana, 1968).

10. Alonso, p. 24.

11. Jaime Concha, "Observaciones sobre algunas imágenes de *Residencia en la Tierra*," *Simposio Pablo Neruda* (Long Island City, New York: Las Américas, 1975), pp. 116–17.

12. Quoted by Rodríguez Monegal, p. 77.

13. Quoted by Aguirre, p. 232.

14. Ibid.

15. Quoted by Rodríguez Monegal, p. 154.

16. Quoted by Aguirre, p. 234.

17. Quoted by Rodríguez Monegal, p. 147.

18. Ibid., p. 155.

19. Ibid., p. 161.

20. *Memoirs,* p. 161.

21. *Dictionario Literario Bompiani-González Porto,* vol. 8 (Barcelona: Montaner y Simón, 1959), p. 371.

22. "Infancia y Poesía," *Obras Completas,* vol. 1, 3d ed. (Buenos Aires: Losada, 1967), p. 38.

23. Alone, *El Mercurio,* Santiago, 30 January 1955, pp. 7–8.

24. Rodríguez Monegal, p. 275.

25. Eduardo Camacho Guizado, *Pablo Neruda: naturaleza, historia y poética* (Madrid: Sociedad Espanola de Librería, 1978), p. 235.

26. "Las Piedras de Chile," *Obras Completas,* vol. 2, 3d ed. (Buenos Aires: Losada, 1968), pp. 345–46.

27. *Las piedras del cielo* (Buenos Aires: Losada, 1970).
28. Quoted by Aguirre, p. 233.

Chapter 3. The Public Poet

1. Rodríguez Monegal, p. 93.
2. Preface to *Las furias y las penas* (Santiago: Editorial Nascimento, 1939).
3. *Memoirs,* p. 126.
4. Yglesias, p. 18.
5. *Chile en el corazón: Homenaje a Pablo Neruda,* ed. Aurora de Albornoz and Elena Andrés (Barcelona: Península, 1975).
6. Quoted by Selden Rodman, *Tongues of Falling Angels* (New York: Grove Press, 1975), p. 69–70.
7. Quoted by Rodríguez Monegal, p. 142.
8. *Princeton Encyclopedia of Poetry and Poetics,* ed. Alex Preminger (Princeton: Princeton University Press, 1972), p. 242.
9. Rodríguez Monegal, p. 238ff.
10. *Satyricon,* Loeb Classics ed., p. 297.
11. *Princeton Encyclopedia,* p. 243.
12. Rodríguez Monegal, p. 235.
13. Ibid., p. 245.
14. Frank Reiss, *The Word and the Stone: Language and Imagery in Neruda's "Canto General"* (London and New York: Oxford University Press, 1972), p. 136.
15. Ibid, p. 137.
16. Ibid., pp. 134–35.
17. Rodríguez Monegal, p. 246.
18. Ibid., p. 248.
19. Ibid., pp. 146–47.
20. Riess, p. 37.
21. Quoted by Camacho Guizado, p. 194.
22. *Memoirs,* p. 295.
23. *Canción de gesta* (Havana: Casa de las Américas, 1960).
24. *Memoirs,* pp. 320–21.
25. *Princeton Encyclopedia,* p. 113.
26. Preface to *Canción de gesta* (Havana: Casa de las Américas, 1960).
27. Camacho Guizado, p. 233.
28. *Memoirs,* p. 326.
29. Ibid., p. 328.
30. "Referencias," *Obras completas,* vol. 2, 3d ed. (Buenos Aires: Losada, 1968), p. 1311.
31. *La espada encendida* (Buenos Aires: Losada, 1970).
32. Preface to *La espada encendida* (Buenos Aires: Losada, 1970).
33. Camacho Guizado, p. 262.
34. *Incitación al Nixonicidio y alabanza de la revolución chilena* (Barcelona: Grijalbo, 1974). The first edition, now rare, was published in Santiago in 1973 by Quimantú.
35. Preface to *Incitación al Nixonicidio y alabanza de la revolución chilena* (Barcelona: Grijalbo, 1974).
36. Ibid.

Chapter 4. The Personal Poet

1. Rodríguez Monegal, p. 323.
2. Ibid.
3. Alastair Reid Translator's note, *Extravagaria* (New York: Farrar, Straus and Giroux, 1974).
4. Camacho Guizado, pp. 215–16.
5. Ibid., p. 219.
6. Ben Belitt, Introduction to *New Poems (1968–1970)*, by Pablo Neruda, ed. and tr. Ben Belitt (New York: Grove Press, 1972.)
7. *Memoirs*, p. 295.
8. Rodríguez Monegal, p. 314.
9. Emir Rodríguez Monegal, *Narradores de esta América*, vol. 2 (Buenos Aires: Alfa Argentina, 1974), p. 173.
10. Ben Belitt, Introduction to *A New Decade. Poems 1958–67*, by Pablo Neruda, ed. Ben Belitt, tr. Ben Belitt and Alastair Reid (New York: Grove Press, 1969).
11. Ben Belitt, "The Burning Sarcophagus: A Revaluation of Pablo Neruda," *The Southern Review*, n. 4 (Summer 1968): 614.
12. Luis González-Cruz, *Memorial de Isla Negra: Integración de la visión poética de Pablo Neruda* (Miami: Ediciones Universal, 1972), p. 21.
13. Belitt, "The Burning Sarcophagus," p. 605.
14. Ibid., pp. 613–15.
15. Neruda, *O Cruzeiro Internacional*, Rio de Janeiro, 16 January 1962.
16. Camacho Guizado, p. 246.
17. Quoted by Margarita Aguirre, p. 277.
18. Camacho Guizado, p. 250.
19. Loyola, p. 33.
20. Several different publication dates exist for this book. Neruda's *Memoirs* speak of its being written in 1965. Hernán Loyola in the *Antología* gives the date of 1968, but then lists a 1969 edition in his bibliography. The version we have consulted appears as an appendix to *Obras Completas*, vol. 2, 3d ed. (Buenos Aires: Losada, 1968). To our knowledge this is in fact the first Spanish publication of the work.
21. Camacho Guizado, p. 258.
22. *Aún* (Santiago: Nascimento, 1969).
23. Robert Pring-Mill, "A Poet and His Roots," *Times Literary Supplement*, London, 16 April 1970.
24. Camacho Guizado, p. 260.
25. Jaime Alazraki, "Para una poética de la poesía póstuma de Pablo Neruda," *Simposio Pablo Neruda* (Long Island City, New York: Las Américas, 1975), p. 68.
26. *Fin de mundo*, 4th ed. (Buenos Aires: Losada, 1976). First edition, 1969.
27. Loyola, p. 35.
28. *Geografía infructuosa* (Buenos Aires: Losada, 1972).
29. *Memoirs*, pp. 338–39.
30. Camacho Guizado, p. 265.
31. Alazraki, "Para una poética . . . ," pp. 52–53.
32. Robert Pring-Mill, "The Winter of Pablo Neruda," *Times Literary Sup-*

plement, London, 3 October 1975. (We are grateful to Robert Pring-Mill for providing us with his working copy of this article.)

33. Alazraki, "Para una poética . . . ," p. 47.
34. Ibid., p. 48.
35. Pring-Mill, "A Poet and His Roots."

Chapter 5. The Posthumous Poetry

1. Pring-Mill, "The Winter of Pablo Neruda."
2. *La rosa separada* (Barcelona: Seix Barral, 1977). First edition Buenos Aires: Losada, 1973. Robert Pring-Mill reports that a limited edition of this book was published in Paris in 1972 by Editions du Dragon ("Pablo Neruda: A Brief Bibliographical Guide," *Bulletin of the Society for Latin American Studies,* no. 22 [January 1975]: 22). Neither Losada nor Neruda's usual French publisher, Gallimard, which published the book in 1979, makes any reference to the existence of an earlier edition, and *The Separate Rose* is universally treated by publishers, critics, and bibliographers alike as one of the posthumous books. All efforts to contact Editions du Dragon or to find a copy of the 1972 edition Pring-Mill cites have proved fruitless, and we are, to date, unable to verify whether this private edition is identical with the "official" edition published posthumously.
3. Pring-Mill, "The Winter of Pablo Neruda."
4. *Jardín de invierno* (Barcelona: Seix Barral, 1977). First edition Buenos Aires: Losada, 1974.
5. Alazraki, "Para una poética . . . ," pp. 51–52.
6. Ibid., p. 59.
7. Georges Bataille, *L'érotisme* (Paris: Minuit, 1957).
8. *2000,* 2d ed. (Buenos Aires: Losada, 1976). First edition 1974.
9. *El corazón amarillo* (Buenos Aires: Losada, 1974).
10. Camacho Guizado, p. 270.
11. *Libro de las preguntas* (Barcelona: Seix Barral, 1977). First edition Buenos Aires: Losada, 1974.
12. *Elegía* (Barcelona: Seix Barral, 1976). First edition Buenos Aires: Losada, 1974.
13. Camacho Guizado, p. 273.
14. *El mar y las campanas,* 2d ed. (Buenos Aires: Losada, 1974). First edition, 1973.
15. Camacho Guizado, p. 275.
16. Alazraki, "Para una poética . . . ," p. 64.
17. Ibid., p. 65.
18. Octavio Paz, "Fábula," *Libertad bajo palabra* (México: Fondo de Cultura, 1968), p. 122; quoted by Alazraki, "Para una poética . . . ," p. 66.
19. Ibid.
20. Ibid., p. 64.
21. Camacho Guizado, p. 274.
22. *Defectos escogidos* (Buenos Aires: Losada, 1974).
23. "Défauts choisis," *La rose détachée et autres poèmes* (Paris: Gallimard, 1979), pp. 333–36.
24. Camacho Guizado, p. 277.
25. Ibid., pp. 276–77.
26. Ibid., p. 274.